Praise for *Ansible: Up and Running*

I devoured the manuscript for the first edition of *Ansible: Up and Running* within a few hours: Lorin did an amazing job describing all of Ansible's facets, and I was excited to hear he'd joined forces with René for a second edition. In this, the two authors have done an outstanding job of showing us how to put an incredibly useful utility to good use, and I cannot think of anything they haven't covered in depth.

—*Jan-Piet Mens, consultant*

Impressive coverage of Ansible. It's not only great for getting started, but also for understanding how to use the more advanced features. Fantastic resource for leveling up your Ansible skills.

—*Matt Jaynes, Chief Engineer, High Velocity Ops*

The nice thing about Ansible is that you can start by doing, and that it lends itself for easy prototyping, which is great to make quick progress and get things done. However, over time this tends to lead to gaps in knowledge and understanding, which is hard to come by.

Ansible: Up and Running is a very useful resource because it can fill those gaps, as it explains Ansible from the very basics up to the complexities of working with YAML and Jinja2. And because it is packed with many off-the-shelf examples to learn from and build on, it gives insight into how others are automating their environments.

During training sessions and hands-on missions over the past few years, I always recommend this book to colleagues and customers.

—*Dag Wieers, freelance Linux system engineer,*
long-time Ansible contributor and consultant

This book gives everyone an easy start, but also a deep dive into Ansible configuration management. There are a lot of hints and how-tos and it covers a wide range of use cases like AWS, Windows, and Docker.

—Ingo Jochim, Manager Cloud Implementation,
itelligence GMS/CIS

Lorin and René did an amazing job by writing this book. The authors take the user by the hand and lead him/her through all the important steps of creating and managing a properly designed Ansible project. The book is much more than a simple Ansible reference, as it covers several important conceptual topics missing from the official docs. It is an excellent resource for Ansible beginners, but it also includes many practical concepts and tricks for existing Ansiblers.

—Dominique Barton, DevOps engineer at confirm IT solutions

Ansible: Up and Running brilliantly covers what you need to know, not only as a novice but also as someone who already knows their way around Ansible and wants to expand their repertoire. Its differentiator is that it takes real world examples and explains both how to achieve tasks and why it works the way it does, leading to a much deeper understanding.

—Paul Angus, VP Technology, ShapeBlue

SECOND EDITION

Ansible: Up and Running

Automating Configuration Management and Deployment the Easy Way

Lorin Hochstein and René Moser

Beijing · Boston · Farnham · Sebastopol · Tokyo

Ansible: Up and Running

by Lorin Hochstein and René Moser

Copyright © 2017 Lorin Hochstein and René Moser. All rights reserved.

Printed in the United States of America.

Published by O'Reilly Media, Inc., 1005 Gravenstein Highway North, Sebastopol, CA 95472.

O'Reilly books may be purchased for educational, business, or sales promotional use. Online editions are also available for most titles (*http://oreilly.com/safari*). For more information, contact our corporate/institutional sales department: 800-998-9938 or *corporate@oreilly.com*.

Editor: Brian Anderson	**Indexer:** Ellen Troutman-Zaig
Production Editor: Kristen Brown	**Interior Designer:** David Futato
Copyeditor: Sharon Wilkey	**Cover Designer:** Karen Montgomery
Proofreader: James Fraleigh	**Illustrator:** Rebecca Demarest

December 2014:   First Edition
August 2017:   Second Edition

Revision History for the Second Edition

2017-07-20:   First Release
2017-09-28:   Second Release

978-1-491-97980-8

[LSI]

Table of Contents

Foreword

Ansible started as a simple side project in February of 2012, and its rapid growth has been a pleasant surprise. It is now the work product of about a thousand people (and the ideas of many more than that), and it is widely deployed in almost every country. It's not unusual in a computer meet-up to find a handful (at least) of people who use it.

Ansible is exciting perhaps because it really isn't. Ansible doesn't attempt to break new ground, but rather to distill a lot of existing ideas that other smart folks had already figured out and make them more accessible.

In creating Ansible, I sought a middle ground between somewhat computer-sciencey IT automation approaches (themselves a reaction to tedious large commercial suites) and hack-and-slash scripting that just gets things done. I also wondered, how can we replace a configuration management system, a deployment project, an orchestration project, and our library of arbitrary but important shell scripts with a single system? That was the idea.

Could we remove major architectural components from the IT automation stack? Eliminating management daemons and relying instead on OpenSSH meant the system could start managing a computer fleet immediately, without having to set up anything on the managed machines. Further, the system was apt to be more reliable and secure.

I had noticed that in trying to automate systems previously, things that should be simple were often hard, and that writing automation content could often create a time-sucking force that kept me from things I wanted to spend more time doing. And I didn't want the system to require months to learn, either.

In particular, I personally enjoyed writing new software, but piloting automation systems, a bit less. In short, I wanted to make automation quicker and leave more time for the things I cared about. Ansible was not something you were meant to use all day long, but to get in, get out, and get back to doing the things you care about. I hope you will like Ansible for many of the same reasons.

Although I spent a lot of time making sure Ansible's docs were comprehensive, there's always a strong advantage to seeing material presented in a variety of ways, and often in seeing actual practice applied alongside the reference material. In *Ansible: Up and Running*, Lorin presents Ansible in a very idiomatic way, in exactly the right order in which you might wish to explore it. Lorin has been around Ansible since almost the very beginning, and I'm grateful for his contributions and input.

I'm also immensely thankful for everyone who has been a part of this project to date, and everyone who will be in the future. Enjoy the book, and enjoy managing your computer fleet! And remember to install cowsay!

— Michael DeHaan
Creator of Ansible (software)
Former CTO of Ansible, Inc. (company)
April 2015

Preface to the Second Edition

In the time since the first edition of the book was written (back in 2014), there have been big changes in the world of Ansible. The Ansible project completed a major release, hitting 2.0. Big changes happened outside the project as well: Ansible, Inc., the company that backs the Ansible project, was acquired by Red Hat. Red Hat's acquisition hasn't slowed the Ansible project at all: it's still in active development and gaining users.

We've made multiple changes in this edition. The most significant change is the addition of five new chapters. The book now covers callback plugins, Windows hosts, network hardware, and Ansible Tower. We added so much content to the "Complex Playbooks" chapter that we expanded to a second chapter called "Customizing Hosts, Runs and Handlers." We also rewrote the "Docker" chapter to cover the new Docker modules.

We've updated all of the example code for compatibility with Ansible 2.3. In particular, the deprecated `sudo` clause has been replaced everywhere with `become`. We also removed references to deprecated modules such as `docker`, `ec2_vpc`, and `ec2_ami_search` and replaced them with examples that use newer modules. The "Vagrant" chapter now covers the Ansible local provisioner, the "Amazon EC2" chapter now covers the Packer Ansible remote provisioner, the "Making Ansible Go Even Faster" chapter now covers asynchronous tasks, and the "Debugging Ansible Playbooks" chapter now covers the debugger that was introduced in version 2.1.

There are also minor changes. For example, OpenSSH switched from using hexadecimal-encoded MD5 fingerprints to base64-encoded SHA256 fingerprints, and we updated examples accordingly. Finally, we fixed errata submitted by readers.

A Note About Language

The first edition of the book had a single author, and often used the first-person singular *I*. Since this edition has two authors, the use of first-person singular might seem odd in some places. However, we decided to keep it because it is typically used to express the opinion of one of the authors.

Acknowledgments

From Lorin

Thanks to Jan-Piet Mens, Matt Jaynes, and John Jarvis for reviewing drafts of the book and providing feedback. Thanks to Isaac Saldana and Mike Rowan at SendGrid for being so supportive of this endeavor. Thanks to Michael DeHaan for creating Ansible and shepherding the community that sprang up around it, as well as for providing feedback on the book, including an explanation of why he chose to use the name *Ansible*. Thanks to my editor, Brian Anderson, for his endless patience in working with me.

Thanks to Mom and Dad for their unfailing support; my brother Eric, the actual writer in the family; and my two sons, Benjamin and Julian. Finally, thanks to my wife, Stacy, for everything.

From René

Thanks to my family, my wife Simone for the support and love, my three children, Gil, Sarina and Léanne, for the joy they brought into my life; to all those people contributing to Ansible, thank you for your work; and a special thanks to Matthias Blaser who introduced Ansible to me.

Preface to the First Edition

Why I Wrote This Book

When I was writing my first web application, using Django, the popular Python-based framework, I remember the sense of accomplishment when the app was finally working on my desktop. I would run `django manage.py runserver`, point my browser to *http://localhost:8000*, and there was my web application in all its glory.

Then I discovered there were all of these…*things* I had to do, just to get the darned app to run on the Linux server. In addition to installing Django and my app onto the server, I had to install Apache and the `mod_python` module so that Apache could run Django apps. Then I had to figure out the right Apache configuration file incantation so that it would run my application and serve up the static assets properly.

None of it was hard; it was just a pain to get all of those details right. I didn't want to muck about with configuration files; I just wanted my app to run. Once I got it working, everything was fine…until, several months later, I had to do it again, on a different server, at which point I had to start the process all over again.

Eventually, I discovered that this process was Doing It Wrong. The right way to do this sort of thing has a name, and that name is *configuration management*. The great thing about using configuration management is that it's a way to capture knowledge that always stays up-to-date. No more hunting for the right doc page or searching through your old notes.

Recently, a colleague at work was interested in trying out Ansible for deploying a new project, and he asked me for a reference on how to apply the Ansible concepts in practice, beyond what was available in the official docs. I didn't know what else to recommend, so I decided to write something to fill the gap—and here it is. Alas, this book comes too late for him, but I hope you'll find it useful.

Who Should Read This Book

This book is for anyone who needs to deal with Linux or Unix-like servers. If you've ever used the terms *systems administration*, *operations*, *deployment*, *configuration management*, or (sigh) *DevOps*, then you should find some value here.

Although I have managed my share of Linux servers, my background is in software engineering. This means that the examples in this book tend toward the deployment end of the spectrum, although I'm in agreement with Andrew Clay Shafer that the distinction between deployment and configuration is unresolved.

Navigating This Book

I'm not a big fan of book outlines: Chapter 1 covers so and so, Chapter 2 covers such and such, that sort of thing. I strongly suspect that nobody ever reads them (I never do), and the table of contents is much easier to scan.

This book is written to be read start to finish, with later chapters building on the earlier ones. It's written largely in a tutorial style, so you should be able to follow along on your own machine. Most of the examples are focused on web applications.

Conventions Used in This Book

The following typographical conventions are used in this book:

Italic
Indicates new terms, URLs, email addresses, filenames, and file extensions.

`Constant width`
Used for program listings, as well as within paragraphs to refer to program elements such as variable or function names, databases, data types, environment variables, statements, and keywords.

`Constant width bold`
Shows commands or other text that should be typed literally by the user.

`Constant width italic`
Shows text that should be replaced with user-supplied values or by values determined by context.

 This icon signifies a general note.

This icon signifies a tip or suggestion.

 This icon indicates a warning or caution.

Online Resources

Code samples from this book are available at this book's GitHub page (*http://github.com/ansiblebook/ansiblebook*). There is ample official Ansible documentation (*http://docs.ansible.com*) available for reference.

I maintain a few Ansible quick reference pages on GitHub (*https://github.com/lorin/ansible-quickref*) as well.

The Ansible code is on GitHub (*https://github.com/ansible/ansible*). It was previously spread out across three repositories, but as of Ansible 2.3, all of the code is maintained in a single repository.

Bookmark the Ansible module index (*http://bit.ly/1Dt75tg*); you'll be referring to it constantly as you use Ansible. Ansible Galaxy (*https://galaxy.ansible.com*) is a repository of Ansible roles contributed by the community. The Ansible Project Google Group (*http://bit.ly/1Dt79ZT*) is the place to go if you have any questions about Ansible.

If you're interested in contributing to Ansible development, check out the Ansible Development Google Group (*http://bit.ly/1Dt79ZT*).

For real-time help with Ansible, there's an active *#ansible* IRC channel on *irc.freenode.net*.

Supplemental material (code examples, exercises, etc.) is available for download at *https://github.com/ansiblebook/ansiblebook*.

This book is here to help you get your job done. In general, you may use the example code offered with this book in your programs and documentation. You do not need to contact us for permission unless you're reproducing a significant portion of the code. For example, writing a program that uses several chunks of code from this book does not require permission. Selling or distributing a CD-ROM of examples from O'Reilly books does require permission. Answering a question by citing this book and quoting example code does not require permission. Incorporating a significant amount of example code from this book into your product's documentation does require permission.

We appreciate, but do not require, attribution. An attribution usually includes the title, author, publisher, and ISBN. For example: "*Ansible: Up and Running* by Lorin Hochstein and René Moser (O'Reilly). Copyright 2017 O'Reilly Media, Inc., 978-1-491-97980-8."

If you feel your use of code examples falls outside fair use or the permission given above, feel free to contact us at *permissions@oreilly.com*.

Safari® Books Online

 *Safari Books Online* is an on-demand digital library that delivers expert content in both book and video form from the world's leading authors in technology and business.

Technology professionals, software developers, web designers, and business and creative professionals use Safari Books Online as their primary resource for research, problem solving, learning, and certification training.

Safari Books Online offers a range of plans and pricing for enterprise, government, education, and individuals.

Members have access to thousands of books, training videos, and prepublication manuscripts in one fully searchable database from publishers like O'Reilly Media, Prentice Hall Professional, Addison-Wesley Professional, Microsoft Press, Sams, Que, Peachpit Press, Focal Press, Cisco Press, John Wiley & Sons, Syngress, Morgan Kaufmann, IBM Redbooks, Packt, Adobe Press, FT Press, Apress, Manning, New Riders, McGraw-Hill, Jones & Bartlett, Course Technology, and hundreds more. For more information about Safari Books Online, please visit us online.

How to Contact Us

Please address comments and questions concerning this book to the publisher:

O'Reilly Media, Inc.
1005 Gravenstein Highway North
Sebastopol, CA 95472
800-998-9938 (in the United States or Canada)
707-829-0515 (international or local)
707-829-0104 (fax)

To comment or ask technical questions about this book, send email to *bookquestions@oreilly.com*.

For more information about our books, courses, conferences, and news, see our website at *http://www.oreilly.com*.

Find us on Facebook: *http://facebook.com/oreilly*

Follow us on Twitter: *http://twitter.com/oreillymedia*

Watch us on YouTube: *http://www.youtube.com/oreillymedia*

## CHAPTER 1

Introduction

It's an interesting time to be working in the IT industry. We don't deliver software to our customers by installing a program on a single machine and calling it a day.[1] Instead, we are all slowly turning into system engineers.

We now deploy software applications by stringing together services that run on a distributed set of computing resources and communicate over different networking protocols. A typical application can include web servers, application servers, memory-based caching systems, task queues, message queues, SQL databases, NoSQL datastores, and load balancers.

We also need to make sure we have the appropriate redundancies in place, so that when failures happen (and they will), our software systems will handle these failures gracefully. Then there are the secondary services that we also need to deploy and maintain, such as logging, monitoring, and analytics, as well as third-party services we need to interact with, such as infrastructure-as-a-service (IaaS) endpoints for managing virtual machine instances.[2]

You can wire up these services by hand: spinning up the servers you need, SSHing to each one, installing packages, editing config files, and so forth, but it's a pain. It's time-consuming, error-prone, and just plain dull to do this kind of work manually, especially around the third or fourth time. And for more complex tasks, like standing up an OpenStack cloud inside your application, doing it by hand is madness. There's a better way.

---

1 OK, nobody ever really delivered software like that.

2 Check out *The Practice of Cloud System Administration* and *Designing Data-Intensive Applications* for excellent books on building and maintaining these types of distributed systems.

If you're reading this, you're probably already sold on the idea of configuration management and considering adopting Ansible as your configuration management tool. Whether you're a developer deploying your code to production, or you're a systems administrator looking for a better way to automate, I think you'll find Ansible to be an excellent solution to your problem.

A Note About Versions

The example code in this book was tested against version 2.3.0.0 of Ansible, which is the most recent release as of this writing. As backward compatibility is a major goal of the Ansible project, these examples should work unmodified in future versions of Ansible.

What's with the Name *Ansible*?

It's a science-fiction reference. An *ansible* is a fictional communication device that can transfer information faster than the speed of light. Ursula K. Le Guin invented the concept in her book *Rocannon's World*, and other sci-fi authors have since borrowed the idea from Le Guin.

More specifically, Michael DeHaan took the name Ansible from the book *Ender's Game* by Orson Scott Card. In that book, the ansible was used to control many remote ships at once, over vast distances. Think of it as a metaphor for controlling remote servers.

Ansible: What Is It Good For?

Ansible is often described as a *configuration management* tool, and is typically mentioned in the same breath as *Chef*, *Puppet*, and *Salt*. When we talk about configuration management, we are typically talking about writing some kind of state description for our servers, and then using a tool to enforce that the servers are, indeed, in that state: the right packages are installed, configuration files contain the expected values and have the expected permissions, the right services are running, and so on. Like other configuration management tools, Ansible exposes a domain-specific language (DSL) that you use to describe the state of your servers.

These tools can be used for *deployment* as well. When people talk about deployment, they are usually referring to the process of taking software that was written in-house, generating binaries or static assets (if necessary), copying the required files to the server(s), and then starting up the services. *Capistrano* and *Fabric* are two examples of open source deployment tools. Ansible is a great tool for deployment as well as configuration management. Using a single tool for both configuration management and deployment makes life simpler for the folks responsible for operations.

Some people talk about the need for *orchestration* of deployment. This is where multiple remote servers are involved, and things have to happen in a specific order. For example, you need to bring up the database before bringing up the web servers, or you need to take web servers out of the load balancer one at a time in order to upgrade them without downtime. Ansible is good at this as well, and is designed from the ground up for performing actions on multiple servers. Ansible has a refreshingly simple model for controlling the order in which actions happen.

Finally, you'll hear people talk about *provisioning* new servers. In the context of public clouds such as Amazon EC2, this refers to spinning up a new virtual machine instance. Ansible has got you covered here, with a number of modules for talking to clouds, including EC2, Azure, Digital Ocean, Google Compute Engine, Linode, and Rackspace, as well as any clouds that support the OpenStack APIs.

 Confusingly, the *Vagrant* tool, covered later in this chapter, uses the term *provisioner* to refer to a tool that does the configuration management. So, Vagrant refers to Ansible as a kind of provisioner, whereas I think of Vagrant as a provisioner, since Vagrant is responsible for starting up virtual machines.

How Ansible Works

Figure 1-1 shows a sample use case of Ansible in action. A user we'll call Stacy is using Ansible to configure three Ubuntu-based web servers to run Nginx. She has written an Ansible script called *webservers.yml*. In Ansible, a script is called a *playbook*. A playbook describes which *hosts* (what Ansible calls *remote servers*) to configure, and an ordered list of *tasks* to perform on those hosts. In this example, the hosts are web1, web2, and web3, and the tasks are things such as these:

- Install Nginx
- Generate an Nginx configuration file
- Copy over the security certificate
- Start the Nginx service

In the next chapter, we'll discuss what's in this playbook. Stacy executes the playbook by using the `ansible-playbook` command. In the example, the playbook is named *webservers.yml*, and is executed by typing the following:

```
$ ansible-playbook webservers.yml
```

Ansible will make SSH connections in parallel to web1, web2, and web3. It will execute the first task on the list on all three hosts simultaneously. In this example, the first task is installing the Nginx apt package (since Ubuntu uses the apt package manager), so the task in the playbook would look something like this:

```
- name: Install nginx
  apt: name=nginx
```

Ansible will do the following:

1. Generate a Python script that installs the Nginx package
2. Copy the script to web1, web2, and web3
3. Execute the script on web1, web2, and web3
4. Wait for the script to complete execution on all hosts

Ansible will then move to the next task in the list, and go through these same four steps. It's important to note the following:

- Ansible runs each task in parallel across all hosts.
- Ansible waits until all hosts have completed a task before moving to the next task.
- Ansible runs the tasks in the order that you specify them.

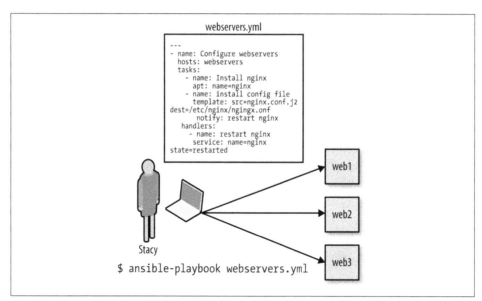

Figure 1-1. Running an Ansible playbook to configure three web servers

What's So Great About Ansible?

There are several open source configuration management tools out there to choose from. Here are some of the things that drew me to Ansible.

Easy-to-Read Syntax

Recall that Ansible configuration management scripts are called *playbooks*. Ansible's playbook syntax is built on top of YAML, which is a data format language that was designed to be easy for humans to read and write. In a way, YAML is to JSON what Markdown is to HTML.

I like to think of Ansible playbooks as *executable documentation*. It's like the README file that describes the commands you had to type out to deploy your software, except that the instructions will never go out-of-date because they are also the code that gets executed directly.

Nothing to Install on the Remote Hosts

To manage a server with Ansible, the server needs to have SSH and Python 2.5 or later installed, or Python 2.4 with the Python *simplejson* library installed. There's no need to preinstall an agent or any other software on the host.

The control machine (the one that you use to control remote machines) needs to have Python 2.6 or later installed.

 Some modules might require Python 2.5 or later, and some might have additional prerequisites. Check the documentation for each module to see whether it has specific requirements.

Push Based

Some configuration management systems that use agents, such as Chef and Puppet, are *pull based* by default. Agents installed on the servers periodically check in with a central service and pull down configuration information from the service. Making configuration management changes to servers goes something like this:

1. You: make a change to a configuration management script.
2. You: push the change up to a configuration management central service.
3. Agent on server: wakes up after periodic timer fires.
4. Agent on server: connects to configuration management central service.

5. Agent on server: downloads new configuration management scripts.

6. Agent on server: executes configuration management scripts locally that change server state.

In contrast, Ansible is *push based* by default. Making a change looks like this:

1. You: make a change to a playbook.

2. You: run the new playbook.

3. Ansible: connects to servers and executes modules, which changes server state.

As soon as you run the `ansible-playbook` command, Ansible connects to the remote server and does its thing.

The push-based approach has a significant advantage: you control when the changes happen to the servers. You don't need to wait around for a timer to expire. Advocates of the pull-based approach claim that pull is superior for scaling to large numbers of servers and for dealing with new servers that can come online anytime. However, as we'll discuss later in the book, Ansible has been used successfully in production with thousands of nodes, and has excellent support for environments where servers are dynamically added and removed.

If you really prefer using a pull-based model, Ansible has official support for pull mode, using a tool it ships with called *ansible-pull*. I don't cover pull mode in this book, but you can read more about it in the official documentation (*http://docs.ansi ble.com/playbooks_intro.html#ansible-pull*).

Ansible Scales Down

Yes, Ansible can be used to manage hundreds or even thousands of nodes. But what got me hooked is how it scales down. Using Ansible to configure a single node is easy; you simply write a single playbook. Ansible obeys Alan Kay's maxim: "Simple things should be simple; complex things should be possible."

Built-in Modules

You can use Ansible to execute arbitrary shell commands on your remote servers, but Ansible's real power comes from the collection of modules it ships with. You use modules to perform tasks such as installing a package, restarting a service, or copying a configuration file.

As you'll see later, Ansible modules are *declarative*; you use them to describe the state you want the server to be in. For example, you would invoke the user module like this to ensure there was an account named `deploy` in the `web` group:

```
user: name=deploy group=web
```

Modules are also *idempotent*. If the `deploy` user doesn't exist, Ansible will create it. If it does exist, Ansible won't do anything. Idempotence is a nice property because it means that it's safe to run an Ansible playbook multiple times against a server. This is a big improvement over the homegrown shell script approach, where running the shell script a second time might have a different (and likely unintended) effect.

What About Convergence?

Books on configuration management often mention the concept of *convergence*. Convergence in configuration management is most closely associated with Mark Burgess and the *CFEngine* configuration management system he authored. If a configuration management system is convergent, the system may run multiple times to put a server into its desired state, with each run bringing the server closer to that state.

This idea of convergence doesn't really apply to Ansible, as Ansible doesn't have a notion of running multiple times to configure servers. Instead, Ansible modules are implemented in such a way that running an Ansible playbook a single time should put each server into the desired state.

If you're interested in what Ansible's author thinks of the idea of convergence, see Michael DeHaan's post (*http://bit.ly/1InGh1A*) in the Ansible Project newsgroup, titled "Idempotence, convergence, and other silly fancy words we use too often."

Very Thin Layer of Abstraction

Some configuration management tools provide a layer of abstraction so that you can use the same configuration management scripts to manage servers running different operating systems. For example, instead of having to deal with a specific package manager like yum or apt, the configuration management tool exposes a "package" abstraction that you use instead.

Ansible isn't like that. You have to use the apt module to install packages on apt-based systems and the yum module to install packages on yum-based systems.

Although this might sound like a disadvantage, in practice I've found that it makes Ansible easier to work with. Ansible doesn't require that I learn a new set of abstractions that hide the differences between operating systems. This makes Ansible's surface area smaller; there's less you need to know before you can start writing playbooks.

If you really want to, you can write your Ansible playbooks to take different actions, depending on the operating system of the remote server. But I try to avoid that when I can, and instead I focus on writing playbooks that are designed to run on a specific operating system, such as Ubuntu.

The primary unit of reuse in the Ansible community is the module. Because the scope of a module is small and can be operating-system specific, it's straightforward to implement well-defined, shareable modules. The Ansible project is very open to accepting modules contributed by the community. I know because I've contributed a few.

Ansible playbooks aren't really intended to be reused across different contexts. In Chapter 7, we'll discuss *roles*, which is a way of collecting playbooks together so they are more reusable, as well as Ansible Galaxy, which is an online repository of these roles.

In practice, though, every organization sets up its servers a little bit differently, and you're best off writing playbooks for your organization rather than trying to reuse generic playbooks. I believe the primary value of looking at other people's playbooks is for examples to see how things are done.

What Is Ansible, Inc.'s Relationship to Ansible?

The name *Ansible* refers to both the software and the company that runs the open source project. Michael DeHaan, the creator of Ansible the software, is the former CTO of Ansible the company. To avoid confusion, I refer to the software as *Ansible* and to the company as *Ansible, Inc.*

Ansible, Inc. sells training and consulting services for Ansible, as well as a proprietary web-based management tool called *Ansible Tower*, which is covered in Chapter 19. In October 2015, Red Hat acquired Ansible, Inc.

Is Ansible Too Simple?

When I was working on this book, my editor mentioned to me that "some folks who use the XYZ configuration management tool call Ansible a for-loop over SSH scripts." If you're considering switching over from another config management tool, you might be concerned at this point about whether Ansible is powerful enough to meet your needs.

As you'll soon learn, Ansible provides a lot more functionality than shell scripts. As I mentioned, Ansible's modules provide idempotence, and Ansible has excellent support for templating, as well as defining variables at different scopes. Anybody who thinks Ansible is equivalent to working with shell scripts has never had to maintain a nontrivial program written in shell. I'll always choose Ansible over shell scripts for config management tasks if given a choice.

And if you're worried about the scalability of SSH? As we'll discuss in Chapter 12, Ansible uses SSH multiplexing to optimize performance, and there are folks out there who are managing thousands of nodes with Ansible.[3]

 I'm not familiar enough with the other tools to describe their differences in detail. If you're looking for a head-to-head comparison of config management tools, check out *Taste Test: Puppet, Chef, Salt, Ansible* by Matt Jaynes. As it happens, Matt prefers Ansible.

What Do I Need to Know?

To be productive with Ansible, you need to be familiar with basic Linux system administration tasks. Ansible makes it easy to automate your tasks, but it's not the kind of tool that "automagically" does things that you otherwise wouldn't know how to do.

For this book, I assumed my readers would be familiar with at least one Linux distribution (e.g., Ubuntu, RHEL/CentOS, SUSE), and that they would know how to

- Connect to a remote machine using SSH
- Interact with the Bash command-line shell (pipes and redirection)
- Install packages
- Use the sudo command
- Check and set file permissions
- Start and stop services
- Set environment variables
- Write scripts (any language)

If these concepts are all familiar to you, you're good to go with Ansible.

I won't assume you have knowledge of any particular programming language. For instance, you don't need to know Python to use Ansible unless you want to write your own module.

Ansible uses the YAML file format and the Jinja2 templating languages, so you'll need to learn some YAML and Jinja2 to use Ansible, but both technologies are easy to pick up.

---

3 For example, see "Using Ansible at Scale to Manage a Public Cloud" (*http://www.slideshare.net/JesseKeating/ ansiblefest-rax*) by Jesse Keating, formerly of Rackspace.

What Isn't Covered

This book isn't an exhaustive treatment of Ansible. It's designed to get you productive in Ansible as quickly as possible and describes how to perform certain tasks that aren't obvious from glancing over the official documentation.

I don't cover the official Ansible modules in detail. There are over 200 of these, and the official Ansible reference documentation on the modules is quite good.

I cover only the basic features of the templating engine that Ansible uses, Jinja2, primarily because I find that I generally need to use only those basic features when I use Ansible. If you need to use more advanced Jinja2 features in your templates, I recommend you check out the official Jinja2 documentation (*http://jinja.pocoo.org/docs/dev/*).

I don't go into detail about some features of Ansible that are mainly useful when you are running Ansible on an older version of Linux. This includes features such as the *Paramiko* SSH client and *accelerated mode*.

Finally, there are several features of Ansible I don't cover simply to keep the book a manageable length. These features include pull mode, logging, connecting to hosts using protocols other than SSH, and prompting the user for passwords or input. I encourage you to check out the official docs to find out more about these features.

Installing Ansible

If you're running on a Linux machine, all of the major Linux distributions package Ansible these days, so you should be able to install it using your native package manager, although this might be an older version of Ansible. If you're running on macOS, I recommend you use the excellent Homebrew package manager to install Ansible.

If all else fails, you can install it using *pip*, Python's package manager. You can install it as root by running the following:

```
$ sudo pip install ansible
```

If you don't want to install Ansible as root, you can safely install it into a Python *virtualenv*. If you're not familiar with virtualenvs, you can use a newer tool called *pipsi* that will automatically install Ansible into a virtualenv for you:

```
$ wget https://raw.githubusercontent.com/mitsuhiko/pipsi/master/get-pipsi.py
$ python get-pipsi.py
$ pipsi install ansible
```

If you go the pipsi route, you need to update your PATH environment variable to include *~/.local/bin*. Some Ansible plugins and modules might require additional Python libraries. If you've installed with pipsi, and you want to install *docker-py* (needed by the Ansible Docker modules) and *boto* (needed by the Ansible EC2 modules), you do it like this:

```
$ cd ~/.local/venvs/ansible
$ source bin/activate
$ pip install docker-py boto
```

If you're feeling adventurous and want to use the bleeding-edge version of Ansible, you can grab the development branch from GitHub:

```
$ git clone https://github.com/ansible/ansible.git --recursive
```

If you're running Ansible from the development branch, you need to run these commands each time to set up your environment variables, including your PATH variable so that your shell knows where the *ansible* and *ansible-playbooks* programs are:

```
$ cd ./ansible
$ source ./hacking/env-setup
```

For more details on installation see these resources:

- Official Ansible install docs (*http://docs.ansible.com/intro_installation.html*)
- Pip (*http://pip.readthedocs.org/*)
- Virtualenv (*http://docs.python-guide.org/en/latest/dev/virtualenvs/*)
- Pipsi (*https://github.com/mitsuhiko/pipsi*)

Setting Up a Server for Testing

You need to have SSH access and root privileges on a Linux server to follow along with the examples in this book. Fortunately, these days it's easy to get low-cost access to a Linux virtual machine through a public cloud service such as Amazon EC2, Google Compute Engine, Microsoft Azure,[4] Digital Ocean, Linode…you get the idea.

Using Vagrant to Set Up a Test Server

If you prefer not to spend the money on a public cloud, I recommend you install Vagrant on your machine. Vagrant is an excellent open source tool for managing virtual machines. You can use Vagrant to boot a Linux virtual machine inside your laptop, and you can use that as a test server.

Vagrant has built-in support for provisioning virtual machines with Ansible, but we'll talk about that in detail in Chapter 3. For now, we'll just manage a Vagrant virtual machine as if it were a regular Linux server.

---

4 Yes, Azure supports Linux servers.

Vagrant needs the VirtualBox virtualizer to be installed on your machine. Download VirtualBox (*http://www.virtualbox.org*) and then download Vagrant (*http://www.vagrantup.com*).

I recommend you create a directory for your Ansible playbooks and related files. In the following example, I've named mine *playbooks*.

Run the following commands to create a Vagrant configuration file (Vagrantfile) for an Ubuntu 14.04 (Trusty Tahr) 64-bit virtual machine image,[5] and boot it:

```
$ mkdir playbooks
$ cd playbooks
$ vagrant init ubuntu/trusty64
$ vagrant up
```

 The first time you use vagrant up, it will download the virtual machine image file, which might take a while, depending on your internet connection.

If all goes well, the output should look like this:

```
Bringing machine 'default' up with 'virtualbox' provider...
==> default: Importing base box 'ubuntu/trusty64'...
==> default: Matching MAC address for NAT networking...
==> default: Checking if box 'ubuntu/trusty64' is up to date...
==> default: Setting the name of the VM: playbooks_default_1474348723697_56934
==> default: Clearing any previously set forwarded ports...
==> default: Clearing any previously set network interfaces...
==> default: Preparing network interfaces based on configuration...
    default: Adapter 1: nat
==> default: Forwarding ports...
    default: 22 (guest) => 2222 (host) (adapter 1)
==> default: Booting VM...
==> default: Waiting for machine to boot. This may take a few minutes...
    default: SSH address: 127.0.0.1:2222
    default: SSH username: vagrant
    default: SSH auth method: private key
    default: Warning: Remote connection disconnect. Retrying...
    default: Warning: Remote connection disconnect. Retrying...
    default:
    default: Vagrant insecure key detected. Vagrant will automatically replace
    default: this with a newly generated keypair for better security.
    default:
    default: Inserting generated public key within guest...
    default: Removing insecure key from the guest if it's present...
    default: Key inserted! Disconnecting and reconnecting using new SSH key...
```

---

5 Vagrant uses the term *machine* to refer to a virtual machine and *box* to refer to a virtual machine image.

```
==> default: Machine booted and ready!
==> default: Checking for guest additions in VM...
    default: The guest additions on this VM do not match the installed version
    default: of VirtualBox! In most cases this is fine, but in rare cases it can
    default: prevent things such as shared folders from working properly. If you
    default: see shared folder errors, please make sure the guest additions
    default: within the virtual machine match the version of VirtualBox you have
    default: installed on your host and reload your VM.
    default:
    default: Guest Additions Version: 4.3.36
    default: VirtualBox Version: 5.0
==> default: Mounting shared folders...
    default: /vagrant => /Users/lorin/dev/ansiblebook/ch01/playbooks
```

You should be able to SSH into your new Ubuntu 14.04 virtual machine by running the following:

```
$ vagrant ssh
```

If this works, you should see a login screen like this:

```
Welcome to Ubuntu 14.04.5 LTS (GNU/Linux 3.13.0-96-generic x86_64)

 * Documentation:  https://help.ubuntu.com/

  System information as of Fri Sep 23 05:13:05 UTC 2016

  System load:  0.76              Processes:          80
  Usage of /:   3.5% of 39.34GB   Users logged in:     0
  Memory usage: 25%               IP address for eth0: 10.0.2.15
  Swap usage:   0%

  Graph this data and manage this system at:
    https://landscape.canonical.com/

  Get cloud support with Ubuntu Advantage Cloud Guest:
    http://www.ubuntu.com/business/services/cloud

0 packages can be updated.
0 updates are security updates.

New release '16.04.1 LTS' available.
Run 'do-release-upgrade' to upgrade to it.
```

Type **exit** to quit the SSH session.

This approach lets us interact with the shell, but Ansible needs to connect to the virtual machine by using the regular SSH client, not the vagrant ssh command.

Tell Vagrant to output the SSH connection details by typing the following:

```
$ vagrant ssh-config
```

On my machine, the output looks like this:

```
Host default
  HostName 127.0.0.1
  User vagrant
  Port 2222
  UserKnownHostsFile /dev/null
  StrictHostKeyChecking no
  PasswordAuthentication no
  IdentityFile /Users/lorin/dev/ansiblebook/ch01/playbooks/.vagrant/
  machines/default/virtualbox/private_key
  IdentitiesOnly yes
  LogLevel FATAL
```

The important lines are shown here:

```
HostName 127.0.0.1
User vagrant
Port 2222
IdentityFile /Users/lorin/dev/ansiblebook/ch01/playbooks/.vagrant/
machines/default/virtualbox/private_key
```

 Vagrant 1.7 changed how it handled private SSH keys. Starting with 1.7, Vagrant generates a new private key for each machine. Earlier versions used the same key, which was in the default location of ~/.vagrant.d/insecure_private_key. The examples in this book use Vagrant 1.7.

In your case, every field should likely be the same except for the path of the identity file.

Confirm that you can start an SSH session from the command line by using this information. In my case, the SSH command is as follows:

```
$ ssh vagrant@127.0.0.1 -p 2222 -i /Users/lorin/dev/ansiblebook/ch01/
playbooks/.vagrant/machines/default/virtualbox/private_key
```

You should see the Ubuntu login screen. Type **exit** to quit the SSH session.

Telling Ansible About Your Test Server

Ansible can manage only the servers it explicitly knows about. You provide Ansible with information about servers by specifying them in an inventory file.

Each server needs a name that Ansible will use to identify it. You can use the hostname of the server, or you can give it an alias and pass additional arguments to tell Ansible how to connect to it. We'll give our Vagrant server the alias of testserver.

Create a file called *hosts* in the *playbooks* directory. This file will serve as the inventory file. If you're using a Vagrant machine as your test server, your *hosts* file should look like Example 1-1. I've broken up the file content across multiple lines so that it fits on the page, but it should be all on one line in your file, without any backslashes.

Example 1-1. playbooks/hosts

```
testserver ansible_host=127.0.0.1 ansible_port=2222 \
 ansible_user=vagrant \
 ansible_private_key_file=.vagrant/machines/default/virtualbox/private_key
```

Here we see one of the drawbacks of using Vagrant: we have to explicitly pass in extra arguments to tell Ansible how to connect. In most cases, we won't need this extra data.

Later in this chapter, you'll see how to use the *ansible.cfg* file to avoid having to be so verbose in the inventory file. In later chapters, you'll see how to use Ansible variables to similar effect.

If you have an Ubuntu machine on Amazon EC2 with a hostname like `ec2-203-0-113-120.compute-1.amazonaws.com`, then your inventory file will look something like this (all on one line):

```
testserver ansible_host=ec2-203-0-113-120.compute-1.amazonaws.com \
 ansible_user=ubuntu ansible_private_key_file=/path/to/keyfile.pem
```

> Ansible supports the ssh-agent program, so you don't need to explicitly specify SSH key files in your inventory files. See "SSH Agent" on page 363 for more details if you haven't used ssh-agent before.

We'll use the `ansible` command-line tool to verify that we can use Ansible to connect to the server. You won't use the `ansible` command often; it's mostly used for ad hoc, one-off things.

Let's tell Ansible to connect to the server named `testserver` described in the inventory file named *hosts* and invoke the `ping` module:

```
$ ansible testserver -i hosts -m ping
```

If your local SSH client has host-key verification enabled, you might see something that looks like this the first time Ansible tries to connect to the server:

```
The authenticity of host '[127.0.0.1]:2222 ([127.0.0.1]:2222)' \
can't be established.
RSA key fingerprint is e8:0d:7d:ef:57:07:81:98:40:31:19:53:a8:d0:76:21.
Are you sure you want to continue connecting (yes/no)?
```

You can just type **yes**.

If it succeeded, output will look like this:

```
testserver | success >> {
    "changed": false,
    "ping": "pong"
}
```

 If Ansible did not succeed, add the -vvvv flag to see more details about the error:

```
$ ansible testserver -i hosts -m ping -vvvv
```

We can see that the module succeeded. The "changed": false part of the output tells us that executing the module did not change the state of the server. The "ping": "pong" text is output that is specific to the ping module.

The ping module doesn't do anything other than check that Ansible can start an SSH session with the servers. It's a useful tool for testing that Ansible can connect to the server.

Simplifying with the ansible.cfg File

We had to type a lot of text in the inventory file to tell Ansible about our test server. Fortunately, Ansible has ways to specify these sorts of variables so we don't have to put them all in one place. Right now, we'll use one such mechanism, the *ansible.cfg* file, to set some defaults so we don't need to type as much.

Where Should I Put My ansible.cfg File?

Ansible looks for an *ansible.cfg* file in the following places, in this order:

1. File specified by the ANSIBLE_CONFIG environment variable
2. *./ansible.cfg* (*ansible.cfg* in the current directory)
3. *~/.ansible.cfg* (*.ansible.cfg* in your home directory)
4. */etc/ansible/ansible.cfg*

I typically put *ansible.cfg* in the current directory, alongside my playbooks. That way, I can check it into the same version-control repository that my playbooks are in.

Example 1-2 shows an *ansible.cfg* file that specifies the location of the inventory file (inventory), the user to SSH (remote_user), and the SSH private key (private_key_file). This assumes you're using Vagrant. If you're using your own server, you'll need to set the remote_user and private_key_file values accordingly.

Our example configuration also disables SSH host-key checking. This is convenient when dealing with Vagrant machines; otherwise, we need to edit our ~/.ssh/known_hosts file every time we destroy and re-create a Vagrant machine. However, disabling host-key checking can be a security risk when connecting to other servers over the network. If you're not familiar with host keys, they are covered in detail in Appendix A.

Example 1-2. ansible.cfg

```
[defaults]
inventory = hosts
remote_user = vagrant
private_key_file = .vagrant/machines/default/virtualbox/private_key
host_key_checking = False
```

Ansible and Version Control

Ansible uses */etc/ansible/hosts* as the default location for the inventory file. However, I never use this because I like to keep my inventory files version-controlled alongside my playbooks.

Although we don't cover the topic of version control in this book, I strongly recommend you use a version-control system such as Git for maintaining all of your playbooks. If you're a developer, you're already familiar with version-control systems. If you're a systems administrator and aren't using version control yet, this is a perfect opportunity to get started.

With our default values set, we no longer need to specify the SSH user or key file in our *hosts* file. Instead, it simplifies to the following:

```
testserver ansible_host=127.0.0.1 ansible_port=2222
```

We can also invoke Ansible without passing the -i hostname arguments, like so:

```
$ ansible testserver -m ping
```

I like to use the `ansible` command-line tool to run arbitrary commands on remote machines, like parallel SSH. You can execute arbitrary commands with the `command` module. When invoking this module, you also need to pass an argument to the module with the -a flag, which is the command to run.

For example, to check the uptime of our server, we can use this:

```
$ ansible testserver -m command -a uptime
```

Output should look like this:

```
testserver | success | rc=0 >>
  17:14:07 up  1:16,  1 user,  load average: 0.16, 0.05, 0.04
```

The command module is so commonly used that it's the default module, so we can
omit it:

```
$ ansible testserver -a uptime
```

If our command contains spaces, we need to quote it so that the shell passes the entire
string as a single argument to Ansible. For example, to view the last several lines of
the */var/log/dmesg* logfile:

```
$ ansible testserver -a "tail /var/log/dmesg"
```

The output from my Vagrant machine looks like this:

```
testserver | success | rc=0 >>
[    5.170544] type=1400 audit(1409500641.335:9): apparmor="STATUS" operation=
"profile_replace" profile="unconfined" name="/usr/lib/NetworkManager/nm-dhcp-c
lient.act on" pid=888 comm="apparmor_parser"
[    5.170547] type=1400 audit(1409500641.335:10): apparmor="STATUS" operation=
"profile_replace" profile="unconfined" name="/usr/lib/connman/scripts/dhclient-
script" pid=888 comm="apparmor_parser"
[    5.222366] vboxvideo: Unknown symbol drm_open (err 0)
[    5.222370] vboxvideo: Unknown symbol drm_poll (err 0)
[    5.222372] vboxvideo: Unknown symbol drm_pci_init (err 0)
[    5.222375] vboxvideo: Unknown symbol drm_ioctl (err 0)
[    5.222376] vboxvideo: Unknown symbol drm_vblank_init (err 0)
[    5.222378] vboxvideo: Unknown symbol drm_mmap (err 0)
[    5.222380] vboxvideo: Unknown symbol drm_pci_exit (err 0)
[    5.222381] vboxvideo: Unknown symbol drm_release (err 0)
```

If we need root access, we pass in the -b flag to tell Ansible to *become* the root user.
For example, accessing */var/log/syslog* requires root access:

```
$ ansible testserver -b -a "tail /var/log/syslog"
```

The output looks something like this:

```
testserver | success | rc=0 >>
Aug 31 15:57:49 vagrant-ubuntu-trusty-64 ntpdate[1465]: /
adjust time server 91.189
94.4 offset -0.003191 sec
Aug 31 16:17:01 vagrant-ubuntu-trusty-64 CRON[1480]: (root) CMD (   cd /
&& run-p
rts --report /etc/cron.hourly)
Aug 31 17:04:18 vagrant-ubuntu-trusty-64 ansible-ping: Invoked with data=None
Aug 31 17:12:33 vagrant-ubuntu-trusty-64 ansible-ping: Invoked with data=None
Aug 31 17:14:07 vagrant-ubuntu-trusty-64 ansible-command: Invoked with executable
None shell=False args=uptime removes=None creates=None chdir=None
Aug 31 17:16:01 vagrant-ubuntu-trusty-64 ansible-command: Invoked with executable
None shell=False args=tail /var/log/messages removes=None creates=None chdir=None
Aug 31 17:17:01 vagrant-ubuntu-trusty-64 CRON[2091]: (root) CMD (    cd /
&& run-pa
```

```
rts --report /etc/cron.hourly)
Aug 31 17:17:09 vagrant-ubuntu-trusty-64 ansible-command: Invoked with /
executable=
N one shell=False args=tail /var/log/dmesg removes=None creates=None chdir=None
Aug 31 17:19:01 vagrant-ubuntu-trusty-64 ansible-command: Invoked with /
executable=
None shell=False args=tail /var/log/messages removes=None creates=None chdir=None
Aug 31 17:22:32 vagrant-ubuntu-trusty-64 ansible-command: Invoked with /
executable=
one shell=False args=tail /var/log/syslog removes=None creates=None chdir=None
```

We can see from this output that Ansible writes to the syslog as it runs.

You aren't just restricted to the ping and command modules when using the ansible command-line tool: you can use any module that you like. For example, you can install Nginx on Ubuntu by using the following command:

```
$ ansible testserver -b -m apt -a name=nginx
```

If installing Nginx fails for you, you might need to update the package lists. To tell Ansible to do the equivalent of apt-get update before installing the package, change the argument from name=nginx to "name=nginx update_cache=yes".

You can restart Nginx as follows:

```
$ ansible testserver -b -m service -a "name=nginx \
    state=restarted"
```

We need the -b argument to become the root user because only root can install the Nginx package and restart services.

Moving Forward

To recap, this introductory chapter covered the basic concepts of Ansible at a high level, including how it communicates with remote servers and how it differs from other configuration management tools. You've also seen how to use the ansible command-line tool to perform simple tasks on a single host.

However, using ansible to run commands against single hosts isn't terribly interesting. The next chapter covers playbooks, where the real action is.

## CHAPTER 2

Playbooks: A Beginning

Most of your time in Ansible will be spent writing playbooks. A *playbook* is the term that Ansible uses for a configuration management script. Let's look at an example: installing the Nginx web server and configuring it for secure communication.

If you're following along in this chapter, you should end up with the files listed here:

- *playbooks/ansible.cfg*
- *playbooks/hosts*
- *playbooks/Vagrantfile*
- *playbooks/web-notls.yml*
- *playbooks/web-tls.yml*
- *playbooks/files/nginx.key*
- *playbooks/files/nginx.crt*
- *playbooks/files/nginx.conf*
- *playbooks/templates/index.html.j2*
- *playbooks/templates/nginx.conf.j2*

Some Preliminaries

Before we can run this playbook against our Vagrant machine, we need to expose ports 80 and 443, so we can access them. As shown in Figure 2-1, we are going to configure Vagrant so that requests to ports 8080 and 8443 on our local machine are forwarded to ports 80 and 443 on the Vagrant machine. This will allow us to access the web server running inside Vagrant at *http://localhost:8080* and *https://localhost: 8443*.

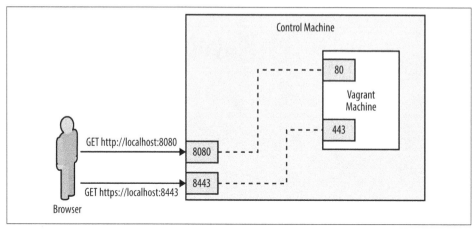

Figure 2-1. Exposing ports on Vagrant machine

Modify your *Vagrantfile* so it looks like this:

```
VAGRANTFILE_API_VERSION = "2"

Vagrant.configure(VAGRANTFILE_API_VERSION) do |config|
  config.vm.box = "ubuntu/trusty64"
  config.vm.network "forwarded_port", guest: 80, host: 8080
  config.vm.network "forwarded_port", guest: 443, host: 8443
end
```

This maps port 8080 on your local machine to port 80 of the Vagrant machine, and port 8443 on your local machine to port 443 on the Vagrant machine. After you make the changes, tell Vagrant to have them go into effect by running this command:

```
$ vagrant reload
```

You should see output that includes the following:

```
==> default: Forwarding ports...
    default: 80 => 8080 (adapter 1)
    default: 443 => 8443 (adapter 1)
    default: 22 => 2222 (adapter 1)
```

A Very Simple Playbook

For our first example playbook, we'll configure a host to run an Nginx web server. For this example, we won't configure the web server to support TLS encryption. This will make setting up the web server simpler. However, a proper website should have Transport Layer Security (TLS) encryption enabled, and we'll cover how to do that later in this chapter.

TLS versus SSL

You might be familiar with the term *SSL* rather than *TLS* in the context of secure web servers. SSL is an older protocol that was used to secure communications between browsers and web servers, and it has been superseded by a newer protocol named TLS. Although many continue to use the term *SSL* to refer to the current secure protocol, in this book, I use the more accurate *TLS*.

First, we'll see what happens when we run the playbook in Example 2-1, and then we'll go over the contents of the playbook in detail.

Example 2-1. web-notls.yml

```
- name: Configure webserver with nginx
  hosts: webservers
  become: True
  tasks:
    - name: install nginx
      apt: name=nginx update_cache=yes

    - name: copy nginx config file
      copy: src=files/nginx.conf dest=/etc/nginx/sites-available/default

    - name: enable configuration
      file: >
        dest=/etc/nginx/sites-enabled/default
        src=/etc/nginx/sites-available/default
        state=link

    - name: copy index.html
      template: src=templates/index.html.j2 dest=/usr/share/nginx/html/index.html
        mode=0644

    - name: restart nginx
      service: name=nginx state=restarted
```

Why Do You Use *True* in One Place and *Yes* in Another?

Sharp-eyed readers might have noticed that Example 2-1 uses True in one spot in the playbook (to enable sudo) and yes in another spot in the playbook (to update the apt cache).

Ansible is pretty flexible in how you represent truthy and falsey values in playbooks. Strictly speaking, module arguments (for example, update_cache=yes) are treated differently from values elsewhere in playbooks (for example, sudo: True). Values elsewhere are handled by the YAML parser and so use the YAML conventions of truthiness:

YAML truthy
> `true, True, TRUE, yes, Yes, YES, on, On, ON, y, Y`

YAML falsey
> `false, False, FALSE, no, No, NO, off, Off, OFF, n, N`

Module arguments are passed as strings and use Ansible's internal conventions:

module arg truthy
> `yes, on, 1, true`

module arg falsey
> `no, off, 0, false`

I tend to follow the examples in the official Ansible documentation. These typically use `yes` and `no` when passing arguments to modules (since that's consistent with the module documentation), and `True` and `False` elsewhere in playbooks.

Specifying an Nginx Config File

This playbook requires two additional files before we can run it. First, we need to define an Nginx configuration file.

Nginx ships with a configuration file that works out of the box if you just want to serve static files. But you'll almost always need to customize this, so we'll overwrite the default configuration file with our own as part of this playbook. As you'll see later, we'll need to modify this configuration file to support TLS. Example 2-2 shows a basic Nginx config file. Put it in *playbooks/files/nginx.conf.*[1]

> An Ansible convention is to keep files in a subdirectory named *files*, and Jinja2 templates in a subdirectory named *templates*. I follow this convention throughout the book.

Example 2-2. files/nginx.conf

```
server {
        listen 80 default_server;
        listen [::]:80 default_server ipv6only=on;
```

---

[1] Note that while we call this file *nginx.conf*, it replaces the *sites-enabled/default* Nginx server block config file, not the main */etc/nginx.conf* config file.

```
        root /usr/share/nginx/html;
        index index.html index.htm;

        server_name localhost;

        location / {
                try_files $uri $uri/ =404;
        }
}
```

Creating a Custom Home Page

Let's add a custom home page. We're going to use Ansible's template functionality so that Ansible will generate the file from a template. Put the content shown in Example 2-3 in *playbooks/templates/index.html.j2*.

Example 2-3. playbooks/templates/index.html.j2

```
<html>
  <head>
    <title>Welcome to ansible</title>
  </head>
  <body>
  <h1>nginx, configured by Ansible</h1>
  <p>If you can see this, Ansible successfully installed nginx.</p>

  <p>Running on {{ inventory_hostname }}</p>
  </body>
</html>
```

This template references a special Ansible variable named `inventory_hostname`. When Ansible renders this template, it will replace this variable with the name of the host as it appears in the hosts file. Figure 2-2 shows a web browser displaying the generated HTML.

Figure 2-2. Rendered HTML

Creating a Webservers Group

Let's create a `webservers` group in our inventory file so that we can refer to this group in our playbook. For now, this group will contain our test server.

Inventory files are in the *.ini* file format. We'll go into this format in detail later in the book. Edit your *playbooks/hosts* file to put a [`webservers`] line above the `testserver` line, as shown in Example 2-4. This indicates that `testserver` is in the `webservers` group.

Example 2-4. playbooks/hosts

```
[webservers]
testserver ansible_host=127.0.0.1 ansible_port=2222
```

You should now be able to ping the `webservers` group by using the `ansible` command-line tool:

```
$ ansible webservers -m ping
```

The output should look like this:

```
testserver | success >> {
    "changed": false,
    "ping": "pong"
}
```

Running the Playbook

The `ansible-playbook` command executes playbooks. To run the playbook, use this command:

```
$ ansible-playbook web-notls.yml
```

Example 2-5 shows what the output should look like.

Example 2-5. Output of ansible-playbook

```
PLAY [Configure webserver with nginx] ********************************

GATHERING FACTS ******************************************************
ok: [testserver]

TASK: [install nginx] ************************************************
changed: [testserver]

TASK: [copy nginx config file] ***************************************
changed: [testserver]

TASK: [enable configuration] *****************************************
```

```
ok: [testserver]

TASK: [copy index.html] ********************************************************
changed: [testserver]

TASK: [restart nginx] **********************************************************
changed: [testserver]

PLAY RECAP *********************************************************************
testserver                 : ok=6    changed=4   unreachable=0   failed=0
```

> ## Cowsay
>
> If you have the *cowsay* program installed on your local machine, Ansible output will
> look like this instead:
>
> ```
>  _____
> < PLAY [Configure webserver with nginx] >
>  ----------------------------------------
>         \   ^__^
>          \  (oo)_____
>             (__)\       )\/\
>                 ||----w |
>                 ||     ||
> ```
>
> If you don't want to see the cows, you can disable cowsay by setting the
> ANSIBLE_NOCOWS environment variable like this:
>
> ```
> $ export ANSIBLE_NOCOWS=1
> ```
>
> You can also disable cowsay by adding the following to your *ansible.cfg* file:
>
> ```
> [defaults]
> nocows = 1
> ```

If you didn't get any errors,[2] you should be able to point your browser to *http://local
host:8080* and see the custom HTML page, as shown in Figure 2-2.

 If your playbook file is marked as executable and starts with a line
that looks like this:[3]

```
#!/usr/bin/env ansible-playbook
```

then you can execute it by invoking it directly, like this:

```
$ ./web-notls.yml
```

---

2 If you encountered an error, you might want to skip to Chapter 16 for assistance on debugging.

3 Colloquially referred to as a *shebang*.

Playbooks Are YAML

Ansible playbooks are written in YAML syntax. *YAML* is a file format similar in intent to JSON, but generally easier for humans to read and write. Before we go over the playbook, let's cover the concepts of YAML that are most important for writing playbooks.

Start of File

YAML files are supposed to start with three dashes to indicate the beginning of the document:

```
---
```

However, if you forget to put those three dashes at the top of your playbook files, Ansible won't complain.

Comments

Comments start with a number sign and apply to the end of the line, the same as in shell scripts, Python, and Ruby:

```
# This is a YAML comment
```

Strings

In general, YAML strings don't have to be quoted, although you can quote them if you prefer. Even if there are spaces, you don't need to quote them. For example, this is a string in YAML:

```
this is a lovely sentence
```

The JSON equivalent is as follows:

```
"this is a lovely sentence"
```

In some scenarios in Ansible, you will need to quote strings. These typically involve the use of {{ braces }} for variable substitution. We'll get to those later.

Booleans

YAML has a native Boolean type, and provides you with a wide variety of strings that can be interpreted as true or false, which we covered in "Why Do You Use *True* in One Place and *Yes* in Another?" on page 23. Personally, I always use True and False in my Ansible playbooks.

For example, this is a Boolean in YAML:

```
True
```

The JSON equivalent is this:

```
true
```

Lists

YAML lists are like arrays in JSON and Ruby, or lists in Python. Technically, these are called *sequences* in YAML, but I call them *lists* here to be consistent with the official Ansible documentation.

They are delimited with hyphens, like this:

```
- My Fair Lady
- Oklahoma
- The Pirates of Penzance
```

The JSON equivalent is shown here:

```
[
  "My Fair Lady",
  "Oklahoma",
  "The Pirates of Penzance"
]
```

(Note again that we don't have to quote the strings in YAML, even though they have spaces in them.)

YAML also supports an inline format for lists, which looks like this:

```
[My Fair Lady, Oklahoma, The Pirates of Penzance]
```

Dictionaries

YAML *dictionaries* are like objects in JSON, dictionaries in Python, or hashes in Ruby. Technically, these are called *mappings* in YAML, but I call them *dictionaries* here to be consistent with the official Ansible documentation.

They look like this:

```
address: 742 Evergreen Terrace
city: Springfield
state: North Takoma
```

The JSON equivalent is shown here:

```
{
  "address": "742 Evergreen Terrace",
  "city": "Springfield",
  "state": "North Takoma"
}
```

YAML also supports an inline format for dictionaries, which looks like this:

```
{address: 742 Evergreen Terrace, city: Springfield, state: North Takoma}
```

Line Folding

When writing playbooks, you'll often encounter situations where you're passing many arguments to a module. For aesthetics, you might want to break this up across multiple lines in your file, but you want Ansible to treat the string as if it were a single line.

You can do this with YAML by using line folding with the greater than (>) character. The YAML parser will replace line breaks with spaces. For example:

```
address: >
    Department of Computer Science,
    A.V. Williams Building,
    University of Maryland
city: College Park
state: Maryland
```

The JSON equivalent is as follows:

```
{
  "address": "Department of Computer Science, A.V. Williams Building,
             University of Maryland",
  "city": "College Park",
  "state": "Maryland"
}
```

Anatomy of a Playbook

Let's take a look at our playbook from the perspective of a YAML file. Here it is again, in Example 2-6.

Example 2-6. web-notls.yml

```
- name: Configure webserver with nginx
  hosts: webservers
  become: True
  tasks:
    - name: install nginx
      apt: name=nginx update_cache=yes

    - name: copy nginx config file
      copy: src=files/nginx.conf dest=/etc/nginx/sites-available/default

    - name: enable configuration
      file: >
        dest=/etc/nginx/sites-enabled/default
        src=/etc/nginx/sites-available/default
        state=link

    - name: copy index.html
```

```
    template: src=templates/index.html.j2 dest=/usr/share/nginx/html/index.html
      mode=0644

  - name: restart nginx
    service: name=nginx state=restarted
```

In Example 2-7, we see the JSON equivalent of this file.

Example 2-7. JSON equivalent of web-notls.yml

```
[
  {
    "name": "Configure webserver with nginx",
    "hosts": "webservers",
    "become": true,
    "tasks": [
      {
        "name": "Install nginx",
        "apt": "name=nginx update_cache=yes"
      },
      {
        "name": "copy nginx config file",
        "template": "src=files/nginx.conf dest=/etc/nginx/
        sites-available/default"
      },
      {
        "name": "enable configuration",
        "file": "dest=/etc/nginx/sites-enabled/default src=/etc/nginx/sites-available
/default state=link"
      },
      {
        "name": "copy index.html",
        "template" : "src=templates/index.html.j2 dest=/usr/share/nginx/html/
        index.html mode=0644"
      },
      {
        "name": "restart nginx",
        "service": "name=nginx state=restarted"
      }
    ]
  }
]
```

 A valid JSON file is also a valid YAML file. This is because YAML allows strings to be quoted, considers true and false to be valid Booleans, and has inline lists and dictionary syntaxes that are the same as JSON arrays and objects. But don't write your playbooks as JSON—the whole point of YAML is that it's easier for people to read.

Plays

Looking at either the YAML or JSON representation, it should be clear that a play-book is a list of dictionaries. Specifically, a playbook is a list of *plays*.

Here's the play[4] from our example:

```
- name: Configure webserver with nginx
  hosts: webservers
  become: True
  tasks:
    - name: install nginx
      apt: name=nginx update_cache=yes

    - name: copy nginx config file
      copy: src=files/nginx.conf dest=/etc/nginx/sites-available/default

    - name: enable configuration
      file: >
        dest=/etc/nginx/sites-enabled/default
        src=/etc/nginx/sites-available/default
        state=link

    - name: copy index.html
      template: src=templates/index.html.j2
                dest=/usr/share/nginx/html/index.html mode=0644


    - name: restart nginx
      service: name=nginx state=restarted
```

Every play must contain the following:

- A set of *hosts* to configure
- A list of *tasks* to be executed on those hosts

Think of a play as the thing that connects hosts to tasks.

In addition to specifying hosts and tasks, plays also support optional settings. We'll get into those later, but here are three common ones:

name
:   A comment that describes what the play is about. Ansible prints this out when the play starts to run.

---

4 Actually, it's a list that contains a single play.

`become`
>   If true, Ansible will run every task by becoming (by default) the root user. This is useful when managing Ubuntu servers, since by default you cannot SSH as the root user.

`vars`
>   A list of variables and values. You'll see this in action later in this chapter.

Tasks

Our example playbook contains one play that has five tasks. Here's the first task of that play:

```
- name: install nginx
  apt: name=nginx update_cache=yes
```

The `name` is optional, so it's perfectly valid to write a task like this:

```
- apt: name=nginx update_cache=yes
```

Even though names are optional, I recommend you use them because they serve as good reminders for the intent of the task. (Names will be very useful when somebody else is trying to understand your playbook, including yourself in six months.) As you've seen, Ansible will print out the name of a task when it runs. Finally, as you'll see in Chapter 16, you can use the `--start-at-task <task name>` flag to tell `ansible-playbook` to start a playbook in the middle of a play, but you need to reference the task by name.

Every task must contain a key with the name of a module and a value with the arguments to that module. In the preceding example, the module name is `apt` and the arguments are `name=nginx update_cache=yes`.

These arguments tell the `apt` module to install the package named *nginx* and to update the package cache (the equivalent of doing an `apt-get update`) before installing the package.

It's important to understand that, from the point of the view of the YAML parser used by the Ansible frontend, the arguments are treated as a string, not as a dictionary. This means that if you want to break arguments into multiple lines, you need to use the YAML folding syntax, like this:

```
- name: install nginx
  apt: >
      name=nginx
      update_cache=yes
```

Ansible also supports a task syntax that will let you specify module arguments as a YAML dictionary, which is helpful when using modules that support complex arguments. We'll cover that in "Complex Arguments in Tasks: A Brief Digression" on page 105.

Ansible also supports an older syntax that uses `action` as the key and puts the name of the module in the value. The preceding example also can be written as follows:

```
- name: install nginx
  action: apt name=nginx update_cache=yes
```

Modules

Modules are scripts that come packaged with Ansible and perform some kind of action on a host.[5] Admittedly, that's a pretty generic description, but there's enormous variety across Ansible modules. The modules we use in this chapter are as follows:

apt
  Installs or removes packages by using the apt package manager

copy
  Copies a file from local machine to the hosts

file
  Sets the attribute of a file, symlink, or directory

service
  Starts, stops, or restarts a service

template
  Generates a file from a template and copies it to the hosts

---

Viewing Ansible Module Documentation

Ansible ships with the `ansible-doc` command-line tool, which shows documentation about modules. Think of it as man pages for Ansible modules. For example, to show the documentation for the `service` module, run this:

```
$ ansible-doc service
```

If you use macOS, there's a wonderful documentation viewer called Dash (*http://kapeli.com/dash*) that has support for Ansible. Dash indexes all of the Ansible module documentation. It's a commercial tool ($24.99 as of this writing), but I find it invaluable.

---

5 The modules that ship with Ansible all are written in Python, but modules can be written in any language.

Recall from the first chapter that Ansible executes a task on a host by generating a custom script based on the module name and arguments, and then copies this script to the host and runs it.

More than 200 modules ship with Ansible, and this number grows with every release. You can also find third-party Ansible modules out there, or write your own.

Putting It All Together

To sum up, a playbook contains one or more plays. A play associates an unordered set of hosts with an ordered list of tasks. Each task is associated with exactly one module.

Figure 2-3 is an entity-relationship diagram that depicts this relationship between playbooks, plays, hosts, tasks, and modules.

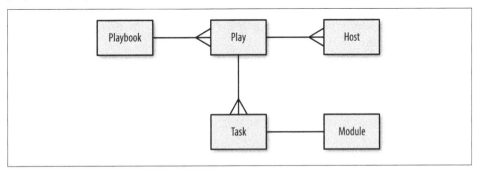

Figure 2-3. Entity-relationship diagram

Did Anything Change? Tracking Host State

When you run `ansible-playbook`, Ansible outputs status information for each task it executes in the play.

Looking back at Example 2-5, notice that the status for some of the tasks is `changed`, and the status for some others is `ok`. For example, the `install nginx` task has status `changed`, which appears as yellow on my terminal:

```
TASK: [install nginx] *******************************************************
changed: [testserver]
```

The `enable configuration`, on the other hand, has status `ok`, which appears as green on my terminal:

```
TASK: [enable configuration] ************************************************
ok: [testserver]
```

Any Ansible task that runs has the potential to change the state of the host in some way. Ansible modules will first check to see whether the state of the host needs to be changed before taking any action. If the state of the host matches the arguments of the module, Ansible takes no action on the host and responds with a state of ok.

On the other hand, if there is a difference between the state of the host and the arguments to the module, Ansible will change the state of the host and return changed.

In the example output just shown, the install nginx task was changed, which meant that before I ran the playbook, the *nginx* package had not previously been installed on the host. The enable configuration task was unchanged, which meant that there was already a configuration file on the server that was identical to the file I was copying over. The reason for this is that the *nginx.conf* file I used in my playbook is the same as the *nginx.conf* file that gets installed by the *nginx* package on Ubuntu.

As you'll see later in this chapter, Ansible's detection of state change can be used to trigger additional actions through the use of *handlers*. But, even without using handlers, it is still a useful form of feedback to see whether your hosts are changing state as the playbook runs.

Getting Fancier: TLS Support

Let's move on to a more complex example: we're going to modify the previous playbook so that our web servers support TLS. The new features here are as follows:

- Variables
- Handlers

Example 2-8 shows what our playbook looks like with TLS support.

Example 2-8. web-tls.yml

```
- name: Configure webserver with nginx and tls
  hosts: webservers
  become: True
  vars:
    key_file: /etc/nginx/ssl/nginx.key
    cert_file: /etc/nginx/ssl/nginx.crt
    conf_file: /etc/nginx/sites-available/default
    server_name: localhost
  tasks:
    - name: Install nginx
      apt: name=nginx update_cache=yes cache_valid_time=3600

    - name: create directories for ssl certificates
      file: path=/etc/nginx/ssl state=directory

    - name: copy TLS key
      copy: src=files/nginx.key dest={{ key_file }} owner=root mode=0600
```

```
    notify: restart nginx

  - name: copy TLS certificate
    copy: src=files/nginx.crt dest={{ cert_file }}
    notify: restart nginx

  - name: copy nginx config file
    template: src=templates/nginx.conf.j2 dest={{ conf_file }}
    notify: restart nginx

  - name: enable configuration
    file: dest=/etc/nginx/sites-enabled/default src={{ conf_file }} state=link
    notify: restart nginx

  - name: copy index.html
    template: src=templates/index.html.j2 dest=/usr/share/nginx/html/index.html
        mode=0644

handlers:
  - name: restart nginx
    service: name=nginx state=restarted
```

Generating a TLS Certificate

We need to manually generate a TLS certificate. In a production environment, you'd purchase your TLS certificate from a certificate authority, or use a free service such as Let's Encrypt, which Ansible supports via the letsencrypt module. We'll use a self-signed certificate, since we can generate those for free.

Create a *files* subdirectory of your *playbooks* directory, and then generate the TLS certificate and key:

```
$ mkdir files
$ openssl req -x509 -nodes -days 3650 -newkey rsa:2048 \
    -subj /CN=localhost \
    -keyout files/nginx.key -out files/nginx.crt
```

This should generate the files *nginx.key* and *nginx.crt* in the *files* directory. The certificate has an expiration date of 10 years (3,650 days) from the day you created it.

Variables

The play in our playbook now has a section called vars:

```
vars:
  key_file: /etc/nginx/ssl/nginx.key
  cert_file: /etc/nginx/ssl/nginx.crt
  conf_file: /etc/nginx/sites-available/default
  server_name: localhost
```

This section defines four variables and assigns a value to each variable.

In our example, each value is a string (e.g., /etc/nginx/ssl/nginx.key), but any valid YAML can be used as the value of a variable. You can use lists and dictionaries in addition to strings and Booleans.

Variables can be used in tasks, as well as in template files. You reference variables by using the {{ braces }} notation. Ansible replaces these braces with the value of the variable.

Consider this task in the playbook:

```
- name: copy TLS key
  copy: src=files/nginx.key dest={{ key_file }} owner=root mode=0600
```

Ansible will substitute {{ key_file }} with /etc/nginx/ssl/nginx.key when it executes this task.

When Quoting Is Necessary

If you reference a variable right after specifying the module, the YAML parser will misinterpret the variable reference as the beginning of an inline dictionary. Consider the following example:

```
- name: perform some task
  command: {{ myapp }} -a foo
```

Ansible will try to parse the first part of {{ myapp }} -a foo as a dictionary instead of a string, and will return an error. In this case, you must quote the arguments:

```
- name: perform some task
  command: "{{ myapp }} -a foo"
```

A similar problem arises if your argument contains a colon. For example:

```
- name: show a debug message
  debug: msg="The debug module will print a message: neat, eh?"
```

The colon in the msg argument trips up the YAML parser. To get around this, you need to quote the entire argument string.

Unfortunately, just quoting the argument string won't resolve the problem, either:

```
- name: show a debug message
  debug: "msg=The debug module will print a message: neat, eh?"
```

This will make the YAML parser happy, but the output isn't what you expect:

```
TASK: [show a debug message] ***********************************************
ok: [localhost] => {
    "msg": "The"
}
```

The debug module's msg argument requires a quoted string to capture the spaces. In this particular case, we need to quote both the whole argument string and the msg argument. Ansible supports alternating single and double quotes, so you can do this:

```
- name: show a debug message
  debug: "msg='The debug module will print a message: neat, eh?'"
```

This yields the expected output:

```
TASK: [show a debug message] **************************************************
ok: [localhost] => {
    "msg": "The debug module will print a message: neat, eh?"
}
```

Ansible is pretty good at generating meaningful error messages if you forget to put quotes in the right places and end up with invalid YAML.

Generating the Nginx Configuration Template

If you've done web programming, you've likely used a template system to generate HTML. In case you haven't, a *template* is just a text file that has special syntax for specifying variables that should be replaced by values. If you've ever received an automated email from a company, it's probably using an email template, as shown in Example 2-9.

Example 2-9. An email template

```
Dear {{ name }},

You have {{ num_comments }} new comments on your blog: {{ blog_name }}.
```

Ansible's use case isn't HTML pages or emails—it's configuration files. You don't want to hand-edit configuration files if you can avoid it. This is especially true if you have to reuse the same bits of configuration data (say, the IP address of your queue server or your database credentials) across multiple configuration files. It's much better to take the info that's specific to your deployment, record it in one location, and then generate all of the files that need this information from templates.

Ansible uses the Jinja2 template engine to implement templating. If you've ever used a templating library such as Mustache, ERB, or the Django template system, Jinja2 will feel very familiar.

Nginx's configuration file needs information about where to find the TLS key and certificate. We're going to use Ansible's templating functionality to define this configuration file so that we can avoid hardcoding values that might change.

In your *playbooks* directory, create a *templates* subdirectory and create the file *templates/nginx.conf.j2*, as shown in Example 2-10.

Example 2-10. templates/nginx.conf.j2

```
server {
        listen 80 default_server;
        listen [::]:80 default_server ipv6only=on;

        listen 443 ssl;

        root /usr/share/nginx/html;
        index index.html index.htm;

        server_name {{ server_name }};
        ssl_certificate {{ cert_file }};
        ssl_certificate_key {{ key_file }};

        location / {
                try_files $uri $uri/ =404;
        }
}
```

We use the `.j2` extension to indicate that the file is a Jinja2 template. However, you can use a different extension if you like; Ansible doesn't care.

In our template, we reference three variables:

server_name
> The hostname of the web server (e.g., `www.example.com`)

cert_file
> The path to the TLS certificate

key_file
> The path to the TLS private key

We define these variables in the playbook.

Ansible also uses the Jinja2 template engine to evaluate variables in playbooks. Recall that we saw the `{{ conf_file }}` syntax in the playbook itself.

 Early versions of Ansible used a dollar sign (`$`) to do variable interpolation in playbooks instead of the braces. You used to dereference the variable *foo* by writing `$foo`, whereas now you write `{{ foo }}`. The dollar sign syntax has been deprecated; if you encounter it in an example playbook you find on the internet, then you're looking at older Ansible code.

You can use all of the Jinja2 features in your templates, but we won't cover them in detail here. Check out the Jinja2 Template Designer Documentation (*http://jinja.pocoo.org/docs/dev/templates/*) for more details. You probably won't need to use those advanced templating features, though. One Jinja2 feature you probably will use with Ansible is filters; we'll cover those in a later chapter.

Handlers

Looking back at our *web-tls.yml* playbook, note that there are two new playbook elements we haven't discussed yet. There's a handlers section that looks like this:

```
handlers:
 - name: restart nginx
   service: name=nginx state=restarted
```

In addition, several of the tasks contain a notify key. For example:

```
 - name: copy TLS key
   copy: src=files/nginx.key dest={{ key_file }} owner=root mode=0600
   notify: restart nginx
```

Handlers are one of the conditional forms that Ansible supports. A handler is similar to a task, but it runs only if it has been notified by a task. A task will fire the notification if Ansible recognizes that the task has changed the state of the system.

A task notifies a handler by passing the handler's name as the argument. In the preceding example, the handler's name is restart nginx. For an Nginx server, we'd need to restart it if any of the following happens:[6]

- The TLS key changes.
- The TLS certificate changes.
- The configuration file changes.
- The contents of the *sites-enabled* directory change.

We put a notify statement on each of the tasks to ensure that Ansible restarts Nginx if any of these conditions are met.

A few things to keep in mind about handlers

Handlers usually run after all of the tasks are run at the end of the play. They run only once, even if they are notified multiple times. If a play contains multiple handlers, the handlers always run in the order that they are defined in the handlers section, not the notification order.

The official Ansible docs mention that the only common uses for handlers are for restarting services and for reboots. Personally, I've always used them only for restarting services. Even then, it's a pretty small optimization, since we can always just

---

6 Alternatively, we could reload the configuration file by using state=reloaded instead of restarting the service.

unconditionally restart the service at the end of the playbook instead of notifying it on change, and restarting a service doesn't usually take very long.

Another pitfall with handlers that I've encountered is that they can be troublesome when debugging a playbook. It goes something like this:

1. I run a playbook.

2. One of my tasks with a notify on it changes state.

3. An error occurs on a subsequent task, stopping Ansible.

4. I fix the error in my playbook.

5. I run Ansible again.

6. None of the tasks report a state change the second time around, so Ansible doesn't run the handler.

Read more about advanced handler usages and applications in "Advanced Handlers" on page 180.

Running the Playbook

As before, we use the ansible-playbook command to run the playbook:

```
$ ansible-playbook web-tls.yml
```

The output should look something like this:

```
PLAY [Configure webserver with nginx and tls] ********************************

GATHERING FACTS **************************************************************
ok: [testserver]

TASK: [Install nginx] ********************************************************
changed: [testserver]

TASK: [create directories for tls certificates] *****************************
changed: [testserver]

TASK: [copy TLS key] *********************************************************
changed: [testserver]

TASK: [copy TLS certificate] *************************************************
changed: [testserver]

TASK: [copy nginx config file] ***********************************************
changed: [testserver]

TASK: [enable configuration] *************************************************
ok: [testserver]
```

```
NOTIFIED: [restart nginx] ************************************************
changed: [testserver]

PLAY RECAP ************************************************************
testserver                : ok=8    changed=6    unreachable=0    failed=0
```

Point your browser to *https://localhost:8443* (don't forget the *s* on *https*). If you're using Chrome, as I am, you'll get a ghastly message that says something like, "Your connection is not private" (see Figure 2-4).

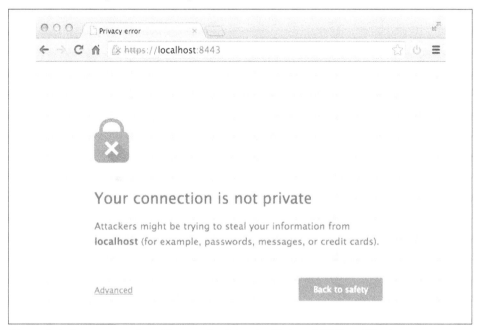

Figure 2-4. Browsers such as Chrome don't trust self-signed TLS certificates

Don't worry, though; that error is expected, as we generated a self-signed TLS certificate, and web browsers such as Chrome trust only certificates that have been issued from a proper authority.

We covered a lot of the *what* of Ansible in this chapter, describing what Ansible will do to your hosts. The handlers we discussed here are just one form of control flow that Ansible supports. In a later chapter, we'll see iteration and conditionally running tasks based on the values of variables. In the next chapter, we'll talk about the *who*; in other words, how to describe the hosts that your playbooks will run against.

## CHAPTER 3

Inventory: Describing Your Servers

So far, we've been working with only one server (or *host*, as Ansible calls it). In reality, you're going to be managing multiple hosts. The collection of hosts that Ansible knows about is called the *inventory*. In this chapter, you will learn how to describe a set of hosts as an Ansible inventory.

The Inventory File

The default way to describe your hosts in Ansible is to list them in text files, called *inventory files*. A very simple inventory file might contain only a list of hostnames, as shown in Example 3-1.

Example 3-1. A very simple inventory file

```
ontario.example.com
newhampshire.example.com
maryland.example.com
virginia.example.com
newyork.example.com
quebec.example.com
rhodeisland.example.com
```

 Ansible uses your local SSH client by default, which means that it will understand any aliases that you set up in your SSH config file. This does not hold true if you configure Ansible to use the Paramiko connection plugin instead of the default SSH plugin.

Ansible automatically adds one host to the inventory by default: *localhost*. Ansible understands that localhost refers to your local machine, so it will interact with it directly rather than connecting by SSH.

 Although Ansible adds localhost to your inventory automatically, you have to have at least one other host in your inventory file; otherwise, ansible-playbook will terminate with an error:

```
ERROR: provided hosts list is empty
```

If you have no other hosts in your inventory file, you can explicitly add an entry for localhost like this:

```
localhost ansible_connection=local
```

Preliminaries: Multiple Vagrant Machines

To talk about inventory, we need to interact with multiple hosts. Let's configure Vagrant to bring up three hosts. We'll unimaginatively call them vagrant1, vagrant2, and vagrant3.

Before you modify your existing Vagrantfile, make sure you destroy your existing virtual machine by running the following:

```
$ vagrant destroy --force
```

If you don't include the --force option, Vagrant will prompt you to confirm that you want to destroy the virtual machine.

Next, edit your Vagrantfile so it looks like Example 3-2.

Example 3-2. Vagrantfile with three servers

```
VAGRANTFILE_API_VERSION = "2"

Vagrant.configure(VAGRANTFILE_API_VERSION) do |config|
  # Use the same key for each machine
  config.ssh.insert_key = false

  config.vm.define "vagrant1" do |vagrant1|
    vagrant1.vm.box = "ubuntu/trusty64"
    vagrant1.vm.network "forwarded_port", guest: 80, host: 8080
    vagrant1.vm.network "forwarded_port", guest: 443, host: 8443
  end
  config.vm.define "vagrant2" do |vagrant2|
    vagrant2.vm.box = "ubuntu/trusty64"
    vagrant2.vm.network "forwarded_port", guest: 80, host: 8081
    vagrant2.vm.network "forwarded_port", guest: 443, host: 8444
  end
  config.vm.define "vagrant3" do |vagrant3|
```

```
    vagrant3.vm.box = "ubuntu/trusty64"
    vagrant3.vm.network "forwarded_port", guest: 80, host: 8082
    vagrant3.vm.network "forwarded_port", guest: 443, host: 8445
  end
end
```

Vagrant 1.7+ defaults to using a different SSH key for each host. Example 3-2 contains the line to revert to the earlier behavior of using the same SSH key for each host:

```
config.ssh.insert_key = false
```

Using the same key on each host simplifies our Ansible setup because we can specify a single SSH key in the *ansible.cfg* file. You'll need to edit the host_key_checking value in your *ansible.cfg*. Your file should look like Example 3-3.

Example 3-3. ansible.cfg

```
[defaults]
inventory = inventory
remote_user = vagrant
private_key_file = ~/.vagrant.d/insecure_private_key
host_key_checking = False
```

For now, we'll assume that each of these servers can potentially be a web server, so Example 3-2 maps ports 80 and 443 inside each Vagrant machine to a port on the local machine.

You should be able to bring up the virtual machines by running the following:

```
$ vagrant up
```

If all went well, the output should look something like this:

```
Bringing machine 'vagrant1' up with 'virtualbox' provider...
Bringing machine 'vagrant2' up with 'virtualbox' provider...
Bringing machine 'vagrant3' up with 'virtualbox' provider...
...
    vagrant3: 80 => 8082 (adapter 1)
    vagrant3: 443 => 8445 (adapter 1)
    vagrant3: 22 => 2201 (adapter 1)
==> vagrant3: Booting VM...
==> vagrant3: Waiting for machine to boot. This may take a few minutes...
    vagrant3: SSH address: 127.0.0.1:2201
    vagrant3: SSH username: vagrant
    vagrant3: SSH auth method: private key
    vagrant3: Warning: Connection timeout. Retrying...
==> vagrant3: Machine booted and ready!
==> vagrant3: Checking for guest additions in VM...
==> vagrant3: Mounting shared folders...
    vagrant3: /vagrant => /Users/lorin/dev/oreilly-ansible/playbooks
```

Let's create an inventory file that contains these three machines.

First, we need to know what ports on the local machine map to the SSH port (22) inside each VM. Recall that we can get that information by running the following:

```
$ vagrant ssh-config
```

The output should look something like this:

```
Host vagrant1
  HostName 127.0.0.1
  User vagrant
  Port 2222
  UserKnownHostsFile /dev/null
  StrictHostKeyChecking no
  PasswordAuthentication no
  IdentityFile /Users/lorin/.vagrant.d/insecure_private_key
  IdentitiesOnly yes
  LogLevel FATAL

Host vagrant2
  HostName 127.0.0.1
  User vagrant
  Port 2200
  UserKnownHostsFile /dev/null
  StrictHostKeyChecking no
  PasswordAuthentication no
  IdentityFile /Users/lorin/.vagrant.d/insecure_private_key
  IdentitiesOnly yes
  LogLevel FATAL

Host vagrant3
  HostName 127.0.0.1
  User vagrant
  Port 2201
  UserKnownHostsFile /dev/null
  StrictHostKeyChecking no
  PasswordAuthentication no
  IdentityFile /Users/lorin/.vagrant.d/insecure_private_key
  IdentitiesOnly yes
  LogLevel FATAL
```

We can see that `vagrant1` uses port 2222, `vagrant2` uses port 2200, and `vagrant3` uses port 2201.

Modify your *hosts* file so it looks like this:

```
vagrant1 ansible_host=127.0.0.1 ansible_port=2222
vagrant2 ansible_host=127.0.0.1 ansible_port=2200
vagrant3 ansible_host=127.0.0.1 ansible_port=2201
```

Now, make sure that you can access these machines. For example, to get information about the network interface for `vagrant2`, run the following:

```
$ ansible vagrant2 -a "ip addr show dev eth0"
```

On my machine, the output looks like this:

```
vagrant2 | success | rc=0 >>
2: eth0: <BROADCAST,MULTICAST,UP,LOWER_UP> mtu 1500 qdisc pfifo_fast state UP
group default qlen 1000
    link/ether 08:00:27:fe:1e:4d brd ff:ff:ff:ff:ff:ff
    inet 10.0.2.15/24 brd 10.0.2.255 scope global eth0
       valid_lft forever preferred_lft forever
    inet6 fe80::a00:27ff:fefe:1e4d/64 scope link
       valid_lft forever preferred_lft forever
```

Behavioral Inventory Parameters

To describe our Vagrant machines in the Ansible inventory file, we had to explicitly specify the hostname (127.0.0.1) and port (2222, 2200, or 2201) that Ansible's SSH client should connect to. Ansible calls these variables *behavioral inventory parameters*, and there are several of them you can use when you need to override the Ansible defaults for a host (see Table 3-1).

Table 3-1. Behavioral inventory parameters

Name	Default	Description
ansible_host	Name of host	Hostname or IP address to SSH to
ansible_port	22	Port to SSH to
ansible_user	Root	User to SSH as
ansible_password	(*None*)	Password to use for SSH authentication
ansible_connection	smart	How Ansible will connect to host (see the following section)
ansible_private_key_file	(*None*)	SSH private key to use for SSH authentication
ansible_shell_type	sh	Shell to use for commands (see the following section)
ansible_python_interpreter	*/usr/bin/ python*	Python interpreter on host (see the following section)
ansible_*_interpreter	(*None*)	Like ansible_python_interpreter for other languages (see the following section)

For some of these options, the meaning is obvious from the name, but others require additional explanation.

ansible_connection

Ansible supports multiple *transports*, which are mechanisms that Ansible uses to connect to the host. The default transport, smart, will check whether the locally installed SSH client supports a feature called *ControlPersist*. If the SSH client supports ControlPersist, Ansible will use the local SSH client. If the SSH client doesn't support ControlPersist, the smart transport will fall back to using a Python-based SSH client library called *Paramiko*.

ansible_shell_type

Ansible works by making SSH connections to remote machines and then invoking scripts. By default, Ansible assumes that the remote shell is the Bourne shell located at */bin/sh*, and will generate the appropriate command-line parameters that work with Bourne shell.

Ansible also accepts `csh`, `fish`, and (on Windows) `powershell` as valid values for this parameter. I've never encountered a need for changing the shell type.

ansible_python_interpreter

Because the modules that ship with Ansible are implemented in Python 2, Ansible needs to know the location of the Python interpreter on the remote machine. You might need to change this if your remote host does not have a Python 2 interpreter at */usr/bin/python*. For example, if you are managing hosts that run Arch Linux, you will need to change this to */usr/bin/python2*, because Arch Linux installs Python 3 at */usr/bin/python*, and Ansible modules are not (yet) compatible with Python 3.

ansible_*_interpreter

If you are using a custom module that is not written in Python, you can use this parameter to specify the location of the interpreter (e.g., */usr/bin/ruby*). We'll cover this in Chapter 12.

Changing Behavioral Parameter Defaults

You can override some of the behavioral parameter default values in the `defaults` section of the *ansible.cfg* file (Table 3-2). Recall that we used this previously to change the default SSH user.

Table 3-2. Defaults that can be overridden in ansible.cfg

Behavioral inventory parameter	ansible.cfg option
ansible_port	remote_port
ansible_user	remote_user
ansible_private_key_file	private_key_file
ansible_shell_type	executable (see the following paragraph)

The *ansible.cfg* `executable` config option is not exactly the same as the `ansible_shell_type` behavioral inventory parameter. Instead, the executable specifies the full path of the shell to use on the remote machine (e.g., */usr/local/bin/fish*). Ansible will look at the name of the base name of this path (in the case of */usr/local/bin/fish*, the base name is *fish*) and use that as the default value for `ansible_shell_type`.

Groups and Groups and Groups

When performing configuration tasks, we typically want to perform actions on groups of hosts, rather than on an individual host. Ansible automatically defines a group called all (or *), which includes all of the hosts in the inventory. For example, we can check whether the clocks on the machines are roughly synchronized by running the following:

```
$ ansible all -a "date"
```

or

```
$ ansible '*' -a "date"
```

The output on my system looks like this:

```
vagrant3 | success | rc=0 >>
Sun Sep  7 02:56:46 UTC 2014

vagrant2 | success | rc=0 >>
Sun Sep  7 03:03:46 UTC 2014

vagrant1 | success | rc=0 >>
Sun Sep  7 02:56:47 UTC 2014
```

We can define our own groups in the inventory file. Ansible uses the *.ini* file format for inventory files. In the *.ini* format, configuration values are grouped together into sections.

Here's how to specify that our vagrant hosts are in a group called vagrant, along with the other example hosts we mentioned at the beginning of the chapter:

```
ontario.example.com
newhampshire.example.com
maryland.example.com
virginia.example.com
newyork.example.com
quebec.example.com
rhodeisland.example.com

[vagrant]
vagrant1 ansible_host=127.0.0.1 ansible_port=2222
vagrant2 ansible_host=127.0.0.1 ansible_port=2200
vagrant3 ansible_host=127.0.0.1 ansible_port=2201
```

We could have also listed the Vagrant hosts at the top, and then also in a group, like this:

```
maryland.example.com
newhampshire.example.com
newyork.example.com
ontario.example.com
quebec.example.com
```

```
rhodeisland.example.com
vagrant1 ansible_host=127.0.0.1 ansible_port=2222
vagrant2 ansible_host=127.0.0.1 ansible_port=2200
vagrant3 ansible_host=127.0.0.1 ansible_port=2201
virginia.example.com

[vagrant]
vagrant1
vagrant2
vagrant3
```

Example: Deploying a Django App

Imagine you're responsible for deploying a Django-based web application that processes long-running jobs. The app needs to support the following services:

- The actual Django web app itself, run by a Gunicorn HTTP server
- An Nginx web server, which will sit in front of Gunicorn and serve static assets
- A Celery task queue that will execute long-running jobs on behalf of the web app
- A RabbitMQ message queue that serves as the backend for Celery
- A Postgres database that serves as the persistent store

 In later chapters, we will work through a detailed example of
deploying this kind of Django-based application, although our
example won't use Celery or RabbitMQ.

We need to deploy this application into different types of environments: production
(the real thing), staging (for testing on hosts that our team has shared access to), and
Vagrant (for local testing).

When we deploy to production, we want the entire system to respond quickly and be
reliable, so we do the following:

- Run the web application on multiple hosts for better performance and put a load
  balancer in front of them.
- Run task queue servers on multiple hosts for better performance.
- Put Gunicorn, Celery, RabbitMQ, and Postgres all on separate servers.
- Use two Postgres hosts, a primary and a replica.

Assuming we have one load balancer, three web servers, three task queues, one RabbitMQ server, and two database servers, that's 10 hosts we need to deal with.

For our staging environment, imagine that we want to use fewer hosts than we do in production in order to save costs, especially since the staging environment is going to see a lot less activity than production. Let's say we decide to use only two hosts for staging; we'll put the web server and task queue on one staging host, and RabbitMQ and Postgres on the other.

For our local Vagrant environment, we decide to use three servers: one for the web app, one for a task queue, and one that will contain RabbitMQ and Postgres.

Example 3-4 shows a possible inventory file that groups our servers by environment (production, staging, Vagrant) and by function (web server, task queue, etc.).

Example 3-4. Inventory file for deploying a Django app

```
[production]
delaware.example.com
georgia.example.com
maryland.example.com
newhampshire.example.com
newjersey.example.com
newyork.example.com
northcarolina.example.com
pennsylvania.example.com
rhodeisland.example.com
virginia.example.com

[staging]
ontario.example.com
quebec.example.com

[vagrant]
vagrant1 ansible_host=127.0.0.1 ansible_port=2222
vagrant2 ansible_host=127.0.0.1 ansible_port=2200
vagrant3 ansible_host=127.0.0.1 ansible_port=2201

[lb]
delaware.example.com

[web]
georgia.example.com
newhampshire.example.com
newjersey.example.com
ontario.example.com
vagrant1

[task]
newyork.example.com
northcarolina.example.com
maryland.example.com
ontario.example.com
```

```
vagrant2

[rabbitmq]
pennsylvania.example.com
quebec.example.com
vagrant3

[db]
rhodeisland.example.com
virginia.example.com
quebec.example.com
vagrant3
```

We could have first listed all of the servers at the top of the inventory file, without specifying a group, but that isn't necessary, and that would've made this file even longer.

Note that we needed to specify the behavioral inventory parameters for the Vagrant instances only once.

Aliases and Ports

We described our Vagrant hosts like this:

```
[vagrant]
vagrant1 ansible_host=127.0.0.1 ansible_port=2222
vagrant2 ansible_host=127.0.0.1 ansible_port=2200
vagrant3 ansible_host=127.0.0.1 ansible_port=2201
```

The names vagrant1, vagrant2, and vagrant3 here are *aliases*. They are not the real hostnames, but instead are useful names for referring to these hosts.

Ansible supports using <hostname>:<port> syntax when specifying hosts, so we could replace the line that contains vagrant1 with 127.0.0.1:2222. However, we can't actually run what you see in Example 3-5.

Example 3-5. This doesn't work

```
[vagrant]
127.0.0.1:2222
127.0.0.1:2200
127.0.0.1:2201
```

The reason is that Ansible's inventory can associate only a single host with *127.0.0.1*, so the Vagrant group would contain only one host instead of three.

Groups of Groups

Ansible also allows you to define groups that are made up of other groups. For example, both the web servers and the task queue servers will need to have Django and its dependencies. We might find it useful to define a `django` group that contains both of these two groups. You would add this to the inventory file:

```
[django:children]
web
task
```

Note that the syntax changes when you are specifying a group of groups, as opposed to a group of hosts. That's so Ansible knows to interpret `web` and `task` as groups and not as hosts.

Numbered Hosts (Pets versus Cattle)

The inventory file shown in Example 3-4 looks complex. In reality, it describes only 15 hosts, which doesn't sound like a large number in this cloudy scale-out world. However, even dealing with 15 hosts in the inventory file can be cumbersome, because each host has a completely different hostname.

Bill Baker of Microsoft came up with the distinction between treating servers as *pets* versus treating them like *cattle*.[1] We give pets distinctive names, and we treat and care for them as individuals. On the other hand, when we discuss cattle, we refer to them by identification number.

The cattle approach is much more scalable, and Ansible supports it well by supporting numeric patterns. For example, if your 20 servers are named *web1.example.com*, *web2.example.com*, and so on, then you can specify them in the inventory file like this:

```
[web]
web[1:20].example.com
```

If you prefer to have a leading zero (e.g., *web01.example.com*), then specify a leading zero in the range, like this:

```
[web]
web[01:20].example.com
```

Ansible also supports using alphabetic characters to specify ranges. If you want to use the convention *web-a.example.com*, *web-b.example.com*, and so on, for your 20 servers, then you can do this:

---

1 This term has been popularized by Randy Bias of Cloudscaling (*http://bit.ly/1P3nHB2*).

```
[web]
web-[a-t].example.com
```

Hosts and Group Variables: Inside the Inventory

Recall how we specified behavioral inventory parameters for Vagrant hosts:

```
vagrant1 ansible_host=127.0.0.1 ansible_port=2222
vagrant2 ansible_host=127.0.0.1 ansible_port=2200
vagrant3 ansible_host=127.0.0.1 ansible_port=2201
```

Those parameters are variables that have special meaning to Ansible. We can also define arbitrary variable names and associated values on hosts. For example, we could define a variable named color and set it to a value for each server:

```
newhampshire.example.com color=red
maryland.example.com color=green
ontario.example.com color=blue
quebec.example.com color=purple
```

This variable can then be used in a playbook, just like any other variable.

Personally, I don't often attach variables to specific hosts. On the other hand, I often associate variables with groups.

Circling back to our Django example, the web application and task queue service need to communicate with RabbitMQ and Postgres. We'll assume that access to the Postgres database is secured both at the network layer (so only the web application and the task queue can reach the database) as well as by username and password, whereas RabbitMQ is secured only by the network layer.

To set everything up, we need to do the following:

- Configure the web servers with the hostname, port, username, password of the primary Postgres server, and name of the database.
- Configure the task queues with the hostname, port, username, password of the primary Postgres server, and the name of the database.
- Configure the web servers with the hostname and port of the RabbitMQ server.
- Configure the task queues with the hostname and port of the RabbitMQ server.
- Configure the primary Postgres server with the hostname, port, and username and password of the replica Postgres server (production only).

This configuration info varies by environment, so it makes sense to define these as group variables on the production, staging, and Vagrant groups. Example 3-6 shows one way to specify this information as group variables in the inventory file.

Example 3-6. Specifying group variables in inventory

```
[all:vars]
ntp_server=ntp.ubuntu.com

[production:vars]
db_primary_host=rhodeisland.example.com
db_primary_port=5432
db_replica_host=virginia.example.com
db_name=widget_production
db_user=widgetuser
db_password=pFmMxcyD;Fc6)6
rabbitmq_host=pennsylvania.example.com
rabbitmq_port=5672


[staging:vars]
db_primary_host=quebec.example.com
db_primary_port=5432
db_name=widget_staging
db_user=widgetuser
db_password=L@4Ryz8cRUXedj
rabbitmq_host=quebec.example.com
rabbitmq_port=5672

[vagrant:vars]
db_primary_host=vagrant3
db_primary_port=5432
db_name=widget_vagrant
db_user=widgetuser
db_password=password
rabbitmq_host=vagrant3
rabbitmq_port=5672
```

Note how group variables are organized into sections named [<group name>:vars]. Also note how we took advantage of the all group that Ansible creates automatically to specify variables that don't change across hosts.

Host and Group Variables: In Their Own Files

The inventory file is a reasonable place to put host and group variables if you don't have too many hosts. But as your inventory gets larger, it gets more difficult to manage variables this way.

Additionally, though Ansible variables can hold Booleans, strings, lists, and dictionaries, in an inventory file, you can specify only Booleans and strings.

Ansible offers a more scalable approach to keep track of host and group variables: you can create a separate variable file for each host and each group. Ansible expects these variable files to be in YAML format.

Ansible looks for host variable files in a directory called *host_vars* and group variable files in a directory called *group_vars*. Ansible expects these directories to be either in the directory that contains your playbooks or in the directory adjacent to your inventory file. In our case, those two directories are the same.

For example, if I had a directory containing my playbooks at */home/lorin/playbooks/* with an inventory file at */home/lorin/playbooks/hosts*, then I would put variables for the *quebec.example.com* host in the file */home/lorin/playbooks/host_vars/quebec.example.com*, and I would put variables for the production group in the file */home/lorin/playbooks/group_vars/production*.

Example 3-7 shows what the */home/lorin/playbooks/group_vars/production* file would look like.

Example 3-7. group_vars/production

```
db_primary_host: rhodeisland.example.com
db_primary_port=5432
db_replica_host: virginia.example.com
db_name: widget_production
db_user: widgetuser
db_password: pFmMxcyD;Fc6)6
rabbitmq_host:pennsylvania.example.com
rabbitmq_port=5672
```

Note that we could also use YAML dictionaries to represent these values, as shown in Example 3-8.

Example 3-8. group_vars/production, with dictionaries

```
db:
    user: widgetuser
    password: pFmMxcyD;Fc6)6
    name: widget_production
    primary:
        host: rhodeisland.example.com
        port: 5432
    replica:
        host: virginia.example.com
        port: 5432

rabbitmq:
    host: pennsylvania.example.com
    port: 5672
```

If we choose YAML dictionaries, that changes the way we access the variables:

```
{{ db_primary_host }}
```

versus:

```
{{ db.primary.host }}
```

If you want to break things out even further, Ansible will allow you to define *group_vars/production* as a directory instead of a file, and let you place multiple YAML files that contain variable definitions. For example, we could put the database-related variables in one file and the RabbitMQ-related variables in another file, as shown in Examples 3-9 and 3-10.

Example 3-9. group_vars/production/db

```
db:
    user: widgetuser
    password: pFmMxcyD;Fc6)6
    name: widget_production
    primary:
        host: rhodeisland.example.com
        port: 5432
    replica:
        host: virginia.example.com
        port: 5432
```

Example 3-10. group_vars/production/rabbitmq

```
rabbitmq:
    host: pennsylvania.example.com
    port: 6379
```

In general, I find it's better to keep things simple rather than split variables out across too many files.

Dynamic Inventory

Up until this point, we've been explicitly specifying all of our hosts in our hosts inventory file. However, you might have a system external to Ansible that keeps track of your hosts. For example, if your hosts run on Amazon EC2, then EC2 tracks information about your hosts for you, and you can retrieve this information through EC2's web interface, its Query API, or through command-line tools such as awscli. Other cloud providers have similar interfaces. Or, if you're managing your own servers and are using an automated provisioning system such as Cobbler or Ubuntu Metal as a Service (MAAS), then your provisioning system is already keeping track of your servers. Or, maybe you have one of those fancy configuration management databases (CMDBs) where all of this information lives.

You don't want to manually duplicate this information in your hosts file, because eventually that file will not jibe with your external system, which is the true source of information about your hosts. Ansible supports a feature called *dynamic inventory* that allows you to avoid this duplication.

If the inventory file is marked executable, Ansible will assume it is a dynamic inventory script and will execute the file instead of reading it.

 To mark a file as executable, use the `chmod +x` command. For example:

```
$ chmod +x dynamic.py
```

The Interface for a Dynamic Inventory Script

An Ansible dynamic inventory script must support two command-line flags:

- `--host=<hostname>` for showing host details
- `--list` for listing groups

Showing host details

To get the details of the individual host, Ansible will call the inventory script like this:

```
$ ./dynamic.py --host=vagrant2
```

The output should contain any host-specific variables, including behavioral parameters, like this:

```
{ "ansible_host": "127.0.0.1", "ansible_port": 2200,
  "ansible_user": "vagrant"}
```

The output is a single JSON object; the names are variable names, and the values are the variable values.

Listing groups

Dynamic inventory scripts need to be able to list all of the groups, and details about the individual hosts. For example, if our script is called *dynamic.py*, Ansible will call it like this to get a list of all of the groups:

```
$ ./dynamic.py --list
```

The output should look something like this:

```
{"production": ["delaware.example.com", "georgia.example.com",
                "maryland.example.com", "newhampshire.example.com",
                "newjersey.example.com", "newyork.example.com",
                "northcarolina.example.com", "pennsylvania.example.com",
                "rhodeisland.example.com", "virginia.example.com"],
  "staging": ["ontario.example.com", "quebec.example.com"],
```

```
    "vagrant": ["vagrant1", "vagrant2", "vagrant3"],
    "lb": ["delaware.example.com"],
    "web": ["georgia.example.com", "newhampshire.example.com",
            "newjersey.example.com", "ontario.example.com", "vagrant1"]
    "task": ["newyork.example.com", "northcarolina.example.com",
            "ontario.example.com", "vagrant2"],
    "rabbitmq": ["pennsylvania.example.com", "quebec.example.com", "vagrant3"],
    "db": ["rhodeisland.example.com", "virginia.example.com", "vagrant3"]
}
```

The output is a single JSON object; the names are Ansible group names, and the values are arrays of hostnames.

As an optimization, the `--list` command can contain the values of the host variables for all of the hosts, which saves Ansible the trouble of making a separate `--host` invocation to retrieve the variables for the individual hosts.

To take advantage of this optimization, the `--list` command should return a key named `_meta` that contains the variables for each host, in this form:

```
"_meta" :
  { "hostvars" :
    "vagrant1" : { "ansible_host": "127.0.0.1", "ansible_port": 2222,
                   "ansible_user": "vagrant"},
    "vagrant2": { "ansible_host": "127.0.0.1", "ansible_port": 2200,
                  "ansible_user": "vagrant"},
    ...
}
```

Writing a Dynamic Inventory Script

One of the handy features of Vagrant is that you can see which machines are currently running by using the `vagrant status` command. Assuming we have a Vagrant file that looks like Example 3-2, if we run `vagrant status`, the output would look like Example 3-11.

Example 3-11. Output of vagrant status

```
$ vagrant status
Current machine states:

vagrant1                  running (virtualbox)
vagrant2                  running (virtualbox)
vagrant3                  running (virtualbox)

This environment represents multiple VMs. The VMs are all listed
above with their current state. For more information about a specific
VM, run `vagrant status NAME`.
```

Because Vagrant already keeps track of machines for us, there's no need for us to write a list of the Vagrant machines in an Ansible inventory file. Instead, we can write a dynamic inventory script that queries Vagrant about which machines are running. Once we've set up a dynamic inventory script for Vagrant, even if we alter our Vagrantfile to run different numbers of Vagrant machines, we won't need to edit an Ansible inventory file.

Let's work through an example of creating a dynamic inventory script that retrieves the details about hosts from Vagrant.[2] Our dynamic inventory script is going to need to invoke the `vagrant status` command. The output shown in Example 3-11 is designed for humans to read, rather than for machines to parse. We can get a list of running hosts in a format that is easier to parse with the `--machine-readable` flag, like so:

```
$ vagrant status --machine-readable
```

The output looks like this:

```
1474694768,vagrant1,metadata,provider,virtualbox
1474694768,vagrant2,metadata,provider,virtualbox
1474694768,vagrant3,metadata,provider,virtualbox
1410577818,vagrant1,state,running
1410577818,vagrant1,state-human-short,running
1410577818,vagrant1,state-human-long,The VM is running. To stop this VM%!(VAGRANT
_COMMA) you can run `vagrant halt` to\nshut it down forcefully%!(VAGRANT_COMMA)
or you can run `vagrant suspend` to simply\nsuspend the virtual machine. In
either case%!(VAGRANT_COMMA) to restart it again%!(VAGRANT_COMMA)\nsimply run
`vagrant up`.
1410577818,vagrant2,state,running
1410577818,vagrant2,state-human-short,running
1410577818,vagrant2,state-human-long,The VM is running. To stop this VM%!(VAGRANT
_COMMA) you can run `vagrant halt` to\nshut it down forcefully%!(VAGRANT_COMMA)
or you can run `vagrant suspend` to simply\nsuspend the virtual machine. In
either case%!(VAGRANT_COMMA) to restart it again%!(VAGRANT_COMMA)\nsimply run
`vagrant up`.
1410577818,vagrant3,state,running
1410577818,vagrant3,state-human-short,running
1410577818,vagrant3,state-human-long,The VM is running. To stop this VM%!(VAGRANT
_COMMA) you can run `vagrant halt` to\nshut it down forcefully%!(VAGRANT_COMMA)
or you can run `vagrant suspend` to simply\nsuspend the virtual machine. In
either case%!(VAGRANT_COMMA) to restart it again%!(VAGRANT_COMMA)\nsimply
run `vagrant up`.
```

To get details about a particular Vagrant machine, say, `vagrant2`, we would run this:

```
$ vagrant ssh-config vagrant2
```

---

2 Yes, there's a Vagrant dynamic inventory script included with Ansible already, but it's helpful to go through the exercise.

The output looks like this:

```
Host vagrant2
  HostName 127.0.0.1
  User vagrant
  Port 2200
  UserKnownHostsFile /dev/null
  StrictHostKeyChecking no
  PasswordAuthentication no
  IdentityFile /Users/lorin/.vagrant.d/insecure_private_key
  IdentitiesOnly yes
  LogLevel FATAL
```

Our dynamic inventory script will need to call these commands, parse the outputs, and output the appropriate JSON. We can use the Paramiko library to parse the output of `vagrant ssh-config`. Here's an interactive Python session that shows how to use the Paramiko library to do this:

```
>>> import subprocess
>>> import paramiko
>>> cmd = "vagrant ssh-config vagrant2"
>>> p = subprocess.Popen(cmd.split(), stdout=subprocess.PIPE)
>>> config = paramiko.SSHConfig()
>>> config.parse(p.stdout)
>>> config.lookup("vagrant2")
{'identityfile': ['/Users/lorin/.vagrant.d/insecure_private_key'],
 'loglevel': 'FATAL', 'hostname': '127.0.0.1', 'passwordauthentication': 'no',
 'identitiesonly': 'yes', 'userknownhostsfile': '/dev/null', 'user': 'vagrant',
 'stricthostkeychecking': 'no', 'port': '2200'}
```

 You need to install the Python Paramiko library in order to use this script. You can do this with pip:

```
$ sudo pip install paramiko
```

Example 3-12 shows our complete *vagrant.py* script.

Example 3-12. vagrant.py

```
#!/usr/bin/env python
# Adapted from Mark Mandel's implementation
# https://github.com/ansible/ansible/blob/stable-2.1/contrib/inventory/vagrant.py
# License: GNU General Public License, Version 3 <http://www.gnu.org/licenses/>
import argparse
import json
import paramiko
import subprocess
import sys
```

```python
def parse_args():
    parser = argparse.ArgumentParser(description="Vagrant inventory script")
    group = parser.add_mutually_exclusive_group(required=True)
    group.add_argument('--list', action='store_true')
    group.add_argument('--host')
    return parser.parse_args()


def list_running_hosts():
    cmd = "vagrant status --machine-readable"
    status = subprocess.check_output(cmd.split()).rstrip()
    hosts = []
    for line in status.split('\n'):
        (_, host, key, value) = line.split(',')[:4]
        if key == 'state' and value == 'running':
            hosts.append(host)
    return hosts


def get_host_details(host):
    cmd = "vagrant ssh-config {}".format(host)
    p = subprocess.Popen(cmd.split(), stdout=subprocess.PIPE)
    config = paramiko.SSHConfig()
    config.parse(p.stdout)
    c = config.lookup(host)
    return {'ansible_host': c['hostname'],
            'ansible_port': c['port'],
            'ansible_user': c['user'],
            'ansible_private_key_file': c['identityfile'][0]}


def main():
    args = parse_args()
    if args.list:
        hosts = list_running_hosts()
        json.dump({'vagrant': hosts}, sys.stdout)
    else:
        details = get_host_details(args.host)
        json.dump(details, sys.stdout)

if __name__ == '__main__':
    main()
```

Preexisting Inventory Scripts

Ansible ships with several dynamic inventory scripts that you can use. I can never figure out where my package manager installs these files, so I just grab the ones I need
directly off GitHub. You can grab these by going to the Ansible GitHub repo (*https://
github.com/ansible/ansible*) and browsing to the *contrib/inventory* directory.

Many of these inventory scripts have an accompanying configuration file. In Chapter 14, we'll discuss the Amazon EC2 inventory script in more detail.

Breaking the Inventory into Multiple Files

If you want to have both a regular inventory file and a dynamic inventory script (or, really, any combination of static and dynamic inventory files), just put them all in the same directory and configure Ansible to use that directory as the inventory. You can do this either via the `inventory` parameter in *ansible.cfg* or by using the `-i` flag on the command line. Ansible will process all of the files and merge the results into a single inventory.

For example, our directory structure could look like this: *inventory/hosts* and *inventory/vagrant.py*.

Our *ansible.cfg* file would contain these lines:

```
[defaults]
inventory = inventory
```

Adding Entries at Runtime with add_host and group_by

Ansible will let you add hosts and groups to the inventory during the execution of a playbook.

add_host

The `add_host` module adds a host to the inventory. This module is useful if you're using Ansible to provision new virtual machine instances inside an infrastructure-as-a-service cloud.

Why Do I Need add_host if I'm Using Dynamic Inventory?

Even if you're using dynamic inventory scripts, the `add_host` module is useful for scenarios where you start up new virtual machine instances and configure those instances in the same playbook.

If a new host comes online while a playbook is executing, the dynamic inventory script will not pick up this new host. This is because the dynamic inventory script is executed at the beginning of the playbook, so if any new hosts are added while the playbook is executing, Ansible won't see them.

We'll cover a cloud computing example that uses the `add_host` module in Chapter 14.

Invoking the module looks like this:

```
    add_host name=hostname groups=web,staging myvar=myval
```

Specifying the list of groups and additional variables is optional.

Here's the `add_host` command in action, bringing up a new Vagrant machine and then configuring the machine:

```
- name: Provision a vagrant machine
  hosts: localhost
  vars:
    box: trusty64
  tasks:
    - name: create a Vagrantfile
      command: vagrant init {{ box }} creates=Vagrantfile

    - name: Bring up a vagrant machine
      command: vagrant up

    - name: add the vagrant machine to the inventory
      add_host: >
          name=vagrant
          ansible_host=127.0.0.1
          ansible_port=2222
          ansible_user=vagrant
          ansible_private_key_file=/Users/lorin/.vagrant.d/
          insecure_private_key

- name: Do something to the vagrant machine
  hosts: vagrant
  become: yes
  tasks:
    # The list of tasks would go here
    - ...
```

The `add_host` module adds the host only for the duration of the execution of the playbook. It does not modify your inventory file.

When I do provisioning inside my playbooks, I like to split it into two plays. The first play runs against `localhost` and provisions the hosts, and the second play configures the hosts.

Note that we use the `creates=Vagrantfile` parameter in this task:

```
- name: create a Vagrantfile
  command: vagrant init {{ box }} creates=Vagrantfile
```

This tells Ansible that if the *Vagrantfile* file is present, the host is already in the correct state, and there is no need to run the command again. It's a way of achieving idempotence in a playbook that invokes the command module, by ensuring that the (potentially nonidempotent) command is run only once.

group_by

Ansible also allows you to create new groups during execution of a playbook, using the group_by module. This lets you create a group based on the value of a variable that has been set on each host, which Ansible refers to as a *fact*.[3]

If Ansible fact gathering is enabled, Ansible will associate a set of variables with a host. For example, the ansible_machine variable will be i386 for 32-bit x86 machines and x86_64 for 64-bit x86 machines. If Ansible is interacting with a mix of such hosts, we can create i386 and x86_64 groups with the task.

Or, if we want to group our hosts by Linux distribution (e.g., Ubuntu, CentOS), we can use the ansible_distribution fact:

```
- name: create groups based on Linux distribution
  group_by: key={{ ansible_distribution }}
```

In Example 3-13, we use group_by to create separate groups for our Ubuntu hosts and our CentOS hosts, and then we use the apt module to install packages onto Ubuntu and the yum module to install packages into CentOS.

Example 3-13. Creating ad hoc groups based on Linux distribution

```
- name: group hosts by distribution
  hosts: myhosts
  gather_facts: True
  tasks:
    - name: create groups based on distro
      group_by: key={{ ansible_distribution }}

- name: do something to Ubuntu hosts
  hosts: Ubuntu
  tasks:
    - name: install htop
      apt: name=htop
    # ...

- name: do something else to CentOS hosts
  hosts: CentOS
  tasks:
    - name: install htop
      yum: name=htop
    # ...
```

---

3 We cover facts in more detail in Chapter 4.

Although using `group_by` is one way to achieve conditional behavior in Ansible, I've never found much use for it. In Chapter 6, you'll see an example of how to use the `when` task parameter to take different actions based on variables.

That about does it for Ansible's inventory. The next chapter covers how to use variables. See Chapter 11 for more details about *ControlPersist*, also known as SSH multiplexing.

## CHAPTER 4

Variables and Facts

Ansible is not a full-fledged programming language, but it does have several programming language features, and one of the most important of these is variable substitution. This chapter presents Ansible's support for variables in more detail, including a certain type of variable that Ansible calls a *fact*.

Defining Variables in Playbooks

The simplest way to define variables is to put a `vars` section in your playbook with the names and values of variables. Recall from Example 2-8 that we used this approach to define several configuration-related variables, like this:

```
vars:
  key_file: /etc/nginx/ssl/nginx.key
  cert_file: /etc/nginx/ssl/nginx.crt
  conf_file: /etc/nginx/sites-available/default
  server_name: localhost
```

Ansible also allows you to put variables into one or more files, using a section called `vars_files`. Let's say we want to take the preceding example and put the variables in a file named *nginx.yml* instead of putting them right in the playbook. We would replace the `vars` section with a `vars_files` that looks like this:

```
vars_files:
  - nginx.yml
```

The *nginx.yml* file would look like Example 4-1.

Example 4-1. nginx.yml

```
key_file: /etc/nginx/ssl/nginx.key
cert_file: /etc/nginx/ssl/nginx.crt
conf_file: /etc/nginx/sites-available/default
server_name: localhost
```

You'll see an example of `vars_files` in action in Chapter 6 when we use it to separate out the variables that contain sensitive information.

As we discussed in Chapter 3, Ansible also lets you define variables associated with hosts or groups in the inventory file or in separate files that live alongside the inventory file.

Viewing the Values of Variables

For debugging, it's often handy to be able to view the output of a variable. You saw in Chapter 2 how to use the `debug` module to print out an arbitrary message. We can also use it to output the value of the variable. It works like this:

```
- debug: var=myvarname
```

We'll be using this form of the debug module several times in this chapter.

Registering Variables

Often, you'll find that you need to set the value of a variable based on the result of a task. To do so, we create a *registered variable* using the `register` clause when invoking a module. Example 4-2 shows how to capture the output of the `whoami` command to a variable named `login`.

Example 4-2. Capturing the output of a command to a variable

```
- name: capture output of whoami command
  command: whoami
  register: login
```

In order to use the `login` variable later, we need to know the type of value to expect. The value of a variable set using the `register` clause is always a dictionary, but the specific keys of the dictionary are different, depending on the module that was invoked.

Unfortunately, the official Ansible module documentation doesn't contain information about what the return values look like for each module. The module docs do often contain examples that use the `register` clause, which can be helpful. I've found the simplest way to find out what a module returns is to register a variable and then output that variable with the debug module.

Let's say we run the playbook shown in Example 4-3.

Example 4-3. whoami.yml

```
- name: show return value of command module
  hosts: server1
  tasks:
    - name: capture output of id command
      command: id -un
      register: login
    - debug: var=login
```

The output of the debug module looks like this:

```
TASK: [debug var=login] ******************************************************
ok: [server1] => {
    "login": {
        "changed": true, ❶
        "cmd": [ ❷
            "id",
            "-un"
        ],
        "delta": "0:00:00.002180",
        "end": "2015-01-11 15:57:19.193699",
        "invocation": {
            "module_args": "id -un",
            "module_name": "command"
        },
        "rc": 0, ❸
        "start": "2015-01-11 15:57:19.191519",
        "stderr": "", ❹
        "stdout": "vagrant", ❺
        "stdout_lines": [ ❻
            "vagrant"
        ],
        "warnings": []
    }
}
```

❶ The changed key is present in the return value of all Ansible modules, and Ansible uses it to determine whether a state change has occurred. For the command and shell module, this will always be set to true unless overridden with the changed_when clause, which we cover in Chapter 8.

❷ The cmd key contains the invoked command as a list of strings.

❸ The `rc` key contains the return code. If it is nonzero, Ansible will assume the task failed to execute.

❹ The `stderr` key contains any text written to standard error, as a single string.

❺ The `stdout` key contains any text written to standard out, as a single string.

❻ The `stdout_lines` key contains any text written to split by newline. It is a list, and each element of the list is a line of output.

If you're using the `register` clause with the `command` module, you'll likely want access to the `stdout` key, as shown in Example 4-4.

Example 4-4. Using the output of a command in a task

```
- name: capture output of id command
  command: id -un
  register: login
- debug: msg="Logged in as user {{ login.stdout }}"
```

Sometimes it's useful to do something with the output of a failed task. However, if the task fails, Ansible will stop executing tasks for the failed host. We can use the `ignore_errors` clause, as shown in Example 4-5, so Ansible does not stop on the error.

Example 4-5. Ignoring when a module returns an error

```
- name: Run myprog
  command: /opt/myprog
  register: result
  ignore_errors: True
- debug: var=result
```

The `shell` module has the same output structure as the `command` module, but other modules contain different keys. Example 4-6 shows the output of the `apt` module when installing a package that wasn't present before.

Example 4-6. Output of apt module when installing a new package

```
ok: [server1] => {
    "result": {
        "changed": true,
        "invocation": {
            "module_args": "name=nginx",
            "module_name": "apt"
        },
```

```
            "stderr": "",
            "stdout": "Reading package lists...\nBuilding dependency tree...",
            "stdout_lines": [
                "Reading package lists...",
                "Building dependency tree...",
                "Reading state information...",
                "Preparing to unpack .../nginx-common_1.4.6-1ubuntu3.1_all.deb ...",
                ...
                "Setting up nginx-core (1.4.6-1ubuntu3.1) ...",
                "Setting up nginx (1.4.6-1ubuntu3.1) ...",
                "Processing triggers for libc-bin (2.19-0ubuntu6.3) ..."
            ]
        }
    }
}
```

Accessing Dictionary Keys in a Variable

If a variable contains a dictionary, you can access the keys of the dictionary by using
either a dot (.) or a subscript ([]). Example 4-4 has a variable reference that uses dot
notation:

```
{{ login.stdout }}
```

We could have used subscript notation instead:

```
{{ login['stdout'] }}
```

This rule applies to multiple dereferences, so all of the following are equivalent:

```
ansible_eth1['ipv4']['address']
ansible_eth1['ipv4'].address
ansible_eth1.ipv4['address']
ansible_eth1.ipv4.address
```

I generally prefer dot notation, unless the key is a string that contains a character
that's not allowed as a variable name, such as a dot, space, or hyphen.

Ansible uses Jinja2 to implement variable dereferencing, so for more details on this
topic, see the Jinja2 documentation on variables (*http://jinja.pocoo.org/docs/dev/
templates/#variables*).

Example 4-7 shows the output of the apt module when the package is already present
on the host.

Example 4-7. Output of apt module when package already present

```
ok: [server1] => {
    "result": {
        "changed": false,
        "invocation": {
```

```
            "module_args": "name=nginx",
            "module_name": "apt"
        }
    }
}
```

Note that the stdout, stderr, and stdout_lines keys are present in the output only when the package was not previously installed.

 If your playbooks use registered variables, make sure you know the content of those variables, both for cases where the module changes the host's state and for when the module doesn't change the host's state. Otherwise, your playbook might fail when it tries to access a key in a registered variable that doesn't exist.

Facts

As you've already seen, when Ansible runs a playbook, before the first task runs, this happens:

```
GATHERING FACTS ***************************************************
ok: [servername]
```

When Ansible gathers facts, it connects to the host and queries it for all kinds of details about the host: CPU architecture, operating system, IP addresses, memory info, disk info, and more. This information is stored in variables that are called *facts*, and they behave just like any other variable.

Here's a simple playbook that prints out the operating system of each server:

```
- name: print out operating system
  hosts: all
  gather_facts: True
  tasks:
  - debug: var=ansible_distribution
```

Here's what the output looks like for servers running Ubuntu and CentOS:

```
PLAY [print out operating system] *******************************************

GATHERING FACTS *************************************************************
ok: [server1]
ok: [server2]

TASK: [debug var=ansible_distribution] **************************************
ok: [server1] => {
    "ansible_distribution": "Ubuntu"
}
ok: [server2] => {
    "ansible_distribution": "CentOS"
```

```
    }

PLAY RECAP *********************************************************************
server1                     : ok=2   changed=0   unreachable=0   failed=0
server2                     : ok=2   changed=0   unreachable=0   failed=0
```

You can consult the official Ansible documentation (*http://bit.ly/1G9pVfx*) for a list of some of the available facts. I maintain a more comprehensive list of facts on GitHub (*http://bit.ly/1G9pX7a*).

Viewing All Facts Associated with a Server

Ansible implements fact collecting through the use of a special module called the `setup` module. You don't need to call this module in your playbooks because Ansible does that automatically when it gathers facts. However, if you invoke it manually with the `ansible` command-line tool, like this:

```
$ ansible server1 -m setup
```

then Ansible will output all of the facts, as shown in Example 4-8.

Example 4-8. Output of setup module

```
server1 | success >> {
    "ansible_facts": {
        "ansible_all_ipv4_addresses": [
            "10.0.2.15",
            "192.168.4.10"
        ],
        "ansible_all_ipv6_addresses": [
            "fe80::a00:27ff:fefe:1e4d",
            "fe80::a00:27ff:fe67:bbf3"
        ],
(many more facts)
```

Note that the returned value is a dictionary whose key is `ansible_facts` and whose value is a dictionary that contains the name and value of the actual facts.

Viewing a Subset of Facts

Because Ansible collects many facts, the `setup` module supports a `filter` parameter that lets you filter by fact name by specifying a glob.[1] For example:

```
$ ansible web -m setup -a 'filter=ansible_eth*'
```

The output looks like this:

---

1 A *glob* is what shells use to match file patterns (e.g., `*.txt`).

```
web | success >> {
    "ansible_facts": {
        "ansible_eth0": {
            "active": true,
            "device": "eth0",
            "ipv4": {
                "address": "10.0.2.15",
                "netmask": "255.255.255.0",
                "network": "10.0.2.0"
            },
            "ipv6": [
                {
                    "address": "fe80::a00:27ff:fefe:1e4d",
                    "prefix": "64",
                    "scope": "link"
                }
            ],
            "macaddress": "08:00:27:fe:1e:4d",
            "module": "e1000",
            "mtu": 1500,
            "promisc": false,
            "type": "ether"
        },
        "ansible_eth1": {
            "active": true,
            "device": "eth1",
            "ipv4": {
                "address": "192.168.33.10",
                "netmask": "255.255.255.0",
                "network": "192.168.33.0"
            },
            "ipv6": [
                {
                    "address": "fe80::a00:27ff:fe23:ae8e",
                    "prefix": "64",
                    "scope": "link"
                }
            ],
            "macaddress": "08:00:27:23:ae:8e",
            "module": "e1000",
            "mtu": 1500,
            "promisc": false,
            "type": "ether"
        }
    },
    "changed": false
}
```

Any Module Can Return Facts

If you look closely at Example 4-8, you'll see that the output is a dictionary whose key is ansible_facts. The use of ansible_facts in the return value is an Ansible idiom.

If a module returns a dictionary that contains `ansible_facts` as a key, Ansible will create variable names in the environment with those values and associate them with the active host.

For modules that return facts, there's no need to register variables, since Ansible creates these variables for you automatically. For example, the following tasks use the `ec2_facts` module to retrieve Amazon EC2[2] facts about a server and then print out the instance ID:

```
- name: get ec2 facts
  ec2_facts:

- debug: var=ansible_ec2_instance_id
```

The output looks like this.

```
TASK: [debug var=ansible_ec2_instance_id] *************************************
ok: [myserver] => {
    "ansible_ec2_instance_id": "i-a3a2f866"
}
```

Note that we do not need to use the `register` keyword when invoking `ec2_facts`, since the returned values are facts. Several modules ship with Ansible that return facts. You'll see another one of them, the `docker` module, in Chapter 15.

Local Facts

Ansible provides an additional mechanism for associating facts with a host. You can place one or more files on the remote host machine in the */etc/ansible/facts.d* directory. Ansible will recognize the file if it's any of the following:

- In *.ini* format
- In JSON format
- An executable that takes no arguments and outputs JSON on standard out

These facts are available as keys of a special variable named `ansible_local`.

For instance, Example 4-9 shows a fact file in *.ini* format.

Example 4-9. /etc/ansible/facts.d/example.fact

```
[book]
title=Ansible: Up and Running
author=Lorin Hochstein
publisher=O'Reilly Media
```

---

2 We'll cover Amazon EC2 in more detail in Chapter 14.

If we copy this file to */etc/ansible/facts.d/example.fact* on the remote host, we can access the contents of the `ansible_local` variable in a playbook:

```
- name: print ansible_local
  debug: var=ansible_local
- name: print book title
  debug: msg="The title of the book is {{ ansible_local.example.book.title }}"
```

The output of these tasks looks like this:

```
TASK: [print ansible_local] **************************************************
ok: [server1] => {
    "ansible_local": {
        "example": {
            "book": {
                "author": "Lorin Hochstein",
                "publisher": "O'Reilly Media",
                "title": "Ansible: Up and Running"
            }
        }
    }
}

TASK: [print book title] *****************************************************
ok: [server1] => {
    "msg": "The title of the book is Ansible: Up and Running"
}
```

Note the structure of value in the `ansible_local` variable. Because the fact file is named *example.fact*, the `ansible_local` variable is a dictionary that contains a key named `example`.

Using set_fact to Define a New Variable

Ansible also allows you to set a fact (effectively the same as defining a new variable) in a task by using the `set_fact` module. I often like to use `set_fact` immediately after `register` to make it simpler to refer to a variable. Example 4-10 demonstrates how to use `set_fact` so that a variable can be referred to as `snap` instead of `snap_result.stdout`.

Example 4-10. Using set_fact to simplify variable reference

```
- name: get snapshot id
  shell: >
    aws ec2 describe-snapshots --filters
    Name=tag:Name,Values=my-snapshot
    | jq --raw-output ".Snapshots[].SnapshotId"
  register: snap_result

- set_fact: snap={{ snap_result.stdout }}
```

```
- name: delete old snapshot
  command: aws ec2 delete-snapshot --snapshot-id "{{ snap }}"
```

Built-in Variables

Ansible defines several variables that are always available in a playbook; some of these variables are shown in Table 4-1.

Table 4-1. Built-in variables

Parameter	Description
hostvars	A dict whose keys are Ansible hostnames and values are dicts that map variable names to values
inventory_hostname	Fully qualified domain name of the current host as known by Ansible (e.g., `myhost.example.com`)
inventory_hostname_short	Name of the current host as known by Ansible, without the domain name (e.g., `myhost`)
group_names	A list of all groups that the current host is a member of
groups	A dict whose keys are Ansible group names and values are a list of hostnames that are members of the group. Includes `all` and `ungrouped` groups: `{"all": [...], "web": [...], "ungrouped": [...]}`
ansible_check_mode	A boolean that is true when running in check mode (see "Check Mode" on page 313)
ansible_play_batch	A list of the inventory hostnames that are active in the current batch (see "Running on a Batch of Hosts at a Time" on page 175)
ansible_play_hosts	A list of all of the inventory hostnames that are active in the current play
ansible_version	A dict with Ansible version info: `{"full": 2.3.1.0", "major": 2, "minor": 3, "revision": 1, "string": "2.3.1.0"}`

The `hostvars`, `inventory_hostname`, and `groups` variables merit some additional discussion.

hostvars

In Ansible, variables are scoped by host. It only makes sense to talk about the value of a variable relative to a given host.

The idea that variables are relative to a given host might sound confusing, since Ansible allows you to define variables on a group of hosts. For example, if you define a variable in the `vars` section of a play, you are defining the variable for the set of hosts in the play. But what Ansible is really doing is creating a copy of that variable for each host in the group.

Sometimes, a task that's running on one host needs the value of a variable defined on another host. Say you need to create a configuration file on web servers that contains the IP address of the *eth1* interface of the database server, and you don't know in advance what this IP address is. This IP address is available as the *ansible_eth1.ipv4.address* fact for the database server.

The solution is to use the `hostvars` variable. This is a dictionary that contains all of the variables defined on all of the hosts, keyed by the hostname as known to Ansible. If Ansible has not yet gathered facts on a host, you will not be able to access its facts by using the `hostvars` variable, unless fact caching is enabled.[3]

Continuing our example, if our database server is *db.example.com*, then we could put the following in a configuration template:

```
{{ hostvars['db.example.com'].ansible_eth1.ipv4.address }}
```

This evaluates to the *ansible_eth1.ipv4.address* fact associated with the host named *db.example.com*.

inventory_hostname

The `inventory_hostname` is the hostname of the current host, as known by Ansible. If you have defined an alias for a host, this is the alias name. For example, if your inventory contains a line like this:

```
server1 ansible_host=192.168.4.10
```

then `inventory_hostname` would be `server1`.

You can output all of the variables associated with the current host with the help of the `hostvars` and `inventory_hostname` variables:

```
- debug: var=hostvars[inventory_hostname]
```

Groups

The `groups` variable can be useful when you need to access variables for a group of hosts. Let's say we are configuring a load-balancing host, and our configuration file needs the IP addresses of all of the servers in our web group. Our configuration file contains a fragment that looks like this:

```
backend web-backend
{% for host in groups.web %}
  server {{ hostvars[host].inventory_hostname }} \
  {{ hostvars[host].ansible_default_ipv4.address }}:80
{% endfor %}
```

---

3 See Chapter 11 for information about fact caching.

The generated file looks like this:

```
backend web-backend
    server georgia.example.com 203.0.113.15:80
    server newhampshire.example.com 203.0.113.25:80
    server newjersey.example.com 203.0.113.38:80
```

Setting Variables on the Command Line

Variables set by passing `-e var=value` to `ansible-playbook` have the highest precedence, which means you can use this to override variables that are already defined. Example 4-11 shows how to set the variable named `token` to the value `12345`.

Example 4-11. Setting a variable from the command line

```
$ ansible-playbook example.yml -e token=12345
```

Use the `ansible-playbook -e var=value` method when you want to use a playbook as you would a shell script that takes a command-line argument. The `-e` flag effectively allows you to pass variables as arguments.

Example 4-12 shows a very simple playbook that outputs a message specified by a variable.

Example 4-12. greet.yml

```
- name: pass a message on the command line
  hosts: localhost
  vars:
    greeting: "you didn't specify a message"
  tasks:
    - name: output a message
      debug: msg="{{ greeting }}"
```

If we invoke it like this:

```
$ ansible-playbook greet.yml -e greeting=hiya
```

then the output looks like this:

```
PLAY [pass a message on the command line] ************************************

TASK: [output a message] ****************************************************
ok: [localhost] => {
    "msg": "hiya"
}

PLAY RECAP ******************************************************************
localhost                  : ok=1    changed=0    unreachable=0    failed=0
```

If you want to put a space in the variable, you need to use quotes like this:

```
$ ansible-playbook greet.yml -e 'greeting="hi there"'
```

You have to put single quotes around the entire `'greeting="hi there"'` so that the shell interprets that as a single argument to pass to Ansible, and you have to put double quotes around `"hi there"` so that Ansible treats that message as a single string.

Ansible also allows you to pass a file containing the variables instead of passing them directly on the command line by passing `@filename.yml` as the argument to `-e`; for example, say we have a file that looks like Example 4-13.

Example 4-13. greetvars.yml

```
greeting: hiya
```

Then we can pass this file to the command line like this:

```
$ ansible-playbook greet.yml -e @greetvars.yml
```

Precedence

We've covered several ways of defining variables, and it can happen that you define the same variable multiple times for a host, using different values. Avoid this when you can, but if you can't, then keep in mind Ansible's precedence rules. When the same variable is defined in multiple ways, the precedence rules determine which value wins.

The basic rules of precedence are as follows:

1. (Highest) `ansible-playbook -e var=value`
2. Task variables
3. Block variables
4. Role and include variables
5. `set_fact`
6. Registered variables
7. `vars_files`
8. `vars_prompt`
9. Play variables
10. Host facts
11. `host_vars` set on a playbook
12. `group_vars` set on a playbook

13. `host_vars` set in the inventory

14. `group_vars` set in the inventory

15. Inventory variables

16. In *defaults/main.yml* of a role[4]

In this chapter, we covered various ways to define and access variables and facts. The next chapter focuses on a realistic example of deploying an application.

---

4 We'll discuss roles in Chapter 7.

## CHAPTER 5

Introducing Mezzanine: Our Test Application

Chapter 2 covered the basics of writing playbooks. But real life is always messier than introductory chapters of programming books, so in this chapter we're going to work through a complete example of deploying a nontrivial application.

Our example application is an open source content management system (CMS) called Mezzanine (*http://mezzanine.jupo.org*), which is similar in spirit to WordPress. Mezzanine is built on top of Django, the free Python-based framework for writing web applications.

Why Deploying to Production Is Complicated

Let's take a little detour and talk about the differences between running software in development mode on your laptop versus running the software in production. Mezzanine is a great example of an application that is much easier to run in development mode than it is to deploy. Example 5-1 shows all you need to do to get Mezzanine running on your laptop.[1]

Example 5-1. Running Mezzanine in development mode

```
$ virtualenv venv
$ source venv/bin/activate
$ pip install mezzanine
$ mezzanine-project myproject
```

---

[1] This installs the Python packages into a virtualenv. We cover virtualenvs in "Installing Mezzanine and Other Packages into a virtualenv" on page 102.

```
$ cd myproject
$ sed -i.bak 's/ALLOWED_HOSTS = \[\]/ALLOWED_HOSTS = ["127.0.0.1"]/' myproject\
/settings.py
$ python manage.py createdb
$ python manage.py runserver
```

You'll be prompted to answer several questions. I answered "yes" to each yes/no question, and accepted the default answer whenever one was available. This was what my interaction looked like:

```
Operations to perform:
  Apply all migrations: admin, auth, blog, conf, contenttypes, core,
  django_comments, forms, galleries, generic, pages, redirects, sessions, sites,
  twitter
Running migrations:
  Applying contenttypes.0001_initial... OK
  Applying auth.0001_initial... OK
  Applying admin.0001_initial... OK
  Applying admin.0002_logentry_remove_auto_add... OK
  Applying contenttypes.0002_remove_content_type_name... OK
  Applying auth.0002_alter_permission_name_max_length... OK
  Applying auth.0003_alter_user_email_max_length... OK
  Applying auth.0004_alter_user_username_opts... OK
  Applying auth.0005_alter_user_last_login_null... OK
  Applying auth.0006_require_contenttypes_0002... OK
  Applying auth.0007_alter_validators_add_error_messages... OK
  Applying auth.0008_alter_user_username_max_length... OK
  Applying sites.0001_initial... OK
  Applying blog.0001_initial... OK
  Applying blog.0002_auto_20150527_1555... OK
  Applying conf.0001_initial... OK
  Applying core.0001_initial... OK
  Applying core.0002_auto_20150414_2140... OK
  Applying django_comments.0001_initial... OK
  Applying django_comments.0002_update_user_email_field_length... OK
  Applying django_comments.0003_add_submit_date_index... OK
  Applying pages.0001_initial... OK
  Applying forms.0001_initial... OK
  Applying forms.0002_auto_20141227_0224... OK
  Applying forms.0003_emailfield... OK
  Applying forms.0004_auto_20150517_0510... OK
  Applying forms.0005_auto_20151026_1600... OK
  Applying galleries.0001_initial... OK
  Applying galleries.0002_auto_20141227_0224... OK
  Applying generic.0001_initial... OK
  Applying generic.0002_auto_20141227_0224... OK
  Applying pages.0002_auto_20141227_0224... OK
  Applying pages.0003_auto_20150527_1555... OK
  Applying redirects.0001_initial... OK
  Applying sessions.0001_initial... OK
  Applying sites.0002_alter_domain_unique... OK
  Applying twitter.0001_initial... OK
```

```
A site record is required.
Please enter the domain and optional port in the format 'domain:port'.
For example 'localhost:8000' or 'www.example.com'.
Hit enter to use the default (127.0.0.1:8000):

Creating default site record: 127.0.0.1:8000 ...


Creating default account ...

Username (leave blank to use 'lorin'):
Email address: lorin@ansiblebook.com
Password:
Password (again):
Superuser created successfully.
Installed 2 object(s) from 1 fixture(s)

Would you like to install some initial demo pages?
Eg: About us, Contact form, Gallery. (yes/no): yes
```

You should eventually see output on the terminal that looks like this:

```
                   .....
           _d^^^^^^^^^b_
        .d''           ``b.
      .p'                 `q.
     .d'                    `b.
    .d'                      `b.   * Mezzanine 4.2.2
    ::                        ::   * Django 1.10.2
    ::    M E Z Z A N I N E   ::   * Python 3.5.2
    ::                        ::   * SQLite 3.14.1
    `p.                      .q'   * Darwin 16.0.0
     `p.                    .q'
      `b.                  .d'
       `q..              ..p'
         ^q........p^
            ''''
```

```
Performing system checks...

System check identified no issues (0 silenced).
October 04, 2016 - 04:57:44
Django version 1.10.2, using settings 'myproject.settings'
Starting development server at http://127.0.0.1:8000/
Quit the server with CONTROL-C.
```

If you point your browser to *http://127.0.0.1:8000/*, you should see a web page that looks like Figure 5-1.

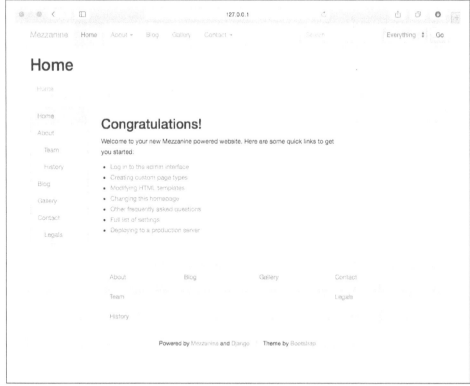

Figure 5-1. Mezzanine after a fresh install

Deploying this application to production is another matter. When you run the `mezzanine-project` command, Mezzanine will generate a Fabric (*http://www.fabfile.org*) deployment script at *myproject/fabfile.py* that you can use to deploy your project to a production server. (Fabric is a Python-based tool that helps automate running tasks via SSH.) The script is almost 700 lines long, and that's not counting the included configuration files that are also involved in deployment. Why is deploying to production so much more complex? I'm glad you asked.

When run in development, Mezzanine provides the following simplifications (see Figure 5-2):

- The system uses SQLite as the backend database, and will create the database file if it doesn't exist.
- The development HTTP server serves up both the static content (images, *.css* files, JavaScript) as well as the dynamically generated HTML.
- The development HTTP server uses the (insecure) HTTP, not (secure) HTTPS.

- The development HTTP server process runs in the foreground, taking over your terminal window.
- The hostname for the HTTP server is always 127.0.0.1 (`localhost`).

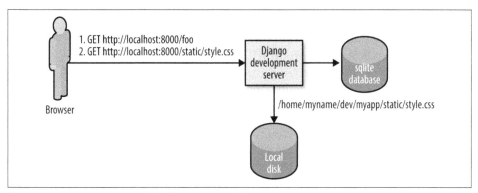

Figure 5-2. Django app in development mode

Now, let's look at what happens when you deploy to production.

PostgreSQL: The Database

SQLite is a serverless database. In production, we want to run a server-based database, because those have better support for multiple, concurrent requests, and server-based databases allow us to run multiple HTTP servers for load balancing. This means we need to deploy a database management system such as MySQL or PostgreSQL (aka Postgres). Setting up one of these database servers requires more work. We need to do the following:

1. Install the database software.
2. Ensure the database service is running.
3. Create the database inside the database management system.
4. Create a database user who has the appropriate permissions for the database system.
5. Configure our Mezzanine application with the database user credentials and connection information.

Gunicorn: The Application Server

Because Mezzanine is a Django-based application, you can run Mezzanine using Django's HTTP server, referred as the *development server* in the Django documentation. Here's what the Django 1.10 docs have to say about the development server (*http://bit.ly/2cPe8X8*).

> [D]on't use this server in anything resembling a production environment. It's intended only for use while developing. (We're in the business of making Web frameworks, not Web servers.)

Django implements the standard Web Server Gateway Interface (WSGI),[2] so any Python HTTP server that supports WSGI is suitable for running a Django application such as Mezzanine. We'll use Gunicorn, one of the most popular HTTP WSGI servers, which is what the Mezzanine deploy script uses.

Nginx: The Web Server

Gunicorn will execute our Django application, just like the development server does. However, Gunicorn won't serve any of the static assets associated with the application. *Static assets* are files such as images, *.css* files, and JavaScript files. They are called static because they never change, in contrast with the dynamically generated web pages that Gunicorn serves up.

Although Gunicorn can handle TLS encryption, it's common to configure Nginx to handle the encryption.[3]

We're going to use Nginx as our web server for serving static assets and for handling the TLS encryption, as shown in Figure 5-3.

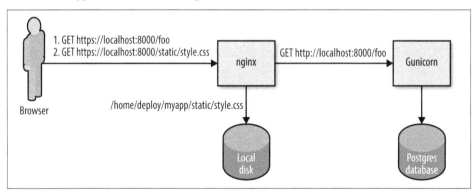

Figure 5-3. Nginx as a reverse proxy

---

2 The WSGI protocol is documented in Python Enhancement Proposal (PEP) 3333 (*https://www.python.org/dev/peps/pep-3333*).

3 Gunicorn 0.17 added support for TLS encryption. Before that, you had to use a separate application such as Nginx to handle the encryption.

We need to configure Nginx as a *reverse proxy* for Gunicorn. If the request is for a static asset, such as a *.css* file, Nginx will serve that file directly from the local filesystem. Otherwise, Nginx will proxy the request to Gunicorn, by making an HTTP request against the Gunicorn service that is running on the local machine. Nginx uses the URL to determine whether to serve a local file or proxy the request to Gunicorn. Note that requests to Nginx will be (encrypted) HTTPS, and all requests that Nginx proxies to Gunicorn will be (unencrypted) HTTP.

Supervisor: The Process Manager

When we run in development mode, we run the application server in the foreground of our terminal. If we were to close our terminal, the program would terminate. For a server application, we need it to run as a background process so it doesn't terminate, even if we close the terminal session we used to start the process.

The colloquial terms for such a process are *daemon* or *service*. We need to run Gunicorn as a daemon, and we'd like to be able to easily stop it and restart it. Numerous service managers can do this job. We're going to use Supervisor, because that's what the Mezzanine deployment scripts use.

At this point, you should have a sense of the steps involved in deploying a web application to production. We'll go over how to implement this deployment with Ansible in Chapter 6.

Deploying Mezzanine with Ansible

It's time to write an Ansible playbook to deploy Mezzanine to a server. We'll go through it step by step, but if you're the type of person who starts off by reading the last page of a book to see how it ends,[1] you can find the full playbook at the end of this chapter as Example 6-28. It's also available on GitHub (*http://bit.ly/19P0OAj*). Check out the README file (*http://bit.ly/1Onko4u*) before trying to run it directly.

I've tried to hew as closely as possible to the original Fabric scripts that Mezzanine author Stephen McDonald wrote.[2]

Listing Tasks in a Playbook

Before we dive into the guts of our playbook, let's get a high-level view. The `ansible-playbook` command-line tool supports a flag called `--list-tasks`. This flag prints out the names of all the tasks in a playbook. It's a handy way to summarize what a playbook is going to do. Here's how you use it:

```
$ ansible-playbook --list-tasks mezzanine.yml
```

Example 6-1 shows the output for the *mezzanine.yml* playbook in Example 6-28.

---

1 My wife, Stacy, is notorious for doing this.

2 You can find the Fabric scripts that ship with Mezzanine on GitHub (*http://bit.ly/19P0T73*).

Example 6-1. List of tasks in Mezzanine playbook

```
playbook: mezzanine.yml

  play #1 (web): Deploy mezzanine       TAGS: []
    tasks:
      install apt packages      TAGS: []
      create project path       TAGS: []
      create a logs directory   TAGS: []
      check out the repository on the host      TAGS: []
      install Python requirements globally via pip       TAGS: []
      create project locale     TAGS: []
      create a DB user  TAGS: []
      create the database       TAGS: []
      ensure config path exists TAGS: []
      create tls certificates   TAGS: []
      remove the default nginx config file      TAGS: []
      set the nginx config file TAGS: []
      enable the nginx config file      TAGS: []
      set the supervisor config file    TAGS: []
      install poll twitter cron job     TAGS: []
      set the gunicorn config file      TAGS: []
      generate the settings file        TAGS: []
      install requirements.txt  TAGS: []
      install required python packages  TAGS: []
      apply migrations to create the database, collect static content   TAGS: []
      set the site id   TAGS: []
      set the admin password    TAGS: []
```

Organization of Deployed Files

As we discussed earlier, Mezzanine is built atop Django. In Django, a web app is called a *project*. We get to choose what to name our project, and I've chosen to name it *mezzanine_example*.

Our playbook deploys into a Vagrant machine, and will deploy the files into the home directory of the Vagrant user's account.

Example 6-2 shows the relevant directories underneath */home/vagrant*:

- */home/vagrant/mezzanine/mezzanine-example* will contain the source code that will be cloned from a source code repository on GitHub.

- */home/vagrant/.virtualenvs/mezzanine_example* is the virtualenv directory, which means that we're going to install all of the Python packages into that directory.

- */home/vagrant/logs* will contain log files generated by Mezzanine.

Example 6-2. Directory structure under /home/vagrant

```
.
├── logs
├── mezzanine
│   └── mezzanine_example
└── .virtualenvs
    └── mezzanine_example
```

Variables and Secret Variables

As you can see in Example 6-3, this playbook defines quite a few variables.

Example 6-3. Defining the variables

```
vars:
  user: "{{ ansible_user }}"
  proj_app: mezzanine_example
  proj_name: "{{ proj_app }}"
  venv_home: "{{ ansible_env.HOME }}/.virtualenvs"
  venv_path: "{{ venv_home }}/{{ proj_name }}"
  proj_path: "{{ ansible_env.HOME }}/mezzanine/{{ proj_name }}"
  settings_path: "{{ proj_path }}/{{ proj_name }}"
  reqs_path: requirements.txt
  manage: "{{ python }} {{ proj_path }}/manage.py"
  live_hostname: 192.168.33.10.xip.io
  domains:
    - 192.168.33.10.xip.io
    - www.192.168.33.10.xip.io
  repo_url: git@github.com:ansiblebook/mezzanine_example.git
  locale: en_US.UTF-8
  # Variables below don't appear in Mezzanine's fabfile.py
  # but I've added them for convenience
  conf_path: /etc/nginx/conf
  tls_enabled: True
  python: "{{ venv_path }}/bin/python"
  database_name: "{{ proj_name }}"
  database_user: "{{ proj_name }}"
  database_host: localhost
  database_port: 5432
  gunicorn_procname: gunicorn_mezzanine
  num_workers: "multiprocessing.cpu_count() * 2 + 1"
vars_files:
  - secrets.yml
```

I've tried for the most part to use the same variable names that the Mezzanine Fabric script uses. I've also added some extra variables to make things a little clearer. For example, the Fabric scripts directly use `proj_name` as the database name and database username. I prefer to define intermediate variables named `database_name` and `data base_user` and define these in terms of `proj_name`.

It's worth noting a few things here. First off, we can define one variable in terms of another. For example, we define `venv_path` in terms of `venv_home` and `proj_name`.

Also, note how we can reference Ansible facts in these variables. For example, `venv_home` is defined in terms of the `ansible_env` fact collected from each host.

Finally, note that we have specified some of our variables in a separate file, called *secrets.yml*, by doing this:

```
vars_files:
  - secrets.yml
```

This file contains credentials such as passwords and tokens that need to remain private. The repository on GitHub does not actually contain this file. Instead, it contains a file called *secrets.yml.example* that looks like this:

```
db_pass: e79c9761d0b54698a83ff3f93769e309
admin_pass: 46041386be534591ad24902bf72071B
secret_key: b495a05c396843b6b47ac944a72c92ed
nevercache_key: b5d87bb4e17c483093296fa321056bdc
# You need to create a Twitter application at https://dev.twitter.com
# in order to get the credentials required for Mezzanine's
# twitter integration.
#
# See http://mezzanine.jupo.org/docs/twitter-integration.html
# for details on Twitter integration
twitter_access_token_key: 80b557a3a8d14cb7a2b91d60398fb8ce
twitter_access_token_secret: 1974cf8419114bdd9d4ea3db7a210d90
twitter_consumer_key: 1f1c627530b34bb58701ac81ac3fad51
twitter_consumer_secret: 36515c2b60ee4ffb9d33d972a7ec350a
```

To use this repo, you need to copy *secrets.yml.example* to *secrets.yml* and edit it so that it contains the credentials specific to your site. Also note that *secrets.yml* is included in the *.gitignore* file in the Git repository to prevent someone from accidentally committing these credentials.

It's best to avoid committing unencrypted credentials into your version-control repository because of the security risks involved. This is just one possible strategy for maintaining secret credentials. We also could have passed them as environment variables. Another option, which we will describe in Chapter 8, is to commit an encrypted version of the *secrets.yml* file by using Ansible's `vault` functionality.

Using Iteration (with_items) to Install Multiple Packages

We're going to need two types of packages for our Mezzanine deployment. We need to install some system-level packages, and because we're going to deploy on Ubuntu, we use apt as our package manager for the system packages. We also need to install some Python packages, and we'll use pip to install the Python packages.

System-level packages are generally easier to deal with than Python packages, because system-level packages are designed specifically to work with the operating system. However, the system package repositories often don't have the newest versions of the Python libraries we need, so we turn to the Python packages to install those. It's a trade-off between stability and running the latest and greatest.

Example 6-4 shows the task we'll use to install the system packages.

Example 6-4. Installing system packages

```
- name: install apt packages
  apt: pkg={{ item }} update_cache=yes cache_valid_time=3600
  become: True
  with_items:
    - git
    - libjpeg-dev
    - libpq-dev
    - memcached
    - nginx
    - postgresql
    - python-dev
    - python-pip
    - python-psycopg2
    - python-setuptools
    - python-virtualenv
    - supervisor
```

Because we're installing multiple packages, we use Ansible's iteration functionality, the with_items clause. We could have installed the packages one at a time, like this:

```
- name: install git
  apt: pkg=git

- name: install libjpeg-dev
  apt: pkg=libjpeg-dev
...
```

However, it's easier to write the playbook if we group the packages in a list. When we invoke the apt module, we pass it {{ item }}. This is a placeholder variable that will be populated by each of the elements in the list of the with_items clause.

> By default, Ansible uses item as the name of the loop iteration variable. In Chapter 8, we'll show how to change this variable name.

In addition, the `apt` module contains an optimization making it more efficient to install multiple packages by using the `with_items` clause. Ansible will pass the entire list of packages to the `apt` module, and the module will invoke the apt program only once, passing it the entire list of packages to be installed. Some modules, like `apt`, have been designed to handle lists intelligently like this. If a module doesn't have native support for lists, Ansible will simply invoke the module multiple times, once for each element of the list.

You can tell that the `apt` module is intelligent enough to handle multiple packages at once, because the output looks like this:

```
TASK: [install apt packages] **************************************************
ok: [web] => (item=[u'git', u'libjpeg-dev', u'libpq-dev', u'memcached',
u'nginx', u'postgresql', u'python-dev', u'python-pip', u'python-psycopg2',
u'python-setuptools', u'python-virtualenv', u'supervisor'])
```

On the other hand, the `pip` module does not handle lists intelligently, so Ansible must invoke it once for each element of the list, and the output looks like this:

```
TASK [install required python packages] ****************************************
ok: [web] => (item=gunicorn)
ok: [web] => (item=setproctitle)
ok: [web] => (item=psycopg2)
ok: [web] => (item=django-compressor)
ok: [web] => (item=python-memcached)
```

Adding the Become Clause to a Task

In the playbook examples of Chapter 2, we wanted the whole playbook to run as root, so we added the `become: True` clause to the play. When we deploy Mezzanine, most of the tasks will be run as the user who is SSHing to the host, rather than root. Therefore, we don't want to run as root for the entire play, only for select tasks.

We can accomplish this by adding `become: True` to the tasks that do need to run as root, such as Example 6-4.

Updating the Apt Cache

 All of the example commands in this subsection are run on the (Ubuntu) remote host, not the control machine.

Ubuntu maintains a cache with the names of all of the *apt* packages that are available in the Ubuntu package archive. Let's say you try to install the package named *libssl-dev*. We can use the `apt-cache` program to query the local cache to see what version it knows about:

```
$ apt-cache policy libssl-dev
```

The output is shown in Example 6-5.

Example 6-5. apt-cache output

```
libssl-dev:
  Installed: (none)
  Candidate: 1.0.1f-1ubuntu2.21
  Version table:
     1.0.1f-1ubuntu2.21 0
        500 http://archive.ubuntu.com/ubuntu/ trusty-updates/main amd64 Packages
        500 http://security.ubuntu.com/ubuntu/ trusty-security/main amd64 Packages
     1.0.1f-1ubuntu2 0
        500 http://archive.ubuntu.com/ubuntu/ trusty/main amd64 Packages
```

As we can see, this package is not installed locally. According to the local cache, the latest version is 1.0.1f-1ubuntu2.21. We also see some information about the location of the package archive.

In some cases, when the Ubuntu project releases a new version of a package, it removes the old version from the package archive. If the local apt cache of an Ubuntu server hasn't been updated, then it will attempt to install a package that doesn't exist in the package archive.

To continue with our example, let's say we attempt to install the *libssl-dev* package:

```
$ apt-get install libssl-dev
```

If version 1.0.1f-1ubuntu2.21 is no longer available in the package archive, we'll see the following error:

```
Err http://archive.ubuntu.com/ubuntu/ trusty-updates/main libssl-dev amd64
1.0.1f-1ubuntu2.21
  404  Not Found [IP: 91.189.88.153 80]
Err http://security.ubuntu.com/ubuntu/ trusty-security/main libssl-dev amd64
1.0.1f-1ubuntu2.21
  404  Not Found [IP: 91.189.88.149 80]
Err http://security.ubuntu.com/ubuntu/ trusty-security/main libssl-doc all
1.0.1f-1ubuntu2.21
  404  Not Found [IP: 91.189.88.149 80]
E: Failed to fetch
http://security.ubuntu.com/ubuntu/pool/main/o/openssl/libssl-dev_1.0.1f-1ubuntu2.
21_amd64.deb
  404  Not Found [IP: 91.189.88.149 80]
```

```
E: Failed to fetch
http://security.ubuntu.com/ubuntu/pool/main/o/openssl/libssl-doc_1.0.1f-1ubuntu2.
21_all.deb
404  Not Found [IP: 91.189.88.149 80]

E: Unable to fetch some archives, maybe run apt-get update or try with
--fix-missing?
```

On the command line, the way to bring the local apt cache up-to-date is to run `apt-get update`. When using the `apt` Ansible module, the way to bring the local apt cache up-to-date is to pass the `update_cache=yes` argument when invoking the module, as shown in Example 6-4.

Because updating the cache takes additional time, and because we might be running a playbook multiple times in quick succession in order to debug it, we can avoid paying the cache update penalty by using the `cache_valid_time` argument to the module. This instructs to update the cache only if it's older than a certain threshold. The example in Example 6-4 uses `cache_valid_time=3600`, which updates the cache only if it's older than 3,600 seconds (1 hour).

Checking Out the Project by Using Git

Although Mezzanine can be used without writing any custom code, one of its strengths is that it is written on top of the Django platform, and Django is a great web application platform if you know Python. If you just wanted a CMS, you'd likely just use something like WordPress. But if you're writing a custom application that incorporates CMS functionality, Mezzanine is a good way to go.

As part of the deployment, you need to check out the Git repository that contains your Django applications. In Django terminology, this repository must contain a *project*. I've created a repository on GitHub (*https://github.com/ansiblebook/mezzanine_example*) that contains a Django project with the expected files. That's the project that gets deployed in this playbook.

I created these files using the `mezzanine-project` program that ships with Mezzanine, like this:

```
$ mezzanine-project mezzanine_example
$ chmod +x mezzanine_example/manage.py
```

Note that I don't have any custom Django applications in my repository, just the files that are required for the project. In a real Django deployment, this repository would contain subdirectories that contain additional Django applications.

Example 6-6 shows how we use the `git` module to check out a Git repository onto a remote host.

Example 6-6. Checking out the Git repository

```
- name: check out the repository on the host
  git: repo={{ repo_url }} dest={{ proj_path }} accept_hostkey=yes
```

I've made the project repository public so that readers can access it, but in general, you'll be checking out private Git repositories over SSH. For this reason, I've set the `repo_url` variable to use the scheme that will clone the repository over SSH:

```
repo_url: git@github.com:ansiblebook/mezzanine_example.git
```

If you're following along at home, to run this playbook you must have the following:

- A GitHub account
- A public SSH key associated with your GitHub account
- An SSH agent running on your control machine, with agent forwarding enabled
- Your SSH key added to your SSH agent

Once your SSH agent is running, add your key:

```
$ ssh-add
```

If successful, the following command will output the public key of the SSH you just added:

```
$ ssh-add -l
```

The output should look like something this:

```
2048 SHA256:o7H/I9rRZupXHJ7JnDi10RhSzeAKYiRVrlH9L/JFtfA /Users/lorin/.ssh/id_rsa
```

To enable agent forwarding, add the following to your *ansible.cfg*:

```
[ssh_connection]
ssh_args = -o ControlMaster=auto -o ControlPersist=60s -o ForwardAgent=yes
```

You can verify that agent forwarding is working by using Ansible to list the known keys:

```
$ ansible web -a "ssh-add -l"
```

You should see the same output as when you run `ssh-add -l` on your local machine.

Another useful check is to verify that you can reach GitHub's SSH server:

```
$ ansible web -a "ssh -T git@github.com"
```

If successful, the output should look like this:

```
web | FAILED | rc=1 >>
Hi lorin! You've successfully authenticated, but GitHub does not provide shell
access.
```

Even though the word `FAILED` appears in the output, if the message from GitHub appears, then it was successful.

In addition to specifying the repository URL with the `repo` parameter and the destination path of the repository as the `dest` parameter, we also pass an additional parameter, `accept_hostkey`, which is related to *host-key checking*. We discuss SSH agent forwarding and host-key checking in more detail in Appendix A.

Installing Mezzanine and Other Packages into a virtualenv

As mentioned earlier in this chapter, we're going to install some of the packages as Python packages because we can get more recent versions of those than if we installed the equivalent apt package.

We can install Python packages systemwide as the root user, but it's better practice to install these packages in an isolated environment to avoid polluting the system-level Python packages. In Python, these types of isolated package environments are called *virtualenvs*. A user can create multiple virtualenvs, and can install Python packages into a virtualenv without needing root access.

Ansible's `pip` module has support for installing packages into a virtualenv and for creating the virtualenv if it is not available.

Example 6-7 shows how to use `pip` to install several packages globally. Note that this requires `become: True`.

Example 6-7. Install Python requirements

```
- name: install Python requirements globally via pip
  pip: name={{ item }} state=latest
  with_items:
    - pip
    - virtualenv
    - virtualenvwrapper
  become: True
```

Example 6-8 shows the two tasks that we use to install Python packages into the virtualenv, both of which use the `pip` module, although in different ways.

Example 6-8. Install Python packages

```
- name: install requirements.txt
  pip: requirements={{ proj_path }}/{{ reqs_path }} virtualenv={{ venv_path }}

- name: install required python packages
```

```
    pip: name={{ item }} virtualenv={{ venv_path }}
    with_items:
      - gunicorn
      - setproctitle
      - psycopg2
      - django-compressor
      - python-memcached
```

A common pattern in Python projects is to specify the package dependencies in a file called *requirements.txt*. And, indeed, the repository in our Mezzanine example contains a *requirements.txt* file. It looks like Example 6-9.

Example 6-9. requirements.txt

```
Mezzanine==4.2.2
```

The *requirements.txt* file is missing several other Python packages that we need for the deployment, so we explicitly specify these as a separate task.

Note that the Mezzanine Python package in *requirements.txt* is pinned to a specific version (4.2.2), whereas the other packages aren't pinned; we just grab the latest versions of those. If we did not want to pin Mezzanine, we simply could have added Mezzanine to the list of packages, like this:

```
    - name: install python packages
      pip: name={{ item }} virtualenv={{ venv_path }}
      with_items:
        - mezzanine
        - gunicorn
        - setproctitle
        - south
        - psycopg2
        - django-compressor
        - python-memcached
```

Alternately, if we wanted to pin all of the packages, we have several options. We could have specified all the packages in the *requirements.txt* file. This file contains information about the packages and the dependencies. An example file looks like Example 6-10.

Example 6-10. Example requirements.txt

```
beautifulsoup4==4.5.3
bleach==1.5.0
chardet==2.3.0
Django==1.10.4
django-appconf==1.0.2
django-compressor==2.1
django-contrib-comments==1.7.3
```

```
filebrowser-safe==0.4.6
future==0.16.0
grappelli-safe==0.4.5
gunicorn==19.6.0
html5lib==0.9999999
Mezzanine==4.2.2
oauthlib==2.0.1
olefile==0.43
Pillow==4.0.0
psycopg2==2.6.2
python-memcached==1.58
pytz==2016.10
rcssmin==1.0.6
requests==2.12.4
requests-oauthlib==0.7.0
rjsmin==1.0.12
setproctitle==1.1.10
six==1.10.0
tzlocal==1.3
```

If you have an existing virtualenv with the packages installed, you can use the `pip freeze` command to print out a list of installed packages. For example, if your virtualenv is in *~/mezzanine_example*, you can activate your virtualenv and print out the packages in the virtualenv like this:

```
$ source ~/mezzanine_example/bin/activate
$ pip freeze > requirements.txt
```

Example 6-11 shows how we could have installed all the packages by using a *requirements.txt* file.

Example 6-11. Installing from requirements.txt

```
- name: copy requirements.txt file
  copy: src=files/requirements.txt dest=~/requirements.txt
- name: install packages
  pip: requirements=~/requirements.txt virtualenv={{ venv_path }}
```

Alternatively, we could have specified both the package names and their versions in the list, as shown in Example 6-12. We pass a list of dictionaries, and dereference the elements with `item.name` and `item.version`.

Example 6-12. Specifying package names and version

```
- name: python packages
  pip: name={{ item.name }} version={{ item.version }} virtualenv={{ venv_path }}
  with_items:
    - {name: mezzanine, version: 4.2.2 }
    - {name: gunicorn, version: 19.6.0 }
    - {name: setproctitle, version: 1.1.10 }
```

```
- {name: psycopg2, version: 2.6.2 }
- {name: django-compressor, version: 2.1 }
- {name: python-memcached, version: 1.58 }
```

Complex Arguments in Tasks: A Brief Digression

Up until this point in the book, every time we have invoked a module, we have passed the argument as a string. Taking the pip example from Example 6-12, we passed the `pip` module a string as an argument:

```
- name: install package with pip
  pip: name={{ item.name }} version={{ item.version }} virtualenv={{ venv_path }}
```

If we don't like long lines in our files, we could break up the argument string across multiple lines by using YAML's line folding, which we originally wrote about in "Line Folding" on page 30:

```
- name: install package with pip
  pip: >
    name={{ item.name }}
    version={{ item.version }}
    virtualenv={{ venv_path }}
```

Ansible also provides another option for breaking up a module invocation across multiple lines. Instead of passing a string, we can pass a dictionary in which the keys are the variable names. This means we can invoke Example 6-12 like this instead:

```
- name: install package with pip
  pip:
    name: "{{ item.name }}"
    version: "{{ item.version }}"
    virtualenv: "{{ venv_path }}"
```

The dictionary-based approach to passing arguments is also useful when invoking modules that take complex arguments. A *complex argument* is an argument to a module that is a list or a dictionary. The `ec2` module, which creates new servers on Amazon EC2, is a good example of a module that takes complex arguments. Example 6-13 shows how to call a module that takes a list as an argument for the `group` parameter, and a dictionary as an argument to the `instance_tags` parameter. We'll cover this module in more detail in Chapter 14.

Example 6-13. Calling a module with complex arguments

```
- name: create an ec2 instance
  ec2:
    image: ami-8caa1ce4
    instance_type: m3.medium
    key_name: mykey
    group:
```

```
    - web
    - ssh
instance_tags:
  type: web
  env: production
```

You can even mix it up by passing some arguments as a string and others as a dictionary, by using the `args` clause to specify some of the variables as a dictionary. We could rewrite our preceding example as follows:

```
- name: create an ec2 instance
  ec2: image=ami-8caa1ce4 instance_type=m3.medium key_name=mykey
  args:
    group:
      - web
      - ssh
    instance_tags:
      type: web
      env: production
```

If you're using the `local_action` clause (we'll cover this in more detail in Chapter 9), the syntax for complex args changes slightly. You need to add `module: <modulename>` as shown here:

```
- name: create an ec2 instance
  local_action:
    module: ec2
    image: ami-8caa1ce4
    instance_type: m3.medium
    key_name: mykey
    group:
      - web
      - ssh
    instance_tags:
      type: web
      env: production
```

You can also mix simple arguments and complex arguments when using `local_action`:

```
- name: create an ec2 instance
  local_action: ec2 image=ami-8caa1ce4 instance_type=m3.medium key_name=mykey
  args:
    image: ami-8caa1ce4
    instance_type: m3.medium
    key_name: mykey
    group:
      - web
      - ssh
    instance_tags:
      type: web
      env: production
```

Ansible allows you to specify file permissions, which are used by several modules, including `file`, `copy`, and `template`. If you are specifying an octal value as a complex argument, it must either start the value with a 0 or quote it as a string.

For example, note how the `mode` argument starts with a 0:

```
- name: copy index.html
  copy:
    src: files/index.html
    dest: /usr/share/nginx/html/index.html
    mode: "0644"
```

If you do not start the mode argument with a 0 or quote it as a string, Ansible will interpret the value as a decimal number instead of an octal, and will not set the file permissions the way you expect. For details, see GitHub (*http://bit.ly/1GASfbl*).

If you want to break your arguments across multiple lines, and you aren't passing complex arguments, which form you choose is a matter of taste. I generally prefer dictionaries to multiline strings, but in this book I use both forms.

Configuring the Database

When Django runs in development mode, it uses the SQLite backend. This backend will create the database file if the file does not exist.

When using a database management system such as Postgres, we need to first create the database inside Postgres and then create the user account that owns the database. Later, we will configure Mezzanine with the credentials of this user.

Ansible ships with the `postgresql_user` and `postgresql_db` modules for creating users and databases inside Postgres. Example 6-14 shows how we invoke these modules in our playbook.

When creating the database, we specify locale information through the `lc_ctype` and `lc_collate` parameters. We use the `locale_gen` module to ensure that the locale we are using is installed in the operating system.

Example 6-14. Creating the database and database user

```
- name: create project locale
  locale_gen: name={{ locale }}
  become: True

- name: create a DB user
  postgresql_user:
    name: "{{ database_user }}"
    password: "{{ db_pass }}"
```

```
    become: True
    become_user: postgres

- name: create the database
  postgresql_db:
    name: "{{ database_name }}"
    owner: "{{ database_user }}"
    encoding: UTF8
    lc_ctype: "{{ locale }}"
    lc_collate: "{{ locale }}"
    template: template0
  become: True
  become_user: postgres
```

Note the use of `become: True` and `become_user: postgres` on the last two tasks. When you install Postgres on Ubuntu, the installation process creates a user named `postgres` that has administrative privileges for the Postgres installation. Note that the root account does not have administrative privileges in Postgres by default, so in the playbook, we need to `become` the Postgres user in order to perform administrative tasks, such as creating users and databases.

When we create the database, we set the encoding (`UTF8`) and locale categories (`LC_CTYPE`, `LC_COLLATE`) associated with the database. Because we are setting locale information, we use *template0* as the template.[3]

Generating the local_settings.py File from a Template

Django expects to find project-specific settings in a file called *settings.py*. Mezzanine follows the common Django idiom of breaking these settings into two groups:

- Settings that are the same for all deployments (*settings.py*)
- Settings that vary by deployment (*local_settings.py*)

We define the settings that are the same for all deployments in the *settings.py* file in our project repository. You can find that file on GitHub (*http://bit.ly/2jaw4zf*).

The *settings.py* file contains a Python snippet that loads a *local_settings.py* file that contains deployment-specific settings. The *.gitignore* file is configured to ignore the *local_settings.py* file, since developers will commonly create this file and configure it for local development.

As part of our deployment, we need to create a *local_settings.py* file and upload it to the remote host. Example 6-15 shows the Jinja2 template that we use.

---

3 See the Postgres documentation (*http://bit.ly/1F5AYpN*) for more details about template databases.

Example 6-15. local_settings.py.j2

```
from __future__ import unicode_literals

SECRET_KEY = "{{ secret_key }}"
NEVERCACHE_KEY = "{{ nevercache_key }}"
ALLOWED_HOSTS = [{% for domain in domains %}"{{ domain }}",{% endfor %}]

DATABASES = {
    "default": {
        # Ends with "postgresql_psycopg2", "mysql", "sqlite3" or "oracle".
        "ENGINE": "django.db.backends.postgresql_psycopg2",
        # DB name or path to database file if using sqlite3.
        "NAME": "{{ proj_name }}",
        # Not used with sqlite3.
        "USER": "{{ proj_name }}",
        # Not used with sqlite3.
        "PASSWORD": "{{ db_pass }}",
        # Set to empty string for localhost. Not used with sqlite3.
        "HOST": "127.0.0.1",
        # Set to empty string for default. Not used with sqlite3.
        "PORT": "",
    }
}

SECURE_PROXY_SSL_HEADER = ("HTTP_X_FORWARDED_PROTOCOL", "https")

CACHE_MIDDLEWARE_SECONDS = 60

CACHE_MIDDLEWARE_KEY_PREFIX = "{{ proj_name }}"

CACHES = {
    "default": {
        "BACKEND": "django.core.cache.backends.memcached.MemcachedCache",
        "LOCATION": "127.0.0.1:11211",
    }
}

SESSION_ENGINE = "django.contrib.sessions.backends.cache"
```

Most of this template is straightforward; it uses the {{ variable }} syntax to insert the values of variables such as secret_key, nevercache_key, proj_name, and db_pass. The only nontrivial bit of logic is the line shown in Example 6-16.

Example 6-16. Using a for loop in a Jinja2 template

```
ALLOWED_HOSTS = [{% for domain in domains %}"{{ domain }}",{% endfor %}]
```

If we look back at our variable definition, we have a variable called domains that's defined like this:

```
    domains:
      - 192.168.33.10.xip.io
      - www.192.168.33.10.xip.io
```

Our Mezzanine app is going to respond only to requests that are for one of the host-names listed in the `domains` variable: *http://192.168.33.10.xip.io* or *http://www. 192.168.33.10.xip.io* in our case. If a request reaches Mezzanine but the host header is something other than those two domains, the site will return "Bad Request (400)."

We want this line in the generated file to look like this:

```
    ALLOWED_HOSTS = ["192.168.33.10.xip.io", "www.192.168.33.10.xip.io"]
```

We can achieve this by using a `for` loop, as shown in Example 6-16. Note that it doesn't do exactly what we want. Instead, it will have a trailing comma, like this:

```
    ALLOWED_HOSTS = ["192.168.33.10.xip.io", "www.192.168.33.10.xip.io",]
```

However, Python is perfectly happy with trailing commas in lists, so we can leave it like this.

What's xip.io?

You might have noticed that the domains we are using look a little strange: *192.168.33.10.xip.io* and *www.192.168.33.10.xip.io*. They are domain names, but they have the IP address embedded within them.

When you access a website, you pretty much always point your browser to a domain name such as *http://www.ansiblebook.com*, instead of an IP address such as *http:// 151.101.192.133*. When we write our playbook to deploy Mezzanine to Vagrant, we want to configure the application with the domain name or names that it should be accessible by.

The problem is that we don't have a DNS record that maps to the IP address of our Vagrant box. In this case, that's *192.168.33.10*. There's nothing stopping us from setting up a DNS entry for this. For example, I could create a DNS entry from *mezzanine-internal.ansiblebook.com* that points to *192.168.33.10*.

However, if we want to create a DNS name that resolves to a particular IP address, there's a convenient service called *xip.io*, provided free of charge by Basecamp, that we can use so that we don't have to avoid creating our own DNS records. If *AAA.BBB.CCC.DDD* is an IP address, the DNS entry *AAA.BBB.CCC.DDD.xip.io* will resolve to *AAA.BBB.CCC.DDD*. For example, *192.168.33.10.xip.io* resolves to *192.168.33.10*. In addition, *www.192.168.33.10.xip.io* also resolves to *192.168.33.10*.

I find *xip.io* to be a great tool when I'm deploying web applications to private IP addresses for testing purposes. Alternatively, you can simply add entries to the */etc/ hosts* file on your local machine, which also works when you're offline.

Let's examine the Jinja2 for loop syntax. To make things a little easier to read, we'll break it up across multiple lines, like this:

```
ALLOWED_HOSTS = [
{% for domain in domains %}
                "{{ domain }}",
{% endfor %}
                ]
```

The generated config file looks like this, which is still valid Python.

```
ALLOWED_HOSTS = [
                "192.168.33.10.xip.io",
                "www.192.168.33.10.xip.io",
                ]
```

Note that the for loop has to be terminated by an {% endfor %} statement. Also note that the for statement and the endfor statement are surrounded by {% %} delimiters, which are different from the {{ }} delimiters that we use for variable substitution.

All variables and facts that have been defined in a playbook are available inside Jinja2 templates, so we never need to explicitly pass variables to templates.

Running django-manage Commands

Django applications use a special script called *manage.py* (*http://bit.ly/2iica5a*) that performs administrative actions for Django applications such as the following:

- Creating database tables
- Applying database migrations
- Loading fixtures from files into the database
- Dumping fixtures from the database to files
- Copying static assets to the appropriate directory

In addition to the built-in commands that *manage.py* supports, Django applications can add custom commands. Mezzanine adds a custom command called createdb that is used to initialize the database and copy the static assets to the appropriate place. The official Fabric scripts do the equivalent of this:

```
$ manage.py createdb --noinput --nodata
```

Ansible ships with a django_manage module that invokes manage.py commands. We could invoke it like this:

```
- name: initialize the database
  django_manage:
    command: createdb --noinput --nodata
```

```
    app_path: "{{ proj_path }}"
    virtualenv: "{{ venv_path }}"
```

Unfortunately, the custom `createdb` command that Mezzanine adds isn't idempotent. If invoked a second time, it will fail like this:

```
TASK: [initialize the database] ************************************************
failed: [web] => {"cmd": "python manage.py createdb --noinput --nodata", "failed"
: true, "path": "/home/vagrant/mezzanine_example/bin:/usr/local/sbin:/usr/local/b
in:/usr/sbin: /usr/bin:/sbin:/bin:/usr/games:/usr/local/games", "state": "absent"
, "syspath": ["", "/usr/lib/python2.7", "/usr/lib/python2.7/plat-x86_64-linux-gnu
", "/usr/lib/python2.7/lib-tk", "/usr/lib/python2.7/lib-old", "/usr/lib/python2.7
/lib-dynload", "/usr/local/lib/python2.7/dist-packages", "/usr/lib/python2.7/dist
-packages"]}
msg:
:stderr: CommandError: Database already created, you probably want the syncdb or
migrate command
```

Fortunately, the custom `createdb` command is effectively equivalent to two idempotent built-in `manage.py` commands:

`migrate`
> Create and update database tables for Django models

`collectstatic`
> Copy the static assets to the appropriate directories

By invoking these commands, we get an idempotent task:

```
- name: apply migrations to create the database, collect static content
  django_manage:
    command: "{{ item }}"
    app_path: "{{ proj_path }}"
    virtualenv: "{{ venv_path }}"
  with_items:
    - syncdb
    - collectstatic
```

Running Custom Python Scripts in the Context of the Application

To initialize our application, we need to make two changes to our database:

- We need to create a Site (*http://bit.ly/2hYWztG*) model object that contains the domain name of our site (in our case, that's *192.168.33.10.xip.io*).

- We need to set the administrator username and password.

Although we could make these changes with raw SQL commands or Django data migrations, the Mezzanine Fabric scripts use Python scripts, so that's how we'll do it.

There are two tricky parts here. The Python scripts need to run in the context of the virtualenv that we've created, and the Python environment needs to be set up properly so that the script will import the *settings.py* file that's in *~/mezzanine/mezzanine_example/mezzanine_example*.

In most cases, if we needed some custom Python code, I'd write a custom Ansible module. However, as far as I know, Ansible doesn't let you execute a module in the context of a virtualenv, so that's out.

I used the `script` module instead. This will copy over a custom script and execute it. I wrote two scripts, one to set the Site record, and the other to set the admin username and password.

You can pass command-line arguments to `script` modules and parse them out, but I decided to pass the arguments as environment variables instead. I didn't want to pass passwords via command-line argument (those show up in the process list when you run the `ps` command), and it's easier to parse out environment variables in the scripts than it is to parse command-line arguments.

 You can set environment variables with an `environment` clause on a task, passing it a dictionary that contains the environment variable names and values. You can add an `environment` clause to any task; it doesn't have to be a `script`.

In order to run these scripts in the context of the virtualenv, I also needed to set the `path` variable so that the first Python executable in the `path` would be the one inside the virtualenv. Example 6-17 shows how I invoked the two scripts.

Example 6-17. Using the script module to invoke custom Python code

```
- name: set the site id
  script: scripts/setsite.py
  environment:
    PATH: "{{ venv_path }}/bin"
    PROJECT_DIR: "{{ proj_path }}"
    PROJECT_APP: "{{ proj_app }}"
    WEBSITE_DOMAIN: "{{ live_hostname }}"

- name: set the admin password
  script: scripts/setadmin.py
  environment:
    PATH: "{{ venv_path }}/bin"
    PROJECT_DIR: "{{ proj_path }}"
    PROJECT_APP: "{{ proj_app }}"
    ADMIN_PASSWORD: "{{ admin_pass }}"
```

The scripts themselves are shown in Examples 6-18 and 6-19. I put these in a *scripts* subdirectory.

Example 6-18. scripts/setsite.py

```
#!/usr/bin/env python
# A script to set the site domain
# Assumes two environment variables
#
# WEBSITE_DOMAIN: the domain of the site (e.g., www.example.com)
# PROJECT_DIR: root directory of the project
# PROJECT_APP: name of the project app
import os
import sys

# Add the project directory to system path
proj_dir = os.path.expanduser(os.environ['PROJECT_DIR'])
sys.path.append(proj_dir)

proj_app = os.environ['PROJECT_APP']
os.environ['DJANGO_SETTINGS_MODULE'] = proj_app + '.settings'
import django
django.setup()
from django.conf import settings
from django.contrib.sites.models import Site
domain = os.environ['WEBSITE_DOMAIN']
Site.objects.filter(id=settings.SITE_ID).update(domain=domain)
Site.objects.get_or_create(domain=domain)
```

Example 6-19. scripts/setadmin.py

```
#!/usr/bin/env python
# A script to set the admin credentials
# Assumes two environment variables
#
# PROJECT_DIR: the project directory (e.g., ~/projname)
# PROJECT_APP: name of the project app
# ADMIN_PASSWORD: admin user's password

import os
import sys

# Add the project directory to system path
proj_dir = os.path.expanduser(os.environ['PROJECT_DIR'])
sys.path.append(proj_dir)

proj_app = os.environ['PROJECT_APP']
os.environ['DJANGO_SETTINGS_MODULE'] = proj_app + '.settings'
import django
django.setup()
from django.contrib.auth import get_user_model
```

```
User = get_user_model()
u, _ = User.objects.get_or_create(username='admin')
u.is_staff = u.is_superuser = True
u.set_password(os.environ['ADMIN_PASSWORD'])
u.save()
```

Setting Service Configuration Files

Next, we set the configuration file for Gunicorn (our application server), Nginx (our web server), and Supervisor (our process manager), as shown in Example 6-20. The template for the Gunicorn configuration file is shown in Example 6-22, and the template for the Supervisor configuration file is shown in Example 6-23.

Example 6-20. Setting configuration files

```
- name: set the gunicorn config file
  template:
      src: templates/gunicorn.conf.py.j2
      dest: "{{ proj_path }}/gunicorn.conf.py"

- name: set the supervisor config file
  template:
      src: templates/supervisor.conf.j2
      dest: /etc/supervisor/conf.d/mezzanine.conf
  become: True
  notify: restart supervisor

- name: set the nginx config file
  template:
      src: templates/nginx.conf.j2
      dest: /etc/nginx/sites-available/mezzanine.conf
  notify: restart nginx
  become: True
```

In all three cases, we generate the config files by using templates. The Supervisor and Nginx processes are started by root (although they drop down to nonroot users when running), so we need to sudo so that we have the appropriate permissions to write their configuration files.

If the Supervisor config file changes, Ansible will fire the restart supervisor handler. If the Nginx config file changes, Ansible will fire the restart nginx handler, as shown in Example 6-21.

Example 6-21. Handlers

```
handlers:
  - name: restart supervisor
    supervisorctl: name=gunicorn_mezzanine state=restarted
```

```
    sudo: True

  - name: restart nginx
    service: name=nginx state=restarted
    sudo: True
```

Example 6-22. templates/gunicorn.conf.py.j2

```
from __future__ import unicode_literals
import multiprocessing

bind = "127.0.0.1:{{ gunicorn_port }}"
workers = multiprocessing.cpu_count() * 2 + 1
loglevel = "error"
proc_name = "{{ proj_name }}"
```

Example 6-23. templates/supervisor.conf.j2

```
[program:{{ gunicorn_procname }}]
command={{ venv_path }}/bin/gunicorn -c gunicorn.conf.py -p gunicorn.pid \
    {{ proj_app }}.wsgi:application
directory={{ proj_path }}
user={{ user }}
autostart=true
stdout_logfile = /home/{{ user }}/logs/{{ proj_name }}_supervisor
autorestart=true
redirect_stderr=true
environment=LANG="{{ locale }}",LC_ALL="{{ locale }}",LC_LANG="{{ locale }}"
```

The only template that has any template logic (other than variable substitution) is Example 6-24. It has conditional logic to enable TLS if the `tls_enabled` variable is set to `true`. You'll see some `if` statements scattered about the templates that look like this:

```
{% if tls_enabled %}
...
{% endif %}
```

It also uses the `join` Jinja2 filter here:

```
server_name {{ domains|join(", ") }};
```

This code snippet expects the variable `domains` to be a list. It will generate a string with the elements of `domains` connected together, separated by commas. Recall that in our case, the `domains` list is defined as follows:

```
domains:
  - 192.168.33.10.xip.io
  - www.192.168.33.10.xip.io
```

When the template renders, the line looks like this:

```
server_name 192.168.33.10.xip.io, www.192.168.33.10.xip.io;
```

Example 6-24. templates/nginx.conf.j2

```
upstream {{ proj_name }} {
    server unix:{{ proj_path }}/gunicorn.sock fail_timeout=0;
}

server {

    listen 80;

    {% if tls_enabled %}
    listen 443 ssl;
    {% endif %}
    server_name {{ domains|join(", ") }};
    client_max_body_size 10M;
    keepalive_timeout    15;

    {% if tls_enabled %}
    ssl_certificate        conf/{{ proj_name }}.crt;
    ssl_certificate_key    conf/{{ proj_name }}.key;
    ssl_session_cache      shared:SSL:10m;
    ssl_session_timeout    10m;
    # ssl_ciphers entry is too long to show in this book
    # See https://github.com/ansiblebook/ansiblebook
    #     ch06/playbooks/templates/nginx.conf.j2
    ssl_prefer_server_ciphers on;
    {% endif %}

    location / {
        proxy_redirect      off;
        proxy_set_header    Host                    $host;
        proxy_set_header    X-Real-IP               $remote_addr;
        proxy_set_header    X-Forwarded-For         $proxy_add_x_forwarded_for;
        proxy_set_header    X-Forwarded-Protocol    $scheme;
        proxy_pass          http://{{ proj_name }};
    }

    location /static/ {
        root            {{ proj_path }};
        access_log      off;
        log_not_found   off;
    }

    location /robots.txt {
        root            {{ proj_path }}/static;
        access_log      off;
        log_not_found   off;
    }
```

```
    location /favicon.ico {
        root            {{ proj_path }}/static/img;
        access_log      off;
        log_not_found   off;
    }
}
```

Enabling the Nginx Configuration

The convention with Nginx configuration files is to put your configuration files in */etc/nginx/sites-available* and enable them by symlinking them into */etc/nginx/sites-enabled*.

The Mezzanine Fabric scripts just copy the configuration file directly into *sites-enabled*, but I'm going to deviate from how Mezzanine does it because it gives me an excuse to use the `file` module to create a symlink. We also need to remove the default configuration file that the Nginx package sets up in */etc/nginx/sites-enabled/default*.

As shown in Example 6-25, we use the `file` module to create the symlink and to remove the default config file. This module is useful for creating directories, symlinks, and empty files; deleting files, directories, and symlinks; and setting properties such as permissions and ownership.

Example 6-25. Enabling Nginx configuration

```
- name: enable the nginx config file
  file:
    src: /etc/nginx/sites-available/mezzanine.conf
    dest: /etc/nginx/sites-enabled/mezzanine.conf
    state: link
  become: True

- name: remove the default nginx config file
  file: path=/etc/nginx/sites-enabled/default state=absent
  notify: restart nginx
  become: True
```

Installing TLS Certificates

Our playbook defines a variable named `tls_enabled`. If this variable is set to `true`, the playbook will install TLS certificates. In our example, we use self-signed certificates, so the playbook will create the certificate if it doesn't exist.

In a production deployment, you would copy an existing TLS certificate that you obtained from a certificate authority.

Example 6-26 shows the two tasks involved in configuring for TLS certificates. We use the `file` module to ensure that the directory that will house the TLS certificates exists.

Example 6-26. Installing TLS certificates

```
- name: ensure config path exists
  file: path={{ conf_path }} state=directory
  sudo: True
  when: tls_enabled

- name: create tls certificates
  command: >
    openssl req -new -x509 -nodes -out {{ proj_name }}.crt
    -keyout {{ proj_name }}.key -subj '/CN={{ domains[0] }}' -days 3650
    chdir={{ conf_path }}
    creates={{ conf_path }}/{{ proj_name }}.crt
  sudo: True
  when: tls_enabled
  notify: restart nginx
```

Note that both tasks contain this clause:

```
when: tls_enabled
```

If `tls_enabled` evaluates to `false`, Ansible will skip the task.

Ansible doesn't ship with modules for creating TLS certificates, so we need to use the `command` module to invoke the `openssl` command in order to create the self-signed certificate. Since the command is very long, we use YAML line-folding syntax (see "Line Folding" on page 30) so that we can break the command across multiple lines.

These two lines at the end of the command are additional parameters that are passed to the module; they are not passed to the command line:

```
chdir={{ conf_path }}
creates={{ conf_path }}/{{ proj_name }}.crt
```

The `chdir` parameter changes the directory before running the command. The `creates` parameter implements idempotence: Ansible will first check whether the file `{{ conf_path }}/{{ proj_name }}.crt` exists on the host. If it already exists, Ansible will skip this task.

Installing Twitter Cron Job

If you run `manage.py poll_twitter`, Mezzanine will retrieve tweets associated with the configured accounts and show them on the home page. The Fabric scripts that ship with Mezzanine keep these tweets up-to-date by installing a cron job that runs every five minutes.

If we followed the Fabric scripts exactly, we'd copy a cron script into the */etc/cron.d* directory that had the cron job. We could use the `template` module to do this. However, Ansible ships with a `cron` module that allows us to create or delete cron jobs, which I find more elegant. Example 6-27 shows the task that installs the cron job.

Example 6-27. Installing cron job for polling Twitter

```
- name: install poll twitter cron job
  cron: name="poll twitter" minute="*/5" user={{ user }} job="{{ manage }} \
  poll_twitter"
```

If you manually SSH to the box, you can see the cron job that gets installed by using `crontab -l` to list the jobs. Here's what it looks like for me when I deploy as the Vagrant user:

```
#Ansible: poll twitter
*/5 * * * * /home/vagrant/.virtualenvs/mezzanine_example/bin/python \
/home/vagrant/mezzanine/mezzanine_example/manage.py poll_twitter
```

Notice the comment at the first line. That's how the Ansible module supports deleting cron jobs by name. If you were to do this:

```
- name: remove cron job
    cron: name="poll twitter" state=absent
```

the `cron` module would look for the comment line that matches the name and delete the job associated with that comment.

The Full Playbook

Example 6-28 shows the complete playbook in all its glory.

Example 6-28. mezzanine.yml: the complete playbook

```
---
- name: Deploy mezzanine
  hosts: web
  vars:
    user: "{{ ansible_user }}"
    proj_app: mezzanine_example
    proj_name: "{{ proj_app }}"
    venv_home: "{{ ansible_env.HOME }}/.virtualenvs"
    venv_path: "{{ venv_home }}/{{ proj_name }}"
    proj_path: "{{ ansible_env.HOME }}/mezzanine/{{ proj_name }}"
    settings_path: "{{ proj_path }}/{{ proj_name }}"
    reqs_path: requirements.txt
    manage: "{{ python }} {{ proj_path }}/manage.py"
    live_hostname: 192.168.33.10.xip.io
    domains:
```

```
        - 192.168.33.10.xip.io
        - www.192.168.33.10.xip.io
    repo_url: git@github.com:ansiblebook/mezzanine_example.git
    locale: en_US.UTF-8
    # Variables below don't appear in Mezannine's fabfile.py
    # but I've added them for convenience
    conf_path: /etc/nginx/conf
    tls_enabled: True
    python: "{{ venv_path }}/bin/python"
    database_name: "{{ proj_name }}"
    database_user: "{{ proj_name }}"
    database_host: localhost
    database_port: 5432
    gunicorn_procname: gunicorn_mezzanine
    num_workers: "multiprocessing.cpu_count() * 2 + 1"
  vars_files:
    - secrets.yml
  tasks:
    - name: install apt packages
      apt: pkg={{ item }} update_cache=yes cache_valid_time=3600
      become: True
      with_items:
        - git
        - libjpeg-dev
        - libpq-dev
        - memcached
        - nginx
        - postgresql
        - python-dev
        - python-pip
        - python-psycopg2
        - python-setuptools
        - python-virtualenv
        - supervisor
    - name: create project path
      file: path={{ proj_path }} state=directory
    - name: create a logs directory
      file:
        path: "{{ ansible_env.HOME }}/logs"
        state: directory
    - name: check out the repository on the host
      git: repo={{ repo_url }} dest={{ proj_path }} accept_hostkey=yes
    - name: install Python requirements globally via pip
      pip: name={{ item }} state=latest
      with_items:
        - pip
        - virtualenv
        - virtualenvwrapper
      become: True
    - name: create project locale
      locale_gen: name={{ locale }}
      become: True
```

```yaml
- name: create a DB user
  postgresql_user:
    name: "{{ database_user }}"
    password: "{{ db_pass }}"
  become: True
  become_user: postgres
- name: create the database
  postgresql_db:
    name: "{{ database_name }}"
    owner: "{{ database_user }}"
    encoding: UTF8
    lc_ctype: "{{ locale }}"
    lc_collate: "{{ locale }}"
    template: template0
  become: True
  become_user: postgres
- name: ensure config path exists
  file: path={{ conf_path }} state=directory
  become: True
- name: create tls certificates
  command: >
    openssl req -new -x509 -nodes -out {{ proj_name }}.crt
    -keyout {{ proj_name }}.key -subj '/CN={{ domains[0] }}' -days 3650
    chdir={{ conf_path }}
    creates={{ conf_path }}/{{ proj_name }}.crt
  become: True
  when: tls_enabled
  notify: restart nginx
- name: remove the default nginx config file
  file: path=/etc/nginx/sites-enabled/default state=absent
  notify: restart nginx
  become: True
- name: set the nginx config file
  template:
    src=templates/nginx.conf.j2
    dest=/etc/nginx/sites-available/mezzanine.conf
  notify: restart nginx
  become: True
- name: enable the nginx config file
  file:
    src: /etc/nginx/sites-available/mezzanine.conf
    dest: /etc/nginx/sites-enabled/mezzanine.conf
    state: link
  become: True
  notify: restart nginx
- name: set the supervisor config file
  template:
    src=templates/supervisor.conf.j2
    dest=/etc/supervisor/conf.d/mezzanine.conf
  become: True
  notify: restart supervisor
- name: install poll twitter cron job
```

```
    cron:
      name="poll twitter"
      minute="*/5"
      user={{ user }}
      job="{{ manage }} poll_twitter"
  - name: set the gunicorn config file
    template:
      src=templates/gunicorn.conf.py.j2
      dest={{ proj_path }}/gunicorn.conf.py
  - name: generate the settings file
    template:
      src=templates/local_settings.py.j2
      dest={{ settings_path }}/local_settings.py
  - name: install requirements.txt
    pip: requirements={{ proj_path }}/{{ reqs_path }} virtualenv={{ venv_path }}
  - name: install required python packages
    pip: name={{ item }} virtualenv={{ venv_path }}
    with_items:
      - gunicorn
      - setproctitle
      - psycopg2
      - django-compressor
      - python-memcached
  - name: apply migrations to create the database, collect static content
    django_manage:
      command: "{{ item }}"
      app_path: "{{ proj_path }}"
      virtualenv: "{{ venv_path }}"
    with_items:
      - migrate
      - collectstatic
  - name: set the site id
    script: scripts/setsite.py
    environment:
      PATH: "{{ venv_path }}/bin"
      PROJECT_DIR: "{{ proj_path }}"
      PROJECT_APP: "{{ proj_app }}"
      WEBSITE_DOMAIN: "{{ live_hostname }}"
  - name: set the admin password
    script: scripts/setadmin.py
    environment:
      PATH: "{{ venv_path }}/bin"
      PROJECT_DIR: "{{ proj_path }}"
      PROJECT_APP: "{{ proj_app }}"
      ADMIN_PASSWORD: "{{ admin_pass }}"
handlers:
  - name: restart supervisor
    supervisorctl: "name={{ gunicorn_procname }} state=restarted"
    become: True
  - name: restart nginx
    service: name=nginx state=restarted
    become: True
```

Running the Playbook Against a Vagrant Machine

The `live_hostname` and `domains` variables in our playbook assume that the host we are going to deploy to is accessible at *192.168.33.10*. The Vagrantfile shown in Example 6-29 configures a Vagrant machine with that IP address.

Example 6-29. Vagrantfile

```
VAGRANTFILE_API_VERSION = "2"

Vagrant.configure(VAGRANTFILE_API_VERSION) do |config|
  config.vm.box = "ubuntu/trusty64"
  config.vm.network "private_network", ip: "192.168.33.10"
end
```

Deploy Mezzanine into the Vagrant machine:

```
$ ansible-playbook mezzanine.yml
```

You can then reach your newly deployed Mezzanine site at any of the following URLs:

- *http://192.168.33.10.xip.io*
- *https://192.168.33.10.xip.io*
- *http://www.192.168.33.10.xip.io*
- *https://www.192.168.33.10.xip.io*

Troubleshooting

You might hit a few speed bumps when trying to run this playbook on your local machine. This section describes how to overcome some common obstacles.

Cannot Check Out Git Repository

You may see the task named "check out the repository on the host" fail with this error:

```
fatal: Could not read from remote repository.
```

A likely fix is to remove a preexisting entry for 192.168.33.10 in your *~/.ssh/known_hosts* file. See "A Bad Host Key Can Cause Problems, Even with Key Checking Disabled" on page 371 for more details.

Cannot Reach 192.168.33.10.xip.io

Some WiFi routers ship with DNS servers that won't resolve the hostname *192.168.33.10.xip.io*. You can check whether yours does by typing on the command line:

```
dig +short 192.168.33.10.xip.io
```

The output should be as follows:

```
192.168.33.10
```

If the output is blank, your DNS server is refusing to resolve *xip.io* hostnames. If this is the case, a workaround is to add the following to your */etc/hosts* file:

```
192.168.33.10 192.168.33.10.xip.io
```

Bad Request (400)

If your browser returns the error "Bad Request (400)," it is likely that you are trying to reach the Mezzanine site by using a hostname or IP address that is not in the `ALLOWED_HOSTS` list in the Mezzanine configuration file. This list is populated using the `domains` Ansible variable in the playbook:

```
domains:
  - 192.168.33.10.xip.io
  - www.192.168.33.10.xip.io
```

Deploying Mezzanine on Multiple Machines

In this scenario, we've deployed Mezzanine entirely on a single machine. However, it's common to deploy the database service on a separate host from the web service. In Chapter 7, we'll show a playbook that deploys across the database and web services on separate hosts.

You've now seen what it's like to deploy a real application with Mezzanine. The next chapter covers some more advanced features of Ansible that didn't come up in our example.

Roles: Scaling Up Your Playbooks

One of the things I like about Ansible is how it scales both up and down. I'm not referring to the number of hosts you're managing, but rather the complexity of the jobs you're trying to automate.

Ansible scales down well because simple tasks are easy to implement. It scales up well because it provides mechanisms for decomposing complex jobs into smaller pieces.

In Ansible, the *role* is the primary mechanism for breaking a playbook into multiple files. This simplifies writing complex playbooks, and it makes them easier to reuse. Think of a role as something you assign to one or more hosts. For example, you'd assign a `database` role to the hosts that will act as database servers.

Basic Structure of a Role

An Ansible role has a name, such as `database`. Files associated with the `database` role go in the *roles/database* directory, which contains the following files and directories:

roles/database/tasks/main.yml
> Tasks

roles/database/files/
> Holds files to be uploaded to hosts

roles/database/templates/
> Holds Jinja2 template files

roles/database/handlers/main.yml
> Handlers

roles/database/vars/main.yml
> Variables that shouldn't be overridden

roles/database/defaults/main.yml
> Default variables that can be overridden

roles/database/meta/main.yml
> Dependency information about a role

Each individual file is optional; if your role doesn't have any handlers, there's no need to have an empty *handlers/main.yml* file.

Where Does Ansible Look for My Roles?

Ansible looks for roles in the *roles* directory alongside your playbooks. It also looks for systemwide roles in */etc/ansible/roles*. You can customize the systemwide location of roles by setting the *roles_path* setting in the `defaults` section of your *ansible.cfg* file, as shown in Example 7-1.

Example 7-1. ansible.cfg: overriding default roles path

```
[defaults]
roles_path = ~/ansible_roles
```

You can also override this by setting the `ANSIBLE_ROLES_PATH` environment variable.

Example: Database and Mezzanine Roles

Let's take our Mezzanine playbook and implement it with Ansible roles. We could create a single role called `mezzanine`, but instead I'm going to break out the deployment of the Postgres database into a separate role called `database`. This will make it easier to eventually deploy the database on a host separate from the Mezzanine application.

Using Roles in Your Playbooks

Before we get into the details of how to define roles, let's go over how to assign roles to hosts in a playbook. Example 7-2 shows what our playbook looks like for deploying Mezzanine onto a single host, once we have database and Mezzanine roles defined.

Example 7-2. mezzanine-single-host.yml

```
- name: deploy mezzanine on vagrant
  hosts: web
  vars_files:
    - secrets.yml

  roles:
```

```
  - role: database
    database_name: "{{ mezzanine_proj_name }}"
    database_user: "{{ mezzanine_proj_name }}"

  - role: mezzanine
    live_hostname: 192.168.33.10.xip.io
    domains:
      - 192.168.33.10.xip.io
      - www.192.168.33.10.xip.io
```

When we use roles, we have a `roles` section in our playbook. This section expects a list of roles. In our example, our list contains two roles: `database` and `mezzanine`.

Note that we can pass in variables when invoking the roles. In our example, we pass the `database_name` and `database_user` variables for the `database` role. If these variables have already been defined in the role (either in *vars/main.yml* or *defaults/main.yml*), then the values will be overridden with the variables that were passed in.

If you aren't passing in variables to roles, you can simply specify the names of the roles, like this:

```
roles:
  - database
  - mezzanine
```

With `database` and `mezzanine` roles defined, writing a playbook that deploys the web application and database services to multiple hosts becomes much simpler. Example 7-3 shows a playbook that deploys the database on the db host and the web service on the web host. Note that this playbook contains two separate plays.

Example 7-3. mezzanine-across-hosts.yml

```
- name: deploy postgres on vagrant
  hosts: db
  vars_files:
    - secrets.yml
  roles:
    - role: database
      database_name: "{{ mezzanine_proj_name }}"
      database_user: "{{ mezzanine_proj_name }}"

- name: deploy mezzanine on vagrant
  hosts: web
  vars_files:
    - secrets.yml
  roles:
    - role: mezzanine
      database_host: "{{ hostvars.db.ansible_eth1.ipv4.address }}"
      live_hostname: 192.168.33.10.xip.io
      domains:
```

```
    - 192.168.33.10.xip.io
    - www.192.168.33.10.xip.io
```

Pre-Tasks and Post-Tasks

Sometimes you want to run tasks before or after you invoke your roles. Let's say you want to update the apt cache before you deploy Mezzanine, and you want to send a notification to a Slack channel after you deploy.

Ansible allows you to define a list of tasks that execute before the roles with a `pre_tasks` section, and a list of tasks that execute after the roles with a `post_tasks` section. Example 7-4 shows an example of these in action.

Example 7-4. Using pre-tasks and post-tasks

```
- name: deploy mezzanine on vagrant
  hosts: web
  vars_files:
    - secrets.yml
  pre_tasks:
    - name: update the apt cache
      apt: update_cache=yes
  roles:
    - role: mezzanine
      database_host: "{{ hostvars.db.ansible_eth1.ipv4.address }}"
      live_hostname: 192.168.33.10.xip.io
      domains:
        - 192.168.33.10.xip.io
        - www.192.168.33.10.xip.io
  post_tasks:
    - name: notify Slack that the servers have been updated
      local_action: >
        slack
        domain=acme.slack.com
        token={{ slack_token }}
        msg="web server {{ inventory_hostname }} configured"
```

But enough about using roles; let's talk about writing them.

A database Role for Deploying the Database

The job of our `database` role will be to install Postgres and create the required database and database user.

Our database role comprises the following files:

- *roles/database/tasks/main.yml*
- *roles/database/defaults/main.yml*

- *roles/database/handlers/main.yml*
- *roles/database/files/pg_hba.conf*
- *roles/database/files/postgresql.conf*

This role includes two customized Postgres configuration files:

postgresql.conf
> Modifies the default `listen_addresses` configuration option so that Postgres will accept connections on any network interface. The default for Postgres is to accept connections only from `localhost`, which doesn't work for us if we want our database to run on a separate host from our web application.

pg_hba.conf
> Configures Postgres to authenticate connections over the network by using a username and password.

 These files aren't shown here because they are quite large. You can find them in the code samples on GitHub (*https://github.com/ansiblebook/ansiblebook*) in the *ch08* directory.

Example 7-5 shows the tasks involved in deploying Postgres.

Example 7-5. roles/database/tasks/main.yml

```
- name: install apt packages
  apt: pkg={{ item }} update_cache=yes cache_valid_time=3600
  become: True
  with_items:
    - libpq-dev
    - postgresql
    - python-psycopg2

- name: copy configuration file
  copy: >
    src=postgresql.conf dest=/etc/postgresql/9.3/main/postgresql.conf
    owner=postgres group=postgres mode=0644
  become: True
  notify: restart postgres

- name: copy client authentication configuration file
  copy: >
    src=pg_hba.conf dest=/etc/postgresql/9.3/main/pg_hba.conf
    owner=postgres group=postgres mode=0640
  become: True
  notify: restart postgres
```

```
- name: create project locale
  locale_gen: name={{ locale }}
  become: True

- name: create a user
  postgresql_user:
    name: "{{ database_user }}"
    password: "{{ db_pass }}"
  become: True
  become_user: postgres

- name: create the database
  postgresql_db:
    name: "{{ database_name }}"
    owner: "{{ database_user }}"
    encoding: UTF8
    lc_ctype: "{{ locale }}"
    lc_collate: "{{ locale }}"
    template: template0
  become: True
  become_user: postgres
```

Example 7-6 shows the handlers file.

Example 7-6. roles/database/handlers/main.yml

```
- name: restart postgres
  service: name=postgresql state=restarted
  become: True
```

The only default variable we are going to specify is the database port, shown in Example 7-7.

Example 7-7. roles/database/defaults/main.yml

```
database_port: 5432
```

Note that our list of tasks refers to several variables that we haven't defined anywhere in the role:

- database_name
- database_user
- db_pass
- locale

In Examples 7-2 and 7-3, we pass in `database_name` and `database_user` when we invoke the role. I'm assuming that `db_pass` is defined in the *secrets.yml* file, which is included in the `vars_files` section. The `locale` variable is likely something that would be the same for every host, and might be used by multiple roles or playbooks, so I defined it in the *group_vars/all* file in the code samples that accompany this book.

Why Are There Two Ways to Define Variables in Roles?

When Ansible first introduced support for roles, there was only one place to define role variables, in *vars/main.yml*. Variables defined in this location have a higher precedence than those defined in the `vars` section of a play, which meant you couldn't override the variable unless you explicitly passed it as an argument to the role.

Ansible later introduced the notion of default role variables that go in *defaults/main.yml*. This type of variable is defined in a role, but has a low precedence, so it will be overridden if another variable with the same name is defined in the playbook.

If you think you might want to change the value of a variable in a role, use a default variable. If you don't want it to change, use a regular variable.

A mezzanine Role for Deploying Mezzanine

The job of our `mezzanine` role will be to install Mezzanine. This includes installing Nginx as the reverse proxy and Supervisor as the process monitor.

Here are the files that the role comprises:

- *roles/mezzanine/defaults/main.yml*
- *roles/mezzanine/handlers/main.yml*
- *roles/mezzanine/tasks/django.yml*
- *roles/mezzanine/tasks/main.yml*
- *roles/mezzanine/tasks/nginx.yml*
- *roles/mezzanine/templates/gunicorn.conf.py.j2*
- *roles/mezzanine/templates/local_settings.py.filters.j2*
- *roles/mezzanine/templates/local_settings.py.j2*
- *roles/mezzanine/templates/nginx.conf.j2*
- *roles/mezzanine/templates/supervisor.conf.j2*
- *roles/mezzanine/vars/main.yml*

Example 7-8 shows the variables we've defined for this role. Note that we've changed the name of the variables so that they all start with *mezzanine*. It's good practice to do this with role variables because Ansible doesn't have any notion of namespace across roles. This means that variables that are defined in other roles, or elsewhere in a playbook, will be accessible everywhere. This can cause some unexpected behavior if you accidentally use the same variable name in two different roles.

Example 7-8. roles/mezzanine/vars/main.yml

```
# vars file for mezzanine
mezzanine_user: "{{ ansible_user }}"
mezzanine_venv_home: "{{ ansible_env.HOME }}"
mezzanine_venv_path: "{{ mezzanine_venv_home }}/{{ mezzanine_proj_name }}"
mezzanine_repo_url: git@github.com:lorin/mezzanine-example.git
mezzanine_proj_dirname: project
mezzanine_proj_path: "{{ mezzanine_venv_path }}/{{ mezzanine_proj_dirname }}"
mezzanine_reqs_path: requirements.txt
mezzanine_conf_path: /etc/nginx/conf
mezzanine_python: "{{ mezzanine_venv_path }}/bin/python"
mezzanine_manage: "{{ mezzanine_python }} {{ mezzanine_proj_path }}/manage.py"
mezzanine_gunicorn_port: 8000
```

Example 7-9 shows the default variables defined in our `mezzanine` role. In this case, we have only a single variable. When I write default variables, I'm less likely to prefix them because I might intentionally want to override them elsewhere.

Example 7-9. roles/mezzanine/defaults/main.yml

```
tls_enabled: True
```

Because the task list is pretty long, I've decided to break it up across several files. Example 7-10 shows the top-level task file for the `mezzanine` role. It installs the apt packages, and then it uses `include` statements to invoke two other task files that are in the same directory, shown in Examples 7-11 and 7-12.

Example 7-10. roles/mezzanine/tasks/main.yml

```
- name: install apt packages
  apt: pkg={{ item }} update_cache=yes cache_valid_time=3600
  become: True
  with_items:
    - git
    - libjpeg-dev
    - libpq-dev
    - memcached
    - nginx
    - python-dev
```

```
    - python-pip
    - python-psycopg2
    - python-setuptools
    - python-virtualenv
    - supervisor

- include: django.yml

- include: nginx.yml
```

Example 7-11. roles/mezzanine/tasks/django.yml

```
- name: create a logs directory
  file: path="{{ ansible_env.HOME }}/logs" state=directory

- name: check out the repository on the host
  git:
    repo: "{{ mezzanine_repo_url }}"
    dest: "{{ mezzanine_proj_path }}"
    accept_hostkey: yes

- name: install Python requirements globally via pip
  pip: name={{ item }} state=latest
  with_items:
    - pip
    - virtualenv
    - virtualenvwrapper

- name: install required python packages
  pip: name={{ item }} virtualenv={{ mezzanine_venv_path }}
  with_items:
    - gunicorn
    - setproctitle
    - psycopg2
    - django-compressor
    - python-memcached

- name: install requirements.txt
  pip: >
    requirements={{ mezzanine_proj_path }}/{{ mezzanine_reqs_path }}
    virtualenv={{ mezzanine_venv_path }}

- name: generate the settings file
  template: src=local_settings.py.j2 dest={{ mezzanine_proj_path }}/local_settings.py

- name: apply migrations to create the database, collect static content
  django_manage:
    command: "{{ item }}"
    app_path: "{{ mezzanine_proj_path }}"
    virtualenv: "{{ mezzanine_venv_path }}"
  with_items:
    - migrate
```

```
    - collectstatic

- name: set the site id
  script: scripts/setsite.py
  environment:
    PATH: "{{ mezzanine_venv_path }}/bin"
    PROJECT_DIR: "{{ mezzanine_proj_path }}"
    PROJECT_APP: "{{ mezzanine_proj_app }}"
    WEBSITE_DOMAIN: "{{ live_hostname }}"

- name: set the admin password
  script: scripts/setadmin.py
  environment:
    PATH: "{{ mezzanine_venv_path }}/bin"
    PROJECT_DIR: "{{ mezzanine_proj_path }}"
    PROJECT_APP: "{{ mezzanine_proj_app }}"
    ADMIN_PASSWORD: "{{ admin_pass }}"

- name: set the gunicorn config file
  template: src=gunicorn.conf.py.j2 dest={{ mezzanine_proj_path }}/gunicorn.conf.py

- name: set the supervisor config file
  template: src=supervisor.conf.j2 dest=/etc/supervisor/conf.d/mezzanine.conf
  become: True
  notify: restart supervisor

- name: ensure config path exists
  file: path={{ mezzanine_conf_path }} state=directory
  become: True
  when: tls_enabled

- name: install poll twitter cron job
  cron: >
    name="poll twitter" minute="*/5" user={{ mezzanine_user }}
    job="{{ mezzanine_manage }} poll_twitter"
```

Example 7-12. roles/mezzanine/tasks/nginx.yml

```
- name: set the nginx config file
  template: src=nginx.conf.j2 dest=/etc/nginx/sites-available/mezzanine.conf
  notify: restart nginx
  become: True

- name: enable the nginx config file
  file:
    src: /etc/nginx/sites-available/mezzanine.conf
    dest: /etc/nginx/sites-enabled/mezzanine.conf
    state: link
  notify: restart nginx
  become: True

- name: remove the default nginx config file
```

```
file: path=/etc/nginx/sites-enabled/default state=absent
notify: restart nginx
become: True

- name: create tls certificates
  command: >
    openssl req -new -x509 -nodes -out {{ mezzanine_proj_name }}.crt
    -keyout {{ mezzanine_proj_name }}.key -subj '/CN={{ domains[0] }}' -days 3650
    chdir={{ mezzanine_conf_path }}
    creates={{ mezzanine_conf_path }}/{{ mezzanine_proj_name }}.crt
  become: True
  when: tls_enabled
  notify: restart nginx
```

There's one important difference between tasks defined in a role and tasks defined in a regular playbook, and that's when using the copy or template modules.

When invoking copy in a task defined in a role, Ansible will first check the *rolename/files/* directory for the location of the file to copy. Similarly, when invoking template in a task defined in a role, Ansible will first check the *rolename/templates* directory for the location of the template to use.

This means that a task that used to look like this in a playbook:

```
- name: set the nginx config file
  template: src=templates/nginx.conf.j2 \
    dest=/etc/nginx/sites-available/mezzanine.conf
```

now looks like this when invoked from inside the role (note the change of the src parameter):

```
- name: set the nginx config file
  template: src=nginx.conf.j2 dest=/etc/nginx/sites-available/mezzanine.conf
  notify: restart nginx
```

Example 7-13 shows the handlers file.

Example 7-13. roles/mezzanine/handlers/main.yml

```
- name: restart supervisor
  supervisorctl: name=gunicorn_mezzanine state=restarted
  become: True

- name: restart nginx
  service: name=nginx state=restarted
  become: True
```

I won't show the template files here, since they're basically the same as in the previous chapter, although some of the variable names have changed. Check out the accompanying code samples (*http://github.com/ansiblebook/ansiblebook*) for details.

Creating Role Files and Directories with ansible-galaxy

Ansible ships with another command-line tool we haven't talked about yet, `ansible-galaxy`. Its primary purpose is to download roles that have been shared by the Ansible community (more on that later in the chapter). But it can also be used to generate *scaffolding*, an initial set of files and directories involved in a role:

```
$ ansible-galaxy init -p playbooks/roles web
```

The `-p` flag tells `ansible-galaxy` where your roles directory is. If you don't specify it, the role files will be created in your current directory.

Running the command creates the following files and directories:

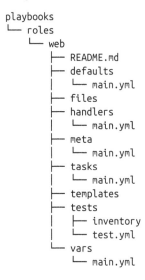

```
playbooks
└── roles
    └── web
        ├── README.md
        ├── defaults
        │   └── main.yml
        ├── files
        ├── handlers
        │   └── main.yml
        ├── meta
        │   └── main.yml
        ├── tasks
        │   └── main.yml
        ├── templates
        ├── tests
        │   ├── inventory
        │   └── test.yml
        └── vars
            └── main.yml
```

Dependent Roles

Imagine that we have two roles, `web` and `database`, that both require an NTP[1] server to be installed on the host. We could specify the installation of the NTP server in both the `web` and `database` roles, but that would result in duplication. We could create a separate `ntp` role, but then we would have to remember that whenever we apply the `web` or `database` role to a host, we have to apply the `ntp` role as well. This would avoid the duplication, but it's error-prone because we might forget to specify the `ntp` role. What we really want is to have an `ntp` role that is always applied to a host whenever we apply the `web` role or the `database` role.

---

1 *NTP* stands for *Network Time Protocol*, used for synchronizing clocks.

Ansible supports a feature called *dependent roles* to deal with this scenario. When you define a role, you can specify that it depends on one or more other roles. Ansible will ensure that roles that are specified as dependencies are executed first.

Continuing with our example, let's say that we create an `ntp` role that configures a host to synchronize its time with an NTP server. Ansible allows us to pass parameters to dependent roles, so let's also assume that we can pass the NTP server as a parameter to that role.

We specify that the `web` role depends on the `ntp` role by creating a *roles/web/meta/main.yml* file and listing `ntp` as a role, with a parameter, as shown in Example 7-14.

Example 7-14. roles/web/meta/main.yml

```
dependencies:
    - { role: ntp, ntp_server=ntp.ubuntu.com }
```

We can also specify multiple dependent roles. For example, if we have a `django` role for setting up a Django web server, and we want to specify `nginx` and `memcached` as dependent roles, then the role metadata file might look like Example 7-15.

Example 7-15. roles/django/meta/main.yml

```
dependencies:
    - { role: web }
    - { role: memcached }
```

For details on how Ansible evaluates the role dependencies, check out the official Ansible documentation on role dependencies (*http://bit.ly/1F6tH9a*).

Ansible Galaxy

If you need to deploy an open source software system onto your hosts, chances are somebody has already written an Ansible role to do it. Although Ansible does make it easier to write scripts for deploying software, some systems are just plain tricky to deploy.

Whether you want to reuse a role somebody has already written, or you just want to see how someone else solved the problem you're working on, Ansible Galaxy can help you out. *Ansible Galaxy* is an open source repository of Ansible roles contributed by the Ansible community. The roles themselves are stored on GitHub.

Web Interface

You can explore the available roles on the Ansible Galaxy site (*http://galaxy.ansi ble.com*). Galaxy supports freetext searching and browsing by category or contributor.

Command-Line Interface

The `ansible-galaxy` command-line tool allows you to download roles from Ansible Galaxy.

Installing a role

Let's say I want to install the role named `ntp`, written by GitHub user *bennojoy*. This is a role that will configure a host to synchronize its clock with an NTP server.

Install the role with the `install` command:

```
$ ansible-galaxy install -p ./roles bennojoy.ntp
```

The `ansible-galaxy` program will install roles to your systemwide location by default (see "Where Does Ansible Look for My Roles?" on page 128), which we overrode in the preceding example with the `-p` flag.

The output should look like this:

```
downloading role 'ntp', owned by bennojoy
no version specified, installing master
- downloading role from https://github.com/bennojoy/ntp/archive/master.tar.gz
- extracting bennojoy.ntp to ./roles/bennojoy.ntp
write_galaxy_install_info!
bennojoy.ntp was installed successfully
```

The `ansible-galaxy` tool will install the role files to *roles/bennojoy.ntp*.

Ansible will install some metadata about the installation to the *./roles/bennojoy.ntp/ meta/.galaxy_install_info* file. On my machine, that file contains the following:

```
{install_date: 'Sat Oct  4 20:12:58 2014', version: master}
```

The *bennojoy.ntp* role does not have a specific version number, so the version is simply listed as `master`. Some roles will have a specific version number, such as 1.2.

Listing installed roles

You can list installed roles as follows:

```
$ ansible-galaxy list
```

Output should look like this:

```
bennojoy.ntp, master
```

Uninstalling a role

Remove a role with the `remove` command:

```
$ ansible-galaxy remove bennojoy.ntp
```

Contributing Your Own Role

See "How To Share Roles You've Written" on the Ansible Galaxy website (*https://galaxy.ansible.com/intro*) for details on how to contribute a role to the community. Because the roles are hosted on GitHub, you need to have a GitHub account to contribute.

At this point, you should have an understanding of how to use roles, how to write your own roles, and how to download roles written by others. Roles are a great way to organize your playbooks. I use them all the time, and I highly recommend them.

## CHAPTER 8

Complex Playbooks

In the preceding chapter, we went over a fully functional Ansible playbook for deploying the Mezzanine CMS. That example used some common Ansible features, but it didn't cover all of them. This chapter touches on those additional features, which makes it a bit of a grab bag.

Dealing with Badly Behaved Commands: changed_when and failed_when

Recall that in Chapter 6, we avoided invoking the custom `createdb manage.py` command, shown in Example 8-1, because the call wasn't idempotent.

Example 8-1. Calling django manage.py createdb

```
- name: initialize the database
  django_manage:
    command: createdb --noinput --nodata
    app_path: "{{ proj_path }}"
    virtualenv: "{{ venv_path }}"
```

We got around this problem by invoking several `django manage.py` commands that were idempotent, and that did the equivalent of `createdb`. But what if we didn't have a module that could invoke equivalent commands? The answer is to use `changed_when` and `failed_when` clauses to change how Ansible identifies that a task has changed state or failed.

First, we need to understand the output of this command the first time it's run, and the output when it's run the second time.

Recall from Chapter 4 that to capture the output of a failed task, you add a `register` clause to save the output to a variable and a `failed_when: False` clause so that the execution doesn't stop even if the module returns failure. Then add a `debug` task to print out the variable, and finally a `fail` clause so that the playbook stops executing, as shown in Example 8-2.

Example 8-2. Viewing the output of a task

```
- name: initialize the database
  django_manage:
    command: createdb --noinput --nodata
    app_path: "{{ proj_path }}"
    virtualenv: "{{ venv_path }}"
  failed_when: False
  register: result

- debug: var=result

- fail:
```

The output of the playbook when invoked the second time is shown in Example 8-3.

Example 8-3. Returned values when database has already been created

```
TASK: [debug var=result] ****************************************************
ok: [default] => {
    "result": {
        "cmd": "python manage.py createdb --noinput --nodata",
        "failed": false,
        "failed_when_result": false,
        "invocation": {
            "module_args": '',
            "module_name": "django_manage"
        },
        "msg": "\n:stderr: CommandError: Database already created, you probably
want the syncdb or migrate command\n",
        "path":
"/home/vagrant/mezzanine_example/bin:/usr/local/sbin:/usr/local/bin:
/usr/sbin:/usr/bin:/sbin:/bin:/usr/games:/usr/local/games",
        "state": "absent",
        "syspath": [
            ``,
            "/usr/lib/python2.7",
            "/usr/lib/python2.7/plat-x86_64-linux-gnu",
            "/usr/lib/python2.7/lib-tk",
            "/usr/lib/python2.7/lib-old",
            "/usr/lib/python2.7/lib-dynload",
            "/usr/local/lib/python2.7/dist-packages",
            "/usr/lib/python2.7/dist-packages"
        ]
    }
}
```

This is what happens when the task has been run multiple times. To see what happens the first time, delete the database and then have the playbook re-create it. The simplest way to do that is to run an Ansible ad hoc task that deletes the database:

```
$ ansible default --become --become-user postgres -m postgresql_db -a \
"name=mezzanine_example state=absent"
```

Now when I run the playbook again, I get the output in Example 8-4.

Example 8-4. Returned values when invoked the first time

```
ASK: [debug var=result] ********************************************************
ok: [default] => {
    "result": {
        "app_path": "/home/vagrant/mezzanine_example/project",
        "changed": false,
        "cmd": "python manage.py createdb --noinput --nodata",
        "failed": false,
        "failed_when_result": false,
        "invocation": {
            "module_args": '',
            "module_name": "django_manage"
        },
        "out": "Creating tables ...\nCreating table auth_permission\nCreating
table auth_group_permissions\nCreating table auth_group\nCreating table
auth_user_groups\nCreating table auth_user_user_permissions\nCreating table
auth_user\nCreating table django_content_type\nCreating table
django_redirect\nCreating table django_session\nCreating table
django_site\nCreating table conf_setting\nCreating table
core_sitepermission_sites\nCreating table core_sitepermission\nCreating table
generic_threadedcomment\nCreating table generic_keyword\nCreating table
generic_assignedkeyword\nCreating table generic_rating\nCreating table
blog_blogpost_related_posts\nCreating table blog_blogpost_categories\nCreating
table blog_blogpost\nCreating table blog_blogcategory\nCreating table
forms_form\nCreating table forms_field\nCreating table forms_formentry\nCreating
table forms_fieldentry\nCreating table pages_page\nCreating table
pages_richtextpage\nCreating table pages_link\nCreating table
galleries_gallery\nCreating table galleries_galleryimage\nCreating table
twitter_query\nCreating table twitter_tweet\nCreating table
south_migrationhistory\nCreating table django_admin_log\nCreating table
django_comments\nCreating table django_comment_flags\n\nCreating default site
record: vagrant-ubuntu-trusty-64 ... \n\nInstalled 2 object(s) from 1
fixture(s)\nInstalling custom SQL ...\nInstalling indexes ...\nInstalled 0
object(s) from 0 fixture(s)\n\nFaking initial migrations ...\n\n",
        "pythonpath": null,
        "settings": null,
        "virtualenv": "/home/vagrant/mezzanine_example"
    }
}
```

Note that `changed` is set to `false` even though it did, indeed, change the state of the database. That's because the `django_manage` module always returns `changed=false` when it runs commands that the module doesn't know about.

We can add a `changed_when` clause that looks for `"Creating tables"` in the `out` return value, as shown in Example 8-5.

Example 8-5. First attempt at adding changed_when

```
- name: initialize the database
  django_manage:
    command: createdb --noinput --nodata
    app_path: "{{ proj_path }}"
    virtualenv: "{{ venv_path }}"
  register: result
  changed_when: '"Creating tables" in result.out'
```

The problem with this approach is that, if we look back at Example 8-3, we see that there is no `out` variable. Instead, there's a `msg` variable. If we executed the playbook, we'd get the following (not terribly helpful) error the second time:

```
TASK: [initialize the database] ********************************************
fatal: [default] => error while evaluating conditional: "Creating tables" in
result.out
```

Instead, we need to ensure that Ansible evaluates `result.out` only if that variable is defined. One way is to explicitly check whether the variable is defined:

```
changed_when: result.out is defined and "Creating tables" in result.out
```

Alternatively, we could provide a default value for `result.out` if it doesn't exist by using the Jinja2 `default` filter:

```
changed_when: '"Creating tables" in result.out|default("")'
```

The final idempotent task is shown in Example 8-6.

Example 8-6. Idempotent manage.py createdb

```
- name: initialize the database
  django_manage:
    command: createdb --noinput --nodata
    app_path: "{{ proj_path }}"
    virtualenv: "{{ venv_path }}"
  register: result
  changed_when: '"Creating tables" in result.out|default("")'
```

Filters

Filters are a feature of the Jinja2 templating engine. Since Ansible uses Jinja2 for evaluating variables, as well as for templates, you can use filters inside `{{ braces }}` in your playbooks, as well as inside your template files. Using filters resembles using Unix pipes, whereby a variable is piped through a filter. Jinja2 ships with a set of built-in filters (*http://bit.ly/1FvOGzI*). In addition, Ansible ships with its own filters to augment the Jinja2 filters (*http://bit.ly/1FvOIrj*).

We'll cover a few sample filters here, but check out the official Jinja2 and Ansible docs for a complete list of the available filters.

The Default Filter

The `default` filter is a useful one. Here's an example of this filter in action:

```
"HOST": "{{ database_host | default('localhost') }}",
```

If the variable `database_host` is defined, the braces will evaluate to the value of that variable. If the variable `database_host` is not defined, the braces will evaluate to the string `localhost`. Some filters take arguments, and some don't.

Filters for Registered Variables

Let's say we want to run a task and print out its output, even if the task fails. However, if the task does fail, we want Ansible to fail for that host after printing the output. Example 8-7 shows how to use the `failed` filter in the argument to the `failed_when` clause.

Example 8-7. Using the failed filter

```
- name: Run myprog
  command: /opt/myprog
  register: result
  ignore_errors: True

- debug: var=result

- debug: msg="Stop running the playbook if myprog failed"
  failed_when: result|failed
# more tasks here
```

Table 8-1 shows a list of filters you can use on registered variables to check the status.

Table 8-1. Task return value filters

Name	Description
failed	True if a registered value is a task that failed
changed	True if a registered value is a task that changed
success	True if a registered value is a task that succeeded
skipped	True if a registered value is a task that was skipped

Filters That Apply to File Paths

Table 8-2 shows filters that are useful when a variable contains the path to a file on the control machine's filesystem.

Table 8-2. File path filters

Name	Description
basename	Base name of file path
dirname	Directory of file path
expanduser	File path with ~ replaced by home directory
realpath	Canonical path of file path, resolves symbolic links

Consider this playbook fragment:

```
vars:
  homepage: /usr/share/nginx/html/index.html
tasks:
- name: copy home page
  copy: src=files/index.html dest={{ homepage }}
```

Note that it references *index.html* twice: once in the definition of the homepage variable, and a second time to specify the path to the file on the control machine.

The basename filter will let us extract the *index.html* part of the filename from the full path, allowing us to write the playbook without repeating the filename:[1]

```
vars:
  homepage: /usr/share/nginx/html/index.html
tasks:
- name: copy home page
  copy: src=files/{{ homepage | basename }} dest={{ homepage }}
```

---

1 Thanks to John Jarvis for this tip.

Writing Your Own Filter

Recall that in our Mezzanine example, we generated the *local_settings.py* file from a template, and a line in the generated file looks like Example 8-8.

Example 8-8. Line from local_settings.py generated by template

```
ALLOWED_HOSTS = ["www.example.com", "example.com"]
```

We had a variable named `domains` that contained a list of the hostnames. We originally used a `for` loop in our template to generate this line, but a filter would be an even more elegant approach.

There is a built-in Jinja2 filter called `join` that will join a list of strings with a delimiter such as a comma. Unfortunately, it doesn't quite give us what we want. If we did this in the template:

```
ALLOWED_HOSTS = [{{ domains|join(", ") }}]
```

then we would end up with the strings unquoted in our file, as shown in Example 8-9.

Example 8-9. Strings incorrectly unquoted

```
ALLOWED_HOSTS = [www.example.com, example.com]
```

If we had a Jinja2 filter that quoted the strings in the list, as shown in Example 8-10, then the template would generate the output depicted in Example 8-8.

Example 8-10. Using a filter to quote the strings in the list

```
ALLOWED_HOSTS = [{{ domains|surround_by_quote|join(", ") }}]
```

Unfortunately, there's no existing `surround_by_quote` filter that does what we want. However, we can write it ourselves. (In fact, Hanfei Sun on Stack Overflow covered this very topic (*http://stackoverflow.com/questions/15514365/*).)

Ansible will look for custom filters in the *filter_plugins* directory, relative to the directory containing your playbooks.

Example 8-11 shows what the filter implementation looks like.

Example 8-11. filter_plugins/surround_by_quotes.py

```
# From http://stackoverflow.com/a/15515929/742

def surround_by_quote(a_list):
    return ['"%s"' % an_element for an_element in a_list]
```

```
class FilterModule(object):
    def filters(self):
        return {'surround_by_quote': surround_by_quote}
```

The `surround_by_quote` function defines the Jinja2 filter. The `FilterModule` class defines a `filters` method that returns a dictionary with the name of the filter function and the function itself. The `FilterModule` class is Ansible-specific code that makes the Jinja2 filter available to Ansible.

You can also place filter plugins in the ~/.*ansible/plugins/filter* directory, or the */usr/ share/ansible/plugins/filter* directory, or you can specify the directory by setting the `ANSIBLE_FILTER_PLUGINS` environment variable to the directory where your plugins are located.

Lookups

In an ideal world, all of your configuration information would be stored as Ansible variables, in the various places that Ansible lets you define variables (e.g., the `vars` section of your playbooks, files loaded by `vars_files`, files in the *host_vars* or *group_vars* directory that we discussed in Chapter 3).

Alas, the world is a messy place, and sometimes a piece of configuration data you need lives somewhere else. Maybe it's in a text file or a *.csv* file, and you don't want to just copy the data into an Ansible variable file because now you have to maintain two copies of the same data, and you believe in the DRY[2] principle. Or maybe the data isn't maintained as a file at all; it's maintained in a key-value storage service such as *etcd*.[3] Ansible has a feature called *lookups* that allows you to read in configuration data from various sources and then use that data in your playbooks and template.

Ansible supports a collection of lookups for retrieving data from different sources. Some of the lookups are shown in Table 8-3.

Table 8-3. Lookups

Name	Description
file	Contents of a file
password	Randomly generate a password
pipe	Output of locally executed command
env	Environment variable

---

2 Don't Repeat Yourself, a term popularized by *The Pragmatic Programmer: From Journeyman to Master*, which is a fantastic book.

3 etcd is a distributed key-value store maintained by the CoreOS project (*https://coreos.com/docs/etcd/*).

Name	Description
template	Jinja2 template after evaluation
csvfile	Entry in a *.csv* file
dnstxt	DNS TXT record
redis_kv	Redis key lookup
etcd	etcd key lookup

You invoke lookups by calling the lookup function with two arguments. The first is a string with the name of the lookup, and the second is a string that contains one or more arguments to pass to the lookup. For example, we call the file lookup like this:

```
lookup('file', '/path/to/file.txt')
```

You can invoke lookups in your playbooks between {{ braces }}, or you can put them in templates.

In this section, I provided only a brief overview of lookups that are available. The Ansible documentation provides more details (*http://docs.ansible.com/playbooks_look ups.html*) on available lookups and how to use them.

All Ansible lookup plugins execute on the control machine, not the remote host.

file

Let's say you have a text file on your control machine that contains a public SSH key that you want to copy to a remote server. Example 8-12 shows how to use the file lookup to read the contents of a file and pass that as a parameter to a module.

Example 8-12. Using the file lookup

```
- name: Add my public key as an EC2 key
  ec2_key: name=mykey key_material="{{ lookup('file', \
  '/Users/lorin/.ssh/id_rsa.pub') }}"
```

You can invoke lookups in templates as well. If we want to use the same technique to create an *authorized_keys* file that contains the contents of a public-key file, we could create a Jinja2 template that invokes the lookup, as shown in Example 8-13, and then call the template module in our playbook, as shown in Example 8-14.

Example 8-13. authorized_keys.j2

```
{{ lookup('file', '/Users/lorin/.ssh/id_rsa.pub') }}
```

Example 8-14. Task to generate authorized_keys

```
- name: copy authorized_host file
  template: src=authorized_keys.j2 dest=/home/deploy/.ssh/authorized_keys
```

pipe

The pipe lookup invokes an external program on the control machine and evaluates to the program's output on standard out.

For example, if our playbooks are version controlled using git, and we want to get the SHA-1 value of the most recent git commit,[4] we could use the pipe lookup:

```
- name: get SHA of most recent commit
  debug: msg="{{ lookup('pipe', 'git rev-parse HEAD') }}"
```

The output looks something like this:

```
TASK: [get the sha of the current commit] ************************************
ok: [myserver] => {
    "msg": "e7748af0f040d58d61de1917980a210df419eae9"
}
```

env

The env lookup retrieves the value of an environment variable set on the control machine. For example, we could use the lookup like this:

```
- name: get the current shell
  debug: msg="{{ lookup('env', 'SHELL') }}"
```

Since I use Zsh as my shell, the output looks like this when I run it:

```
TASK: [get the current shell] ************************************************
ok: [myserver] => {
    "msg": "/bin/zsh"
}
```

password

The password lookup evaluates to a random password, and it will also write the password to a file specified in the argument. For example, if we want to create a Postgres

---

4 If this sounds like gibberish, don't worry about it; it's just an example of running a command.

user named `deploy` with a random password and write that password to *deploy-password.txt* on the control machine, we can do this:

```
- name: create deploy postgres user
  postgresql_user:
    name: deploy
    password: "{{ lookup('password', 'deploy-password.txt') }}"
```

template

The `template` lookup lets you specify a Jinja2 template file, and then returns the result of evaluating the template. Say we have a template that looks like Example 8-15.

Example 8-15. message.j2

```
This host runs {{ ansible_distribution }}
```

If we define a task like this:

```
- name: output message from template
  debug: msg="{{ lookup('template', 'message.j2') }}"
```

then we'll see output that looks like this:

```
TASK: [output message from template] ******************************************
ok: [myserver] => {
    "msg": "This host runs Ubuntu\n"
}
```

csvfile

The `csvfile` lookup reads an entry from a *.csv* file. Assume we have a *.csv* file that looks like Example 8-16.

Example 8-16. users.csv

```
username,email
lorin,lorin@ansiblebook.com
john,john@example.com
sue,sue@example.org
```

If we want to extract Sue's email address by using the `csvfile` lookup plugin, we would invoke the lookup plugin like this:

```
lookup('csvfile', 'sue file=users.csv delimiter=, col=1')
```

The `csvfile` lookup is a good example of a lookup that takes multiple arguments. Here, four arguments are being passed to the plugin:

- sue
- file=users.csv
- delimiter=,
- col=1

You don't specify a name for the first argument to a lookup plugin, but you do specify names for the additional arguments. In the case of `csvfile`, the first argument is an entry that must appear exactly once in column 0 (the first column, 0-indexed) of the table.

The other arguments specify the name of the *.csv* file, the delimiter, and which column should be returned. In our example, we want to look in the file named *users.csv* and locate where the fields are delimited by commas, look up the row where the value in the first column is `sue`, and return the value in the second column (column 1, indexed by 0). This evaluates to *sue@example.org*.

If the username we want to look up is stored in a variable named `username`, we could construct the argument string by using the + sign to concatenate the `username` string with the rest of the argument string:

```
lookup('csvfile', username + ' file=users.csv delimiter=, col=1')
```

dnstxt

 The dnstxt module requires that you install the *dnspython* Python package on the control machine.

If you're reading this book, you're probably aware of what the Domain Name System (DNS) does, but just in case you aren't, DNS is the service that translates hostnames such as *ansiblebook.com* to IP addresses such as *64.99.80.30*.

DNS works by associating one or more records with a hostname. The most commonly used types of DNS records are *A* records and *CNAME* records, which associate a hostname with an IP address (A record) or specify that a hostname is an alias for another hostname (CNAME record).

The DNS protocol supports another type of record that you can associate with a hostname, called a *TXT* record. A TXT record is just an arbitrary string that you can attach to a hostname. Once you've associated a TXT record with a hostname, anybody can retrieve the text by using a DNS client.

For example, I own the *ansiblebook.com* domain, so I can create TXT records associated with any hostnames in that domain.[5] I associated a TXT record with the *ansiblebook.com* hostname that contains the ISBN number for this book. You can look up the TXT record by using the `dig` command-line tool, as shown in Example 8-17.

Example 8-17. Using the dig tool to look up a TXT record

```
$ dig +short ansiblebook.com TXT
"isbn=978-1491979808"
```

The `dnstxt` lookup queries the DNS server for the TXT record associated with the host. If we create a task like this in a playbook:

```
- name: look up TXT record
  debug: msg="{{ lookup('dnstxt', 'ansiblebook.com') }}"
```

the output will look like this:

```
TASK: [look up TXT record] ***************************************************
ok: [myserver] => {
    "msg": "isbn=978-1491979808"
}
```

If multiple TXT records are associated with a host, the module will concatenate them together, and it might do this in a different order each time it is called. For example, if there were a second TXT record on *ansiblebook.com* with this text:

```
author=lorin
```

then the *dnstxt* lookup would randomly return one of the two:

- `isbn=978-1491979808author=lorin`
- `author=lorinisbn=978-1491979808`

redis_kv

The `redis_kv` module requires that you install the *redis* Python package on the control machine.

---

5 DNS service providers typically have web interfaces to let you perform DNS-related tasks such as creating TXT records.

Redis is a popular key-value store, commonly used as a cache, as well as a data store for job queue services such as Sidekiq. You can use the redis_kv lookup to retrieve the value of a key. The key must be a string, as the module does the equivalent of calling the Redis GET command.

For example, let's say that we have a Redis server running on our control machine, and we set the key weather to the value sunny, by doing something like this:

```
$ redis-cli SET weather sunny
```

If we define a task in our playbook that invokes the Redis lookup:

```
- name: look up value in Redis
  debug: msg="{{ lookup('redis_kv', 'redis://localhost:6379,weather') }}"
```

the output will look like this:

```
TASK: [look up value in Redis] *************************************************
ok: [myserver] => {
    "msg": "sunny"
}
```

The module will default to *redis://localhost:6379* if the URL isn't specified, so we could invoke the module like this instead (note the comma before the key):

```
lookup('redis_kv', ',weather')
```

etcd

Etcd is a distributed key-value store, commonly used for keeping configuration data and for implementing service discovery. You can use the etcd lookup to retrieve the value of a key.

For example, let's say that we have an etcd server running on our control machine, and we set the key weather to the value cloudy by doing something like this:

```
$ curl -L http://127.0.0.1:4001/v2/keys/weather -XPUT -d value=cloudy
```

If we define a task in our playbook that invokes the etcd plugin:

```
- name: look up value in etcd
  debug: msg="{{ lookup('etcd', 'weather') }}"
```

The output looks like this:

```
TASK: [look up value in etcd] **************************************************
ok: [localhost] => {
    "msg": "cloudy"
}
```

By default, the etcd lookup looks for the etcd server at *http://127.0.0.1:4001*, but you can change this by setting the ANSIBLE_ETCD_URL environment variable before invoking ansible-playbook.

Writing Your Own Lookup Plugin

You can also write your own lookup plugin if you need functionality not provided by the existing plugins. Writing a custom lookup plugin is out of scope for this book, but if you're really interested, I suggest that you take a look at the source code for the lookup plugins that ship with Ansible (*https://github.com/ansible/ansible/tree/devel/lib/ansible/plugins/lookup*).

Once you've written your lookup plugin, place it in one of the following directories:

- The *lookup_plugins* directory next to your playbook
- *~/.ansible/plugins/lookup*
- */usr/share/ansible/plugins/lookup*
- The directory specified in your ANSIBLE_LOOKUP_PLUGINS environment variable

More Complicated Loops

Up until this point, whenever we've written a task that iterates over a list of items, we've used the with_items clause to specify a list of items. Although this is the most common way to do loops, Ansible supports other mechanisms for iteration. Table 8-4 provides a summary of the constructs that are available.

Table 8-4. Looping constructs

Name	Input	Looping strategy
with_items	List	Loop over list elements
with_lines	Command to execute	Loop over lines in command output
with_fileglob	Glob	Loop over filenames
with_first_found	List of paths	First file in input that exists
with_dict	Dictionary	Loop over dictionary elements
with_flattened	List of lists	Loop over flattened list
with_indexed_items	List	Single iteration
with_nested	List	Nested loop
with_random_choice	List	Single iteration
with_sequence	Sequence of integers	Loop over sequence
with_subelements	List of dictionaries	Nested loop
with_together	List of lists	Loop over zipped list
with_inventory_hostnames	Host pattern	Loop over matching hosts

The official documentation (*http://bit.ly/1F6kfCP*) covers these quite thoroughly, so I'll show examples from just a few of them to give you a sense of how they work.

with_lines

The `with_lines` looping construct lets you run an arbitrary command on your control machine and iterate over the output, one line at a time.

Imagine you have a file that contains a list of names, and you want to send a Slack message for each name, something like this:

```
Leslie Lamport
Silvio Micali
Shafi Goldwasser
Judea Pearl
```

Example 8-18 shows how to use `with_lines` to read a file and iterate over its contents line by line.

Example 8-18. Using with_lines as a loop

```
- name: Send out a slack message
  slack:
    domain: example.slack.com
    token: "{{ slack_token }}"
    msg: "{{ item }} was in the list"
  with_lines:
    - cat files/turing.txt
```

with_fileglob

The `with_fileglob` construct is useful for iterating over a set of files on the control machine.

Example 8-19 shows how to iterate over files that end in *.pub* in the */var/keys* directory, as well as a *keys* directory next to your playbook. It then uses the `file` lookup plugin to extract the contents of the file, which are passed to the `authorized_key` module.

Example 8-19. Using with_fileglob to add keys

```
- name: add public keys to account
  authorized_key: user=deploy key="{{ lookup('file', item) }}"
  with_fileglob:
    - /var/keys/*.pub
    - keys/*.pub
```

with_dict

The `with_dict` construct lets you iterate over a dictionary instead of a list. When you use this looping construct, the `item` loop variable is a dictionary with two keys:

key

One of the keys in the dictionary

value

The value in the dictionary that corresponds to *key*

For example, if your host has an `eth0` interface, there will be an Ansible fact named `ansible_eth0`, with a key named `ipv4` that contains a dictionary that looks something like this:

```
{
  "address": "10.0.2.15",
  "netmask": "255.255.255.0",
  "network": "10.0.2.0"
}
```

We could iterate over this dictionary and print out the entries one at a time:

```
- name: iterate over ansible_eth0
  debug: msg={{ item.key }}={{ item.value }}
  with_dict: "{{ ansible_eth0.ipv4 }}"
```

The output looks like this:

```
TASK: [iterate over ansible_eth0] *********************************************
ok: [myserver] => (item={'key': u'netmask', 'value': u'255.255.255.0'}) => {
    "item": {
        "key": "netmask",
        "value": "255.255.255.0"
    },
    "msg": "netmask=255.255.255.0"
}
ok: [myserver] => (item={'key': u'network', 'value': u'10.0.2.0'}) => {
    "item": {
        "key": "network",
        "value": "10.0.2.0"
    },
    "msg": "network=10.0.2.0"
}
ok: [myserver] => (item={'key': u'address', 'value': u'10.0.2.15'}) => {
    "item": {
        "key": "address",
        "value": "10.0.2.15"
    },
    "msg": "address=10.0.2.15"
}
```

Looping Constructs as Lookup Plugins

Ansible implements looping constructs as lookup plugins. You just slap a `with` at the beginning of a lookup plugin to use it in its loop form. For example, we can rewrite Example 8-12 by using the `with_file` form in Example 8-20.

Example 8-20. Using the file lookup as a loop

```
- name: Add my public key as an EC2 key
  ec2_key: name=mykey key_material="{{ item }}"
  with_file: /Users/lorin/.ssh/id_rsa.pub
```

Typically, you use a lookup plugin as a looping construct only if it returns a list, which is how I was able to separate out the plugins into Table 8-3 (return strings) and Table 8-4 (return lists).

Loop Controls

With version 2.1, Ansible provides users with more control over loop handling.

Setting the Variable Name

The `loop_var` control allows us to give the iteration variable a different name than the default name, `item`, as shown in Example 8-21.

Example 8-21. Use user as loop variable

```
- user:
    name: "{{ user.name }}"
  with_items:
    - { name: gil }
    - { name: sarina }
    - { name: leanne }
  loop_control:
    loop_var: user
```

Although in Example 8-21 `loop_var` provides only a cosmetic improvement, it can be essential for more advanced loops.

In Example 8-22, we would like to loop over multiple tasks at once. One way to achieve that is to use `include` with `with_items`.

However, the *vhosts.yml* file that is going to be included may also contain `with_items` in some tasks. This would produce a conflict, as the default `loop_var item` is used for *both* loops at the same time.

To prevent a naming collision, we specify a different name for `loop_var` in the outer loop.

Example 8-22. Use vhost as loop variable

```
- name: run a set of tasks in one loop
  include: vhosts.yml
```

```
with_items:
  - { domain: www1.example.com }
  - { domain: www2.example.com }
  - { domain: www3.example.com }
loop_control:
  loop_var: vhost ❶
```

❶   Change the loop variable name for outer loops to prevent name collisions.

In the included task file *vhosts.yml* you see in Example 8-23, we are now able to use the default `loop_var` name `item` as we used to do.

Example 8-23. Included file can contain a loop

```
- name: create nginx directories
  file:
    path: /var/www/html/{{ vhost.domain }}/{{ item }} ❶
  state: directory
  with_items:
    - logs
    - public_http
    - public_https
    - includes

- name: create nginx vhost config
  template:
    src: "{{ vhost.domain }}.j2"
    dest: /etc/nginx/conf.d/{{ vhost.domain }}.conf
```

❶   We keep the default loop variable in the inner loop.

Labeling the Output

The `label` control was added in Ansible 2.2 and provides some control over how the loop output will be shown to the user during execution.

The following example contains an ordinary list of dictionaries:

```
- name: create nginx vhost configs
  template:
    src: "{{ item.domain }}.conf.j2"
    dest: "/etc/nginx/conf.d/{{ item.domain }}.conf"
  with_items:
    - { domain: www1.example.com, ssl_enabled: yes }
    - { domain: www2.example.com }
    - { domain: www3.example.com,
        aliases: [ edge2.www.example.com, eu.www.example.com ] }
```

By default, Ansible prints the entire dictionary in the output. For larger dictionaries, the output can be difficult to read without a `loop_control` clause that specifies a label:

```
TASK [create nginx vhost configs] *********************************************
ok: [localhost] => (item={u'domain': u'www1.example.com', u'ssl_enabled': True})
ok: [localhost] => (item={u'domain': u'www2.example.com'})
ok: [localhost] => (item={u'domain': u'www3.example.com', u'aliases':
[u'edge2.www.example.com', u'eu.www.example.com']})
```

Since we are interested only in the domain names, we can simply add a *label* in the `loop_control` clause describing what should be printed when we iterate over the items:

```
- name: create nginx vhost configs
  template:
    src: "{{ item.domain }}.conf.j2"
    dest: "/etc/nginx/conf.d/{{ item.domain }}.conf"
  with_items:
    - { domain: www1.example.com, ssl_enabled: yes }
    - { domain: www2.example.com }
    - { domain: www3.example.com,
        aliases: [ edge2.www.example.com, eu.www.example.com ] }
  loop_control:
    label: "for domain {{ item.domain }}" ❶
```

❶ Adding a custom `label`

This results in much more readable output:

```
TASK [create nginx vhost configs] *********************************************
ok: [localhost] => (item=for domain www1.example.com)
ok: [localhost] => (item=for domain www2.example.com)
ok: [localhost] => (item=for domain www3.example.com)
```

 Keep in mind that running in verbose mode -v will show the full dictionary; don't use it to hide your passwords! Set `no_log: true` on the task instead.

Includes

The `include` feature allows you to include tasks or even whole playbooks, depending on where you define an include. It is often used in roles to separate or even group tasks and task arguments to each task in the included file.

Let's consider an example. Example 8-24 contains two tasks of a play that share an identical `tag`, a `when` condition, and a `become` argument.

Example 8-24. Identical arguments

```
- name: install nginx
  package:
    name: nginx
  tags: nginx ❶
  become: yes ❷
  when: ansible_os_family == 'RedHat' ❸

- name: ensure nginx is running
  service:
    name: nginx
    state: started
    enabled: yes
  tags: nginx ❶
  become: yes ❷
  when: ansible_os_family == 'RedHat' ❸
```

❶ Identical `tags`

❷ Identical `become`

❸ Identical condition

When we separate these two tasks in a file as in Example 8-25 and use `include` as in Example 8-26, we can simplify the play by adding the task arguments only to the `include` task.

Example 8-25. Separate tasks into a different file

```
- name: install nginx
  package:
    name: nginx

- name: ensure nginx is running
  service:
    name: nginx
    state: started
    enabled: yes
```

Example 8-26. Using an include for the tasks file applying the arguments in common

```
- include: nginx_include.yml
  tags: nginx
  become: yes
  when: ansible_os_family == 'RedHat'
```

Dynamic Includes

A common pattern in roles is to define tasks specific to a particular operating system into separate task files. Depending on the number of operating systems supported by the role, this can lead to a lot of boilerplate for the `include` tasks.

```
- include: Redhat.yml
  when: ansible_os_family == 'Redhat'

- include: Debian.yml
  when: ansible_os_family == 'Debian'
```

Since version 2.0, Ansible allows us to dynamically include a file by using variable substitution:

```
- include: "{{ ansible_os_family }}.yml"
  static: no
```

However, there is a drawback to using dynamic includes: `ansible-playbook --list-tasks` might not list the tasks from a dynamic include if Ansible does not have enough information to populate the variables that determine which file will be included. For example, fact variables (see Chapter 4) are not populated when the `--list-tasks` argument is used.

Role Includes

A special include is the `include_role` clause. In contrast with the `role` clause, which will use all parts of the role, the `include_role` not only allows us to selectively choose what parts of a role will be included and used, but also where in the play.

Similarly to the `include` clause, the mode can be static or dynamic, and Ansible does a best guess as to what is needed. However, we can always append `static` to enforce the desired mode.

```
- name: install nginx
  yum:
    pkg: nginx

- name: install php
  include_role:
    name: php ❶

- name: configure nginx
  template:
    src: nginx.conf.j2
    dest: /etc/nginx/nginx.conf
```

❶ Include and run *main.yml* from the php role.

The `include_role` clause makes the handlers available as well.

The `include_role` clause can also help to avoid the hassle of parts of roles depending on each other. Imagine that in the role dependency, which runs before the main role, a file task changes the owner of a file. But the system user used as the owner does not yet exist at that point. It will be created later in the main role during a package installation.

```
- name: install nginx
  yum:
    pkg: nginx

- name: install php
  include_role:
    name: php
    tasks_from: install ❶

- name: configure nginx
  template:
    src: nginx.conf.j2
    dest: /etc/nginx/nginx.conf

- name: configure php
  include_role:
    name: php
    tasks_from: configure ❷
```

❶ Include and run *install.yml* from the `php` role.

❷ Include and run *configure.yml* from the `php` role.

 At the time of writing, the `include_role` clause is still labeled as *preview*, which means there is no guarantee of a backward-compatible interface.

Blocks

Much like the `include` clause, the `block` clause provides a mechanism for grouping tasks. The `block` clause allows you to set conditions or arguments for all tasks within a block at once:

```
  - block:
    - name: install nginx
      package:
        name: nginx
    - name: ensure nginx is running
      service:
        name: nginx
        state: started
        enabled: yes
    become: yes
    when: "ansible_os_family == 'RedHat'"
```

 Unlike an include clause, looping over a block clause is currently not supported.

The block clause has an even more interesting application: error handling.

Error Handling with Blocks

Dealing with error scenarios has always been a challenge. Historically, Ansible has been error agnostic in the sense that errors and failures may occur on a host. Ansible's default error-handling behavior is to take a host out of the play if a task fails and continue as long as there are hosts remaining that haven't encountered errors.

In combination with the serial and max_fail_percentage clause, Ansible gives you some control over when a play has to be declared as failed.

With the blocks clause as shown in Example 8-27, Ansible advances error handling a bit further and lets us automate recovery and rollback of tasks in case of a failure.

Example 8-27. app-upgrade.yml

```
---
- block: ❶
  - debug: msg="You will see a failed tasks right after this"
  - command: /bin/false
  - debug: "You won't see this message"
  rescue: ❷
  - debug: "You only see this message in case of an failure in the block"
  always: ❸
  - debug: "This will be always executed"
```

❶   Start of the block clause

❷   Tasks to be executed in case of a failure in block clause

---

❸ Tasks to always be executed

If you have some programming experience, the way error handling is implemented may remind you of the *try-catch-finally* paradigm, and it works much the same way.

To demonstrate how this can work, we start with a daily business job: upgrading an application. The application is distributed in a cluster of virtual machines (VMs) and deployed on an IaaS cloud (Apache CloudStack (*http://cloudstack.apache.org*)). Furthermore, the cloud provides the functionality to snapshot a VM. The simplified playbook looks like the following:

1. Take VM out of the load balancer.
2. Create a VM snapshot before the app upgrade.
3. Upgrade the application.
4. Run smoke tests.
5. Roll back when something goes wrong.
6. Move VM back to the load balancer.
7. Clean up and remove the VM snapshot.

Let's put these tasks into a playbook, still simplified and not yet runnable, as shown in Example 8-28.

Example 8-28. app-upgrade.yml

```
---
- hosts: app-servers
  serial: 1
  tasks:
  - name: Take VM out of the load balancer
  - name: Create a VM snapshot before the app upgrade

  - block:
    - name: Upgrade the application
    - name: Run smoke tests

    rescue:
    - name: Revert a VM to the snapshot after a failed upgrade

    always:
    - name: Re-add webserver to the loadbalancer
    - name: Remove a VM snapshot
```

In this playbook, we will most certainly end up with a running VM being a member of a load balancer cluster, even if the upgrade fails.

The tasks under the `always` clause will be executed even if an error occurred in the `rescue` clause! Be careful what you put in the `always` clause.

In case we want to get only upgraded VMs back to the load balancer cluster, the play would look a bit different, as shown in Example 8-29.

Example 8-29. app-upgrade.yml

```
---
- hosts: app-servers
  serial: 1
  tasks:
  - name: Take VM out of the load balancer
  - name: Create a VM snapshot before the app upgrade

  - block:
      - name: Upgrade the application
      - name: Run smoke tests

    rescue:
      - name: Revert a VM to the snapshot after a failed upgrade

  - name: Re-add webserver to the loadbalancer
  - name: Remove a VM snapshot
```

We removed the `always` clause and put the two tasks at the end of the play. This ensures that the two tasks will be executed only if the rescue went through. As a result, we get only upgraded VMs back to the load balancer.

The final playbook looks like Example 8-30.

Example 8-30. Error-agnostic application-upgrade playbook

```
---
- hosts: app-servers
  serial: 1
  tasks:
  - name: Take app server out of the load balancer
    local_action:
      module: cs_loadbalancer_rule_member
      name: balance_http
      vm: "{{ inventory_hostname_short }}"
      state: absent
  - name: Create a VM snapshot before an upgrade
    local_action:
      module: cs_vmsnapshot
      name: Snapshot before upgrade
```

```
      vm: "{{ inventory_hostname_short }}"
      snapshot_memory: yes

- block:
  - name: Upgrade the application
    script: upgrade-app.sh
  - name: Run smoke tests
    script: smoke-tests.sh

  rescue:
  - name: Revert the VM to a snapshot after a failed upgrade
    local_action:
      module: cs_vmsnapshot
      name: Snapshot before upgrade
      vm: "{{ inventory_hostname_short }}"
      state: revert

- name: Re-add app server to the loadbalancer
  local_action:
    module: cs_loadbalancer_rule_member
    name: balance_http
    vm: "{{ inventory_hostname_short }}"
    state: present
- name: Remove a VM snapshot after successful upgrade or successful rollback
  local_action:
    module: cs_vmsnapshot
    name: Snapshot before upgrade
    vm: "{{ inventory_hostname_short }}"
    state: absent
```

Encrypting Sensitive Data with Vault

Our Mezzanine playbook requires access to sensitive information, such as database and administrator passwords. We dealt with this in Chapter 6 by putting all of the sensitive information in a separate file called *secrets.yml* and making sure that we didn't check this file into our version-control repository.

Ansible provides an alternative solution: instead of keeping the *secrets.yml* file out of version control, we can commit an encrypted version. That way, even if our version-control repository were compromised, the attacker would not have access to the contents of the *secrets.yml* file unless he also had the password used for the encryption.

The `ansible-vault` command-line tool allows you to create and edit an encrypted file that `ansible-playbook` will recognize and decrypt automatically, given the password.

We can encrypt an existing file like this:

```
$ ansible-vault encrypt secrets.yml
```

Alternately, we can create a new encrypted *secrets.yml* file:

```
$ ansible-vault create secrets.yml
```

You will be prompted for a password, and then `ansible-vault` will launch a text editor so that you can populate the file. It launches the editor specified in the `$EDITOR` environment variable. If that variable is not defined, it defaults to `vim`.

Example 8-31 shows an example of the contents of a file encrypted using `ansible-vault`.

Example 8-31. Contents of file encrypted with ansible-vault

```
$ANSIBLE_VAULT;1.1;AES256
34306434353230663665653353936373635383633393638393131643434303031636665333136326 2
66306333663831353862663330303039363430366461366235a6238376634623930316262333 76232
31613735376632333323162666166376662623933337383565323931623038633930333036 66383530
...
62346633343464313330383832646531623338633438336465323166626335623639383363 643438
64636665366538343038383830316564616136656632656633066396438333165653436
```

You can use the `vars_files` section of a play to reference a file encrypted with `ansible-vault` the same way you would access a regular file: we would not need to modify Example 6-28 at all if we encrypted the *secrets.yml* file.

We do need to tell `ansible-playbook` to prompt us for the password of the encrypted file, or it will simply error out. Do so by using the `--ask-vault-pass` argument:

```
$ ansible-playbook mezzanine.yml --ask-vault-pass
```

You can also store the password in a text file and tell `ansible-playbook` the location of this password file by using the `--vault-password-file` flag:

```
$ ansible-playbook mezzanine --vault-password-file ~/password.txt
```

If the argument to `--vault-password-file` has the executable bit set, Ansible will execute it and use the contents of `standard out` as the vault password. This allows you to use a script to provide the password to Ansible.

Table 8-5 shows the available `ansible-vault` commands.

Table 8-5. ansible-vault commands

Command	Description
ansible-vault encrypt *file.yml*	Encrypt the plain-text *file.yml* file
ansible-vault decrypt *file.yml*	Decrypt the encrypted *file.yml* file
ansible-vault view *file.yml*	Print the contents of the encrypted *file.yml* file
ansible-vault create *file.yml*	Create a new encrypted *file.yml* file
ansible-vault edit *file.yml*	Edit an encrypted *file.yml* file
ansible-vault rekey *file.yml*	Change the password on an encrypted *file.yml* file

## CHAPTER 9

Customizing Hosts, Runs, and Handlers

Sometimes Ansible's default behaviors don't quite fit your use case. In this chapter, we cover Ansible features that provide customization by controlling which hosts to run against, how tasks are run, and how handlers are run.

Patterns for Specifying Hosts

So far, the `host` parameter in our plays has specified a single host or group, like this:

```
hosts: web
```

Instead of specifying a single host or group, you can specify a *pattern*. You've already seen the `all` pattern, which will run a play against all known hosts:

```
hosts: all
```

You can specify a union of two groups with a colon. You specify all dev and staging machines as follows:

```
hosts: dev:staging
```

You can specify an intersection by using a colon and ampersand. For example, to specify all of the database servers in your staging environment, you might do this:

```
hosts: staging:&database
```

Table 9-1 shows the patterns that Ansible supports. Note that the regular expression pattern always starts with a tilde.

Table 9-1. Supported patterns

Action	Example usage
All hosts	`all`
All hosts	`*`
Union	`dev:staging`
Intersection	`staging:&database`
Exclusion	`dev:!queue`
Wildcard	`*.example.com`
Range of numbered servers	`web[5:10]`
Regular expression	`~web\d+\.example\.(com|org)`

Ansible supports multiple combinations of patterns—for example:

```
hosts: dev:staging:&database:!queue
```

Limiting Which Hosts Run

Use the `-l hosts` or `--limit hosts` flag to tell Ansible to limit the hosts to run the playbook against the specified list of hosts, as shown in Example 9-1.

Example 9-1. Limiting which hosts run

```
$ ansible-playbook -l hosts playbook.yml
$ ansible-playbook --limit hosts playbook.yml
```

You can use the pattern syntax just described to specify arbitrary combinations of hosts. For example:

```
$ ansible-playbook -l 'staging:&database' playbook.yml
```

Running a Task on the Control Machine

Sometimes you want to run a particular task on the control machine instead of on the remote host. Ansible provides the `local_action` clause for tasks to support this.

Imagine that the server we want to install Mezzanine onto has just booted, so that if we run our playbook too soon, it will error out because the server hasn't fully started up yet. We could start off our playbook by invoking the `wait_for` module to wait until the SSH server is ready to accept connections before we execute the rest of the playbook. In this case, we want this module to execute on our laptop, not on the remote host.

The first task of our playbook has to start off like this:

```
- name: wait for ssh server to be running
  local_action: wait_for port=22 host="{{ inventory_hostname }}"
    search_regex=OpenSSH
```

Note that we're referencing `inventory_hostname` in this task, which evaluates to the name of the remote host, not `localhost`. That's because the scope of these variables is still the remote host, even though the task is executing locally.

 If your play involves multiple hosts, and you use `local_action`, the task will be executed multiple times, one for each host. You can restrict this by using `run_once`, as described in "Running on One Host at a Time" on page 174.

Running a Task on a Machine Other Than the Host

Sometimes you want to run a task that's associated with a host, but you want to execute the task on a different server. You can use the `delegate_to` clause to run the task on a different host.

Two common use cases are as follows:

- Enabling host-based alerts with an alerting system such as Nagios
- Adding a host to a load balancer such as HAProxy

For example, imagine we want to enable Nagios alerts for all of the hosts in our `web` group. Assume we have an entry in our inventory named *nagios.example.com* that is running Nagios. Example 9-2 shows an example that uses `delegate_to`.

Example 9-2. Using delegate_to with Nagios

```
- name: enable alerts for web servers
  hosts: web
  tasks:
    - name: enable alerts
      nagios: action=enable_alerts service=web host={{ inventory_hostname }}
      delegate_to: nagios.example.com
```

In this example, Ansible would execute the `nagios` task on *nagios.example.com*, but the `inventory_hostname` variable referenced in the play would evaluate to the web host.

For a more detailed example that uses `delegate_to`, see the *lamp_haproxy/rolling_update.yml* example in the Ansible project's examples GitHub repo (*https://github.com/ansible/ansible-examples*).

Running on One Host at a Time

By default, Ansible runs each task in parallel across all hosts. Sometimes you want to run your task on one host at a time. The canonical example is when upgrading application servers that are behind a load balancer. Typically, you take the application server out of the load balancer, upgrade it, and put it back. But you don't want to take all of your application servers out of the load balancer, or your service will become unavailable.

You can use the `serial` clause on a play to tell Ansible to restrict the number of hosts that a play runs on. Example 9-3 shows an example that removes hosts one at a time from an Amazon EC2 elastic load balancer, upgrades the system packages, and then puts them back into the load balancer. (We cover Amazon EC2 in more detail in Chapter 14.)

Example 9-3. Removing hosts from load balancer and upgrading packages

```
- name: upgrade packages on servers behind load balancer
  hosts: myhosts
  serial: 1
  tasks:

    - name: get the ec2 instance id and elastic load balancer id
      ec2_facts:

    - name: take the host out of the elastic load balancer
      local_action: ec2_elb
      args:
        instance_id: "{{ ansible_ec2_instance_id }}"
        state: absent

    - name: upgrade packages
      apt: update_cache=yes upgrade=yes

    - name: put the host back in the elastic load balancer
      local_action: ec2_elb
      args:
        instance_id: "{{ ansible_ec2_instance_id }}"
        state: present
        ec2_elbs: "{{ item }}"
      with_items: ec2_elbs
```

In our example, we pass 1 as the argument to the `serial` clause, telling Ansible to run on only one host at a time. If we had passed 2, Ansible would have run two hosts at a time.

Normally, when a task fails, Ansible stops running tasks against the host that fails, but continues to run against other hosts. In the load-balancing scenario, you might want

Ansible to fail the entire play before all hosts have failed a task. Otherwise, you might end up with the situation where you have taken each host out of the load balancer, and have it fail, leaving no hosts left inside your load balancer.

You can use a `max_fail_percentage` clause along with the `serial` clause to specify the maximum percentage of failed hosts before Ansible fails the entire play. For example, assume that we specify a maximum fail percentage of 25%, as shown here:

```
- name: upgrade packages on servers behind load balancer
  hosts: myhosts
  serial: 1
  max_fail_percentage: 25
  tasks:
    # tasks go here
```

If we have four hosts behind the load balancer, and one of the hosts fail a task, then Ansible will keep executing the play, because this doesn't exceed the 25% threshold. However, if a second host fails a task, Ansible will fail the entire play, because then 50% of the hosts will have failed a task, exceeding the 25% threshold. If you want Ansible to fail if any of the hosts fail a task, set the `max_fail_percentage` to 0.

Running on a Batch of Hosts at a Time

You can also pass `serial` a percentage value instead of a fixed number. Ansible will apply this percentage to the total number of hosts per play to determine the number of hosts per batch, as shown in Example 9-4.

Example 9-4. Using a percentage value as a serial

```
- name: upgrade 50% of web servers
  hosts: myhosts
  serial: 50%
  tasks:
    # tasks go here
```

We can get even more sophisticated. For example, you might want to run the play on one host first, to verify that the play works as expected, and then run the play on a larger number of hosts in subsequent runs. A possible use case would be managing a large logical cluster of independent hosts; for example, 30 hosts of a content delivery network (CDN).

Since version 2.2, Ansible lets you specify a list of serials to achieve this behavior. The list of serial items can be either a number or a percentage, as shown in Example 9-5.

Example 9-5. Using a list of serials

```
- name: configure CDN servers
  hosts: cdn
  serial:
    - 1
    - 30%
  tasks:
    # tasks go here
```

Ansible will restrict the number of hosts on each run to the next available `serial` item unless the end of the list has been reached or there are no hosts left. This means that the last `serial` will be kept and applied to each batch run as long as there are hosts left in the play.

In the preceding play with 30 CDN hosts, on the first batch run Ansible would run against one host, and on each subsequent batch run it would run against at most 30% of the hosts (e.g., 1, 10, 10, 9).

Running Only Once

Sometimes you might want a task to run only once, even if there are multiple hosts. For example, perhaps you have multiple application servers running behind the load balancer, and you want to run a database migration, but you need to run the migration on only one application server.

You can use the `run_once` clause to tell Ansible to run the command only once:

```
- name: run the database migrations
  command: /opt/run_migrations
  run_once: true
```

Using `run_once` can be particularly useful when using `local_action` if your playbook involves multiple hosts, and you want to run the local task only once:

```
- name: run the task locally, only once
  local_action: command /opt/my-custom-command
  run_once: true
```

Running Strategies

The `strategy` clause on a play level gives you additional control over how Ansible behaves per task for all hosts.

The default behavior we are already familiar with is the `linear` strategy. This is the strategy in which Ansible executes one task on all hosts and waits until the task has completed (of failed) on all hosts before it executes the next task on all hosts. As a result, a task takes as much time as the slowest host takes to complete the task.

Let's create a playbook, shown in Example 9-7, to demonstrate the `strategy` feature. We create a minimalistic `hosts` file, shown in Example 9-6, which contains three hosts, each having a variable `sleep_seconds` with a different value in seconds.

Example 9-6. Host file with three hosts having a different value for sleep_seconds

```
one    sleep_seconds=1
two    sleep_seconds=6
three  sleep_seconds=10
```

Linear

The playbook in Example 9-7, which we execute locally by using `connection: local`, has a play with three identical tasks. In each task, we execute `sleep` with the time specified in `sleep_seconds`.

Example 9-7. Playbook in linear strategy

```
---
- hosts: all
  connection: local
  tasks:
  - name: first task
    shell: sleep "{{ sleep_seconds }}"

  - name: second task
    shell: sleep "{{ sleep_seconds }}"

  - name: third task
    shell: sleep "{{ sleep_seconds }}"
```

Running the playbook in the default `strategy` as `linear` results in the output shown in Example 9-8.

Example 9-8. Result of the linear strategy run

```
$ ansible-playbook strategy.yml -i hosts

PLAY [all] ******************************************************************

TASK [setup] ****************************************************************
ok: [two]
ok: [three]
ok: [one]

TASK [first task] ***********************************************************
changed: [one]
changed: [two]
```

```
changed: [three]

TASK [second task] ********************************************************
changed: [one]
changed: [two]
changed: [three]

TASK [third task] *********************************************************
changed: [one]
changed: [two]
changed: [three]

PLAY RECAP ****************************************************************
one                        : ok=4    changed=3   unreachable=0   failed=0
three                      : ok=4    changed=3   unreachable=0   failed=0
two                        : ok=4    changed=3   unreachable=0   failed=0
```

We get the ordered output we are familiar with. Note the identical order of task results, as host one is always the quickest (as it sleeps the least amount of time) and host three is the slowest (as it sleeps the greatest amount of time).

Free

Another strategy available in Ansible is the free strategy. In contrast to linear, Ansible will not wait for results of the task to execute on all hosts. Instead, if a host completes one task, Ansible will execute the next task on that host.

Depending on the hardware resources and network latency, one host may have executed the tasks faster than other hosts located at the end of the world. As a result, some hosts will already be configured, while others are still in the middle of the play.

If we change the playbook to the free strategy, the output changes as shown in Example 9-9.

Example 9-9. Playbook in free strategy

```
---
- hosts: all
  connection: local
  strategy: free ❶
  tasks:
  - name: first task
    shell: sleep "{{ sleep_seconds }}"

  - name: second task
    shell: sleep "{{ sleep_seconds }}"

  - name: third task
    shell: sleep "{{ sleep_seconds }}"
```

❶ We changed the strategy to free.

As we see in the output in Example 9-10, host one is already finished before host three has even finished its first task.

Example 9-10. Results of running the playbook with the free strategy

```
$ ansible-playbook strategy.yml -i hosts

PLAY [all] ********************************************************************

TASK [setup] *****************************************************************
ok: [one]
ok: [two]
ok: [three]

TASK [first task] ************************************************************
changed: [one]

TASK [second task] ***********************************************************
changed: [one]

TASK [third task] ************************************************************
changed: [one]

TASK [first task] ************************************************************
changed: [two]
changed: [three]

TASK [second task] ***********************************************************
changed: [two]

TASK [third task] ************************************************************
changed: [two]

TASK [second task] ***********************************************************
changed: [three]

TASK [third task] ************************************************************
changed: [three]

PLAY RECAP *******************************************************************
one                        : ok=4    changed=3    unreachable=0    failed=0
three                      : ok=4    changed=3    unreachable=0    failed=0
two                        : ok=4    changed=3    unreachable=0    failed=0
```

In this case, the play will execute in the same amount of time in both strategies. Under certain conditions, a play in strategy `free` may take less time to finish.

Like many core parts in Ansible, `strategy` is implemented as a new type of plugin.

Advanced Handlers

Sometimes you'll find that Ansible's default behavior for handlers doesn't quite fit your particular use case. This subsection describes how you can gain tighter control over when your handlers fire.

Handlers in Pre and Post Tasks

When we covered handlers, you learned that they are usually executed after all tasks, once, and only when they get notified. But keep in mind there are not only `tasks`, but `pre_tasks`, `tasks`, and `post_tasks`.

Each `tasks` section in a playbook is handled separately; any handler notified in `pre_tasks`, `tasks`, or `post_tasks` is executed at the end of each section. As a result, it is possible to execute one handler several times in one play:

```
---
- hosts: localhost
  pre_tasks:
  - command: echo Pre Tasks
    notify: print message

  tasks:
  - command: echo Tasks
    notify: print message

  post_tasks:
  - command: echo Post Tasks
    notify: print message

  handlers:
  - name: print message
    command: echo handler executed
```

When we run the playbook, we see the following results:

```
$ ansible-playbook pre_post_tasks_handlers.yml
PLAY [localhost] ***************************************************************

TASK [setup] ******************************************************************
ok: [localhost]
```

```
TASK [command] *******************************************************************
changed: [localhost]

RUNNING HANDLER [print message] **************************************************
changed: [localhost]

TASK [command] *******************************************************************
changed: [localhost]

RUNNING HANDLER [print message] **************************************************
changed: [localhost]

TASK [command] *******************************************************************
changed: [localhost]

RUNNING HANDLER [print message] **************************************************
changed: [localhost]

PLAY RECAP ***********************************************************************
localhost                  : ok=7    changed=6    unreachable=0    failed=0
```

Flush Handlers

You may be wondering why I wrote *usually* executed after all tasks. *Usually*, because this is the default. However, Ansible lets us control the execution point of the handlers with the help of a special module, meta.

In Example 9-12, we see a part of an nginx role in which we use meta with flush_han dlers in the middle of the tasks.

We do this for two reasons:

1. We would like to clean up some old Nginx vhost data, which we can remove only if no process is using it anymore (e.g., after the service restart).

2. We want to run some *smoke tests* and validate a health check URL returning OK if the application is in a healthy state. But validating the healthy state before the restart of the services would not make that much sense.

Example 9-11 shows the configuration of the nginx role: the host and port of the health check, a list of vhosts with a name and a template, and some deprecated vhosts that we want to ensure have been removed:

Example 9-11. Configuration for the nginx role

```
nginx_healthcheck_host: health.example.com
nginx_healthcheck_port: 8080

vhosts:
```

```
  - name: www.example.com
    template: default.conf.j2

absent_vhosts:
  - obsolete.example.com
  - www2.example.com
```

In the tasks file of the role *roles/nginx/tasks/main.yml* as in Example 9-12, we put the
meta tasks with the corresponding argument flush_handlers between our normal
tasks, but just where we want it to be: before the health check task and the cleanup
task.

Example 9-12. Clean up and validate health checks after the service restart

```
---
- name: install nginx
  yum:
    pkg: nginx
  notify: restart nginx

- name: configure nginx vhosts
  template:
    src: conf.d/{{ item.template | default(item.name) }}.conf.j2
    dest: /etc/nginx/conf.d/{{ item.name }}.conf
  with_items: "{{ vhosts }}"
  when: item.name not in vhosts_absent
  notify: restart nginx

- name: removed unused nginx vhosts
  file:
    path: /etc/nginx/conf.d/{{ item }}.conf
    state: absent
  with_items: "{{ vhosts_absent }}"
  notify: restart nginx

- name: validate nginx config ❶
  command: nginx -t
  changed_when: false
  check_mode: false

- name: flush the handlers
  meta: flush_handlers ❷

- name: remove unused vhost directory
  file:
    path: /srv/www/{{ item }} state=absent
  when: item not in vhosts
  with_items: "{{ vhosts_absent }}"

- name: check healthcheck ❸
  local_action:
```

```
    module: uri
    url: http://{{ nginx_healthcheck_host }}:{{ nginx_healthcheck_port }}/healthcheck
    return_content: true
  retries: 10
  delay: 5
  register: webpage

- fail:
    msg: "fail if healthcheck is not ok"
  when: not webpage|skipped and webpage|success and "ok" not in webpage.content
```

❶ Validating the configuration just before flushing the handlers

❷ Flushing handlers between tasks

❸ Running smoke tests to see if all went well. Note this could be a dynamic page validating that an application has access to a database.

Handlers Listen

Before Ansible 2.2, there was only one way to notify a handler: by calling `notify` on the handler's name. This is simple and works well for most use cases.

Before we go into details about how the handlers listen feature can simplify your playbooks and roles, let's see a quick example of handlers listen:

```
---
- hosts: mailservers
  tasks:
    - copy:
        src: main.conf
        dest: /etc/postfix/main.cnf
      notify: postfix config changed ❶

  handlers:
    - name: restart postfix
      service: name=postfix state=restarted
      listen: postfix config changed ❶
```

❶ You notify like an *event* on which you listen to on one or more handlers.

The `listen` clause defines what we'll call an *event*, on which one or more handlers can listen. This decouples the task notification key from the handler's name. To notify more handlers to the same event, we just let these additional handlers listen on the same event, and they will also get notified.

The scope of all handlers is on the play level. We cannot notify across plays, with or without handlers listen.

Handlers listen: The SSL case

The real benefit of handlers listen is related to role and role dependencies. One of the most obvious use cases I have come across is managing SSL certificates for different services.

Because we use SSL heavily in our hosts and across projects, it makes sense to make an SSL role. It is a simple role whose only purpose is to copy our SSL certificates and keys to the remote host. It does this in a few tasks, as in *roles/ssl/tasks/main.yml* in Example 9-13, and it is prepared to run on Red Hat–based Linux operating systems because it has the appropriate paths set in the variables file *roles/ssl/vars/RedHat.yml* in Example 9-14.

Example 9-13. Role tasks in the SSL role

```
---
- name: include OS specific variables
  include_vars: "{{ ansible_os_family }}.yml"

- name: copy SSL certs
  copy:
    src: "{{ item }}"
    dest: {{ ssl_certs_path }}/
    owner: root
    group: root
    mode: 0644
  with_items: "{{ ssl_certs }}"

- name: copy SSL keys
  copy:
    src: "{{ item }}"
    dest: "{{ ssl_keys_path }}/"
    owner: root
    group: root
    mode: 0644
  with_items: "{{ ssl_keys }}"
  no_log: true
```

Example 9-14. Variables for Red Hat–based systems

```
---
ssl_certs_path: /etc/pki/tls/certs
ssl_keys_path: /etc/pki/tls/private
```

In the definition of the role defaults in Example 9-15, we have empty lists of SSL certificates and keys, so no certificates and keys will be handled. We have options for overwriting these defaults to make the role copy the files.

Example 9-15. Defaults of the SSL role

```
---
ssl_certs: []
ssl_keys: []
```

At this point, we can use the SSL role in other roles as a *dependency*, just as we do in Example 9-16 for an nginx role by modifying the file *roles/nginx/meta/main.yml*. Every role dependency will run before the parent role. This means in our case that the SSL role tasks will be executed before the nginx role tasks. As a result, the SSL certificates and keys are already in place and usable within the nginx role (e.g., in the *vhost* config).

Example 9-16. The nginx role depends on SSL

```
---
dependencies:
  - role: ssl
```

Logically, the dependency would be one way: the nginx role depends on the ssl role, as shown in Figure 9-1.

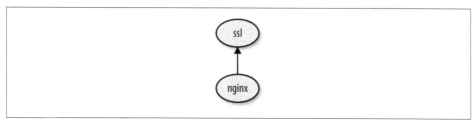

Figure 9-1. One-way dependency

Our nginx role would, of course, handle all aspects of the web server nginx. This role has tasks in *roles/nginx/tasks/main.yml* as in Example 9-17 for templating the *nginx* config and restarting the *nginx* service by notifying the appropriate handler by its name.

Example 9-17. Tasks in the nginx role

```
---
- name: configure nginx
  template:
    src: nginx.conf.j2
    dest: /etc/nginx/nginx.conf
  notify: restart nginx ❶
```

❶ Notify the handler for restarting the *nginx* service.

As you would expect, the corresponding handler for the `nginx` role in *roles/nginx/ handlers/main.yml* looks like Example 9-18.

Example 9-18. Handlers in the nginx role

```
---
- name: restart nginx ❶
  service:
    name: nginx
    state: restarted
```

❶ `Restart nginx` restarts the Nginx service.

That's it, right? Not quite. The SSL certificates need to be replaced once in a while. And when they get replaced, every service consuming an SSL certificate must be restarted to make use of the new certificate.

So how should we do that? Notify to `restart nginx` in the SSL role, I hear you say? OK, let's try.

We edit *roles/ssl/tasks/main.yml* of our SSL role to append the `notify` clause for restarting Nginx to the tasks of copying the certificates and keys, as in Example 9-19.

Example 9-19. Append notify to the tasks to restart Nginx

```
---
- name: include OS specific variables
  include_vars: "{{ ansible_os_family }}.yml"

- name: copy SSL certs
  copy:
    src: "{{ item }}"
    dest: {{ ssl_certs_path }}/
    owner: root
    group: root
    mode: 0644
```

```
  with_items: "{{ ssl_certs }}"
  notify: restart nginx ❶

- name: copy SSL keys
  copy:
    src: "{{ item }}"
    dest: "{{ ssl_keys_path }}/"
    owner: root
    group: root
    mode: 0644
  with_items: "{{ ssl_keys }}"
  no_log: true
  notify: restart nginx ❶
```

❶ Notify the handler in the nginx role.

Great, that works! But wait, we just added a new dependency to our SSL role: the nginx role, as shown in Figure 9-2.

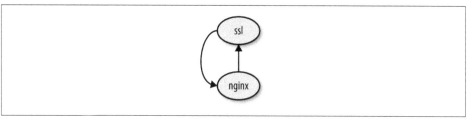

Figure 9-2. The nginx role depends on the SSL role, and the SSL role depends on the nginx role

What are the consequences of this? If we use the SSL role for other roles as a dependency, the way we use it for nginx (e.g., for postfix, dovecot, or ldap, to name just a few possibilities), Ansible will complain about notifying an undefined handler, because restart nginx will not be defined within these roles.

 Ansible in version 1.9 complained about notifying undefined handlers. This behavior was reimplemented in Ansible version 2.2 as it was seen as a regression bug. However, this behavior can be configured in *ansible.cfg* with error_on_missing_handler. The default is error_on_missing_handler = True.

Further, we would need to add more handler names to be notified for every additional role where we use the SSL role as a dependency. This simply wouldn't scale well.

This is the point where handlers listen comes into the game! Instead of notifying a handler's name in the SSL role, we notify an *event*—for example, ssl_certs_changed, as in Example 9-20.

Example 9-20. Notify an event to listen in handlers

```
---
- name: include OS specific variables
  include_vars: "{{ ansible_os_family }}.yml"

- name: copy SSL certs
  copy:
    src: "{{ item }}"
    dest: "{{ ssl_certs_path }}/"
    owner: root
    group: root
    mode: 0644
  with_items: "{{ ssl_certs }}"
  notify: ssl_certs_changed ❶

- name: copy SSL keys
  copy:
    src: "{{ item }}"
    dest: "{{ ssl_keys_path }}/"
    owner: root
    group: root
    mode: 0644
  with_items: "{{ ssl_keys }}"
  no_log: true
  notify: ssl_certs_changed ❶
```

❶ Notify the event ssl_certs_changed

As mentioned, Ansible will still complain about notifying an undefined handler but making Ansible happy again is as simple as adding a no-op handler to the SSL role, as shown in Example 9-21.

Example 9-21. Add a no-op handler to the SSL role to listen to the event

```
---
- name: SSL certs changed
  debug:
    msg: SSL changed event triggered
  listen: ssl_certs_changed ❶
```

❶ Listens to the event ssl_certs_changed

Back to our `nginx` role, where we want to react to the `ssl_certs_changed` event and restart the Nginx service when a certificate has been replaced. Because we already have an appropriate handler that does the job, we simply append the `listen` clause to the corresponding handler, as in Example 9-22.

Example 9-22. Append the listen clause to the existing handler in the nginx role

```
---
- name: restart nginx
  service:
    name: nginx
    state: restarted
  listen: ssl_certs_changed ❶
```

❶ Append the `listen` clause to the existing handler.

When we look back to our dependency graph, things looks a bit different, as shown in Figure 9-3. We restored the one-way dependency and are able to reuse the `ssl` role in other roles just as we use it in the `nginx` role.

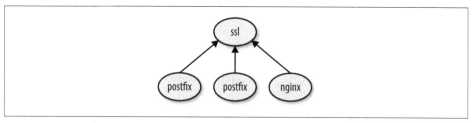

Figure 9-3. Use the ssl role in other roles

One last note for role creators having roles on Ansible Galaxy: consider adding handlers listen and event notification to your Ansible roles where it makes sense.

Manually Gathering Facts

If it's possible that the SSH server wasn't yet running when we started our playbook, we need to turn off explicit fact gathering; otherwise, Ansible will try to SSH to the host to gather facts before running the first tasks. Because we still need access to facts (recall that we use the `ansible_env` fact in our playbook), we can explicitly invoke the `setup` module to get Ansible to gather our facts, as shown in Example 9-23.

Example 9-23. Waiting for SSH server to come up

```
- name: Deploy mezzanine
  hosts: web
  gather_facts: False
```

```
# vars & vars_files section not shown here
tasks:
  - name: wait for ssh server to be running
    local_action: wait_for port=22 host="{{ inventory_hostname }}"
      search_regex=OpenSSH

  - name: gather facts
    setup:
  # The rest of the tasks go here
```

Retrieving the IP Address from the Host

In our playbook, several of the hostnames we use are derived from the IP address of the web server:

```
live_hostname: 192.168.33.10.xip.io
domains:
  - 192.168.33.10.xip.io
  - www.192.168.33.10.xip.io
```

What if we want to use the same scheme but not hardcode the IP addresses into the variables? That way, if the IP address of the web server changes, we don't have to modify our playbook.

Ansible retrieves the IP address of each host and stores it as a fact. Each network interface has an associated Ansible fact. For example, details about network interface eth0 are stored in the ansible_eth0 fact, an example of which is shown in Example 9-24.

Example 9-24. ansible_eth0 fact

```
"ansible_eth0": {
    "active": true,
    "device": "eth0",
    "ipv4": {
        "address": "10.0.2.15",
        "netmask": "255.255.255.0",
        "network": "10.0.2.0"
    },
    "ipv6": [
        {
            "address": "fe80::a00:27ff:fefe:1e4d",
            "prefix": "64",
            "scope": "link"
        }
    ],
    "macaddress": "08:00:27:fe:1e:4d",
    "module": "e1000",
    "mtu": 1500,
    "promisc": false,
```

```
    "type": "ether"
}
```

Our Vagrant box has two interfaces, eth0 and eth1. The eth0 interface is a private interface whose IP address (*10.0.2.15*) we cannot reach. The eth1 interface is the one that has the IP address we've assigned in our Vagrantfile (*192.168.33.10*).

We can define our variables like this:

```
live_hostname: "{{ ansible_eth1.ipv4.address }}.xip.io"
domains:
  - "{{ ansible_eth1.ipv4.address }}.xip.io"
  - "www.{{ ansible_eth1.ipv4.address }}.xip.io"
```

## CHAPTER 10

Callback Plugins

Ansible supports a feature called *callback plugins* that can perform custom actions in response to Ansible events such as a play starting or a task completing on a host. You can use a callback plugin to do things such as send a Slack message or write an entry to a remote logging server. In fact, the output you see in your terminal when you execute an Ansible playbook is implemented as a callback plugin.

Ansible supports two kinds of callback plugins:

- *Stdout plugins* affect the output displayed to the terminal
- *Other plugins* do things other than change displayed output.

Technically, there are three types of callback plugins, not two:

- Stdout
- Notification
- Aggregate

However, since Ansible's implementation makes no distinction between notification and aggregate plugins, we combine notification and aggregate plugins into a single category called *other* plugins.

Stdout Plugins

A *stdout* plugin controls the format of the output displayed to the terminal. Only a single stdout plugin can be active at a time.

You specify a stdout callback by setting the `stdout_callback` parameter in the `defaults` section of *ansible.cfg*. For example, to select the `actionable` plugin:

```
[defaults]
stdout_callback = actionable
```

Ansible supports the stdout plugins in Table 10-1.

Table 10-1. Stdout plugins

Name	Description
actionable	Show only changed or failed
debug	Human-readable stderr and stdout
default	Show default output
dense	Overwrite output instead of scrolling
json	JSON output
minimal	Show task results with minimal formatting
oneline	Like minimal, but on a single line
selective	Show only output for tagged tasks
skippy	Suppress output for skipped hosts

actionable

The `actionable` plugin shows output when a task runs against a host only if the task changes the state of the host or fails. This makes the output less noisy.

debug

The debug plugin makes it easier to read stdout and stderr returned by tasks, which can be helpful for debugging. The default plugin can make it difficult to read the output:

```
TASK [check out the repository on the host] *************************************
fatal: [web]: FAILED! => {"changed": false, "cmd": "/usr/bin/git clone --origin o
rigin '' /home/vagrant/mezzanine/mezzanine_example", "failed": true, "msg": "Clon
ing into '/home/vagrant/mezzanine/mezzanine_example'...\nPermission denied (publi
ckey).\r\nfatal: Could not read from remote repository.\n\nPlease make sure you h
ave the correct access rights\nand the repository exists.", "rc": 128, "stderr":
"Cloning into '/home/vagrant/mezzanine/mezzanine_example'...\nPermission denied (
publickey).\r\nfatal: Could not read from remote repository.\n\nPlease make sure
you have the correct access rights\nand the repository exists.\n", "stderr_lines"
: ["Cloning into '/home/vagrant/mezzanine/mezzanine_example'...", "Permission den
ied (publickey).", "fatal: Could not read from remote repository.", "", "Please m
ake sure you have the correct access rights", "and the repository exists."], "std
out": "", "stdout_lines": []}
```

With the debug plugin, the formatting is much easier to read:

```
TASK [check out the repository on the host] ************************************
fatal: [web]: FAILED! => {
    "changed": false,
    "cmd": "/usr/bin/git clone --origin origin '' /home/vagrant/mezzanine/mezzani
    ne_example",
    "failed": true,
    "rc": 128
}

STDERR:

Cloning into '/home/vagrant/mezzanine/mezzanine_example'...
Permission denied (publickey).
fatal: Could not read from remote repository.

Please make sure you have the correct access rights
and the repository exists.


MSG:

Cloning into '/home/vagrant/mezzanine/mezzanine_example'...
Permission denied (publickey).
fatal: Could not read from remote repository.

Please make sure you have the correct access rights
and the repository exists.
```

dense

The dense plugin (new in Ansible 2.3) always shows only two lines of output. It overwrites the existing lines rather than scrolling:

```
PLAY 1: CONFIGURE WEBSERVER WITH NGINX
task 6: testserver
```

json

The json plugin generates machine-readable JSON as output. This is useful if you want to process the Ansible output by using a script. Note that this callback will not generate output until the entire playbook has finished executing.

The JSON output is too verbose to show here, but here is a partial example:

```
{
  "plays": [
  "play": {
    "id": "a45e60df-95f9-5a33-6619-000000000002"
    "name": "Configure webserver with nginx",
  },
  "tasks": [
```

```
        {
         "task": {
          "name": "install nginx",
          "id": "a45e60df-95f9-5a33-6619-000000000004"
         }
         "hosts": {
          "testserver": {
           "changed": false,
           "invocation": {
            "module_args": { ... }
          }
         }
        }
       ]
      ]
     }
```

minimal

The minimal plugin does very little processing of the result returned from Ansible from an event. For example, whereas the default plugin formats a task like this:

```
TASK [create a logs directory] *********************************************
ok: [web]
```

the minimal plugin outputs this:

```
web | SUCCESS => {
    "changed": false,
    "gid": 1000,
    "group": "vagrant",
    "mode": "0775",
    "owner": "vagrant",
    "path": "/home/vagrant/logs",
    "size": 4096,
    "state": "directory",
    "uid": 1000
}
```

oneline

The oneline plugin is similar to minimal, but prints output on a single line (shown here on multiple lines because the text doesn't fit on one line in the book):

```
web | SUCCESS => {"changed": false, "gid": 1000, "group": "vagrant", "mode":
"0775", "owner": "vagrant", "path": "/home/vagrant/logs", "size": 4096, "state":
"directory", "uid": 1000}
```

selective

The `selective` plugin shows output only for successful tasks that have the `print_action` tag. It always shows output for failed tasks.

skippy

The `skippy` plugin does not show any output for hosts that are skipped. Whereas the `default` plugin shows `skipping: [hostname]` when a host is skipped for a task, the `skippy` plugin suppresses that output.

Other Plugins

The other plugins perform a variety of actions, such as recording execution time or sending a Slack notification. Table 10-2 lists these other plugins.

Unlike with stdout plugins, you can have multiple other plugins enabled at the same time. Enable the other plugins you want in *ansible.cfg* by setting `callback_whitelist` to a comma-separated list; for example:

```
[defaults]
callback_whitelist = mail, slack
```

Many of these plugins have configuration options, which are set via environment variables.

Table 10-2. Other plugins

Name	Description
foreman	Send notifications to Foreman
hipchat	Send notifications to HipChat
jabber	Send notifications to Jabber
junit	Write JUnit-formatted XML file
log_plays	Log playbook results per hosts
logentries	Send notifications to Logentries
logstash	Send results to Logstash
mail	Send email when tasks fail
osx_say	Speak notifications on macOS
profile_tasks	Report execution time for each task
slack	Send notifications to Slack
timer	Report total execution time

foreman

The `foreman` plugin sends notifications to Foreman (*http://theforeman.org*). Table 10-3 lists the environment variables used to configure this plugin.

Table 10-3. foreman plugin environment variables

Environment var	Description	Default
FOREMAN_URL	URL to the Foreman server	`http://localhost:3000`
FOREMAN_SSL_CERT	X509 certificate to authenticate to Foreman if HTTPS is used	`/etc/foreman/client_cert.pem`
FOREMAN_SSL_KEY	The corresponding private key	`/etc/foreman/client_key.pem`
FOREMAN_SSL_VERIFY	Whether to verify the Foreman certificate. It can be set to 1 to verify SSL certificates using the installed CAs or to a path pointing to a CA bundle. Set to 0 to disable certificate checking.	`1`

hipchat

The `hipchat` plugin sends notifications to HipChat (*http://hipchat.com*). Table 10-4 lists the plugin's environment variables used for configuration.

Table 10-4. hipchat plugin environment variables

Environment var	Description	Default
HIPCHAT_TOKEN	HipChat API token	*(None)*
HIPCHAT_ROOM	HipChat room to post in	`ansible`
HIPCHAT_NAME	HipChat name to post as	`ansible`
HIPCHAT_NOTIFY	Add notify flag to important messages	`true`

You must install the Python prettytable library to use the `hipchat` plugin:

```
pip install prettytable
```

jabber

The `jabber` plugin sends notifications to Jabber (*http://jabber.org*). Note that there are no default values for any of the configuration options for the `jabber` plugin. These options are listed in Table 10-5.

Table 10-5. jabber plugin environment variables

Environment var	Description
JABBER_SERV	Hostname of Jabber server
JABBER_USER	Jabber username for auth
JABBER_PASS	Jabber password auth
JABBER_TO	Jabber user to send the notification to

You must install the Python xmpp library to use the `jabber` plugin:

```
pip install git+https://github.com/ArchipelProject/xmpppy
```

junit

The `junit` plugin writes the results of a playbook execution to an XML file in JUnit format. It is configured by using the environment variables listed in Table 10-6. The plugin uses the conventions in Table 10-7 for generating the XML report.

Table 10-6. junit plugin environment variables

Environment var	Description	Default
JUNIT_OUTPUT_DIR	Destination directory for files	`~/.ansible.log`
JUNIT_TASK_CLASS	Configure output: one class per YAML file	`false`

Table 10-7. junit report

Ansible task output	JUnit report
ok	pass
failed with EXPECTED FAILURE in the task name	pass
failed due to an exception	error
failed for other reasons	failure
skipped	skipped

You must install the *junit_xml* library to use the `junit` plugin:

```
pip install junit_xml
```

log_plays

The `log_plays` plugin logs the results to log files in */var/log/ansible/hosts*, one log file per host. The path is not configurable.

 Instead of using the `log_plays` plugin, you can set the `log_path` configuration option in *ansible.cfg*. For example:

```
[defaults]
log_path = /var/log/ansible.log
```

This approach generates a single logfile for all hosts, whereas the plugin generates a separate logfile for each host.

logentries

The `logentries` plugin sends the results to Logentries (*http://logentries.com*). The plugin's environment variables are listed in Table 10-8.

Table 10-8. logentries plugin environment variables

Environment var	Description	Default
LOGENTRIES_ANSIBLE_TOKEN	Logentries token	(*None*)
LOGENTRIES_API	Hostname of Logentries endpoint	`data.logentries.com`
LOGENTRIES_PORT	Logentries port	`80`
LOGENTRIES_TLS_PORT	Logentries TLS port	`443`
LOGENTRIES_USE_TLS	Use TLS with Logentries	`false`
LOGENTRIES_FLATTEN	Flatten results	`false`

 You must install the Python *certifi* and *flctdict* libraries to use the `logentries` plugin:

```
pip install certifi flatdict
```

logstash

The `logstash` plugin writes results to Logstash (*https://www.elastic.co/products/logstash*). It is configured with the environment variables listed in Table 10-9.

Table 10-9. logstash plugin environment variables

Environment var	Description	Default
LOGSTASH_SERVER	Logstash server hostname	localhost
LOGSTASH_PORT	Logstash server port	5000
LOGSTASH_TYPE	Message type	ansible

 You must install the Python *python-logstash* library to use the log
stash plugin:

```
pip install python-logstash
```

mail

The mail plugin sends an email whenever a task fails on a host. Table 10-10 lists the
environment variables for this plugin.

Table 10-10. Mail plugin environment variables

Environment var	Description	Default
SMTPHOST	SMTP server hostname	localhost

osx_say

The osx_say plugin uses the say program to speak notifications on macOS. It has no
configuration options.

profile_tasks

The profile_tasks plugin generates a summary of the execution time of individual
tasks and total execution time for the playbook:

```
Saturday 22 April 2017  20:05:51 -0700 (0:00:01.465)       0:01:02.732 ********
===============================================================================
install nginx ------------------------------------------------------- 57.82s
Gathering Facts ------------------------------------------------------ 1.90s
restart nginx -------------------------------------------------------- 1.47s
copy nginx config file ----------------------------------------------- 0.69s
copy index.html ------------------------------------------------------ 0.44s
enable configuration ------------------------------------------------- 0.35s
```

The plugin also outputs execution time info as the tasks are running, displaying the
following:

- Date and time that the task started
- Execution time of previous task, shown in parentheses
- Cumulative execution time for this play

Here's an example of that output:

```
TASK [install nginx] ************************************************
Saturday 22 April 2017  20:09:31 -0700 (0:00:01.983)      0:00:02.030 ******
ok: [testserver]
```

Table 10-11 lists the environment variables used for configuration.

Table 10-11. profile-tasks plugin environment variables

Environment var	Description	Default
PROFILE_TASKS_SORT_ORDER	Sort output (ascending, none)	none
PROFILE_TASKS_TASK_OUTPUT_LIMIT	Number of tasks to show, or all	20

slack

The slack plugin sends notifications to Slack (*http://slack.com*). Table 10-12 lists the environmental variables used for configuration.

Table 10-12. slack plugin environment variables

Environment var	Description	Default
SLACK_WEBHOOK_URL	Slack webhook URL	(*None*)
SLACK_CHANNEL	Slack room to post in	#ansible
SLACK_USERNAME	Username to post as	ansible
SLACK_INVOCATION	Show command-line invocation details	false

You must install the Python *prettytable* library to use the slack plugin.

timer

The timer plugin outputs the total execution time of the playbook; for example:

```
Playbook run took 0 days, 0 hours, 2 minutes, 16 seconds
```

You're generally better off using the profile_tasks plugin instead, which also shows execution time per task.

## CHAPTER 11

Making Ansible Go Even Faster

Once you start using Ansible on a regular basis, you'll often find yourself wishing that your playbooks could run more quickly. This chapter presents strategies for reducing the time it takes Ansible to execute playbooks.

SSH Multiplexing and ControlPersist

If you've made it this far in the book, you know that Ansible uses SSH as its primary transport mechanism for communicating with servers. In particular, Ansible uses the system SSH program by default.

Because the SSH protocol runs on top of the TCP protocol, when you make a connection to a remote machine with SSH, you need to make a new TCP connection. The client and server have to negotiate this connection before you can actually start doing useful work. The negotiation takes a small amount of time.

When Ansible runs a playbook, it makes many SSH connections, in order to do things such as copy over files and run commands. Each time Ansible makes a new SSH connection to a host, it has to pay this negotiation penalty.

OpenSSH is the most common implementation of SSH and is almost certainly the SSH client you have installed on your local machine if you are on Linux or macOS. OpenSSH supports an optimization called *SSH multiplexing*, which is also referred to as *ControlPersist*. When you use SSH multiplexing, multiple SSH sessions to the same host will share the same TCP connection, so the TCP connection negotiation happens only the first time.

When you enable multiplexing:

- The first time you try to SSH to a host, OpenSSH starts a master connection.
- OpenSSH creates a Unix domain socket (known as the *control socket*) that is associated with the remote host.
- The next time you try to SSH to a host, OpenSSH will use the control socket to communicate with the host instead of making a new TCP connection.

The master connection stays open for a user-configurable amount of time, and then the SSH client will terminate the connection. Ansible uses a default of 60 seconds.

Manually Enabling SSH Multiplexing

Ansible automatically enables SSH multiplexing, but to give you a sense of what's going on behind the scenes, let's work through the steps of manually enabling SSH multiplexing and using it to SSH to a remote machine.

Example 11-1 shows an entry in the *~/.ssh/config* file for *myserver.example.com*, which is configured to use SSH multiplexing.

Example 11-1. ssh/config for enabling ssh multiplexing

```
Host myserver.example.com
  ControlMaster auto
  ControlPath /tmp/%r@%h:%p
  ControlPersist 10m
```

The `ControlMaster auto` line enables SSH multiplexing, and it tells SSH to create the master connection and the control socket if it does not exist yet.

The `ControlPath /tmp/%r@%h:%p` line tells SSH where to put the control Unix domain socket file on the filesystem. `%h` is the target hostname, `%r` is the remote login username, and `%p` is the port. If we SSH as the Ubuntu user:

```
$ ssh ubuntu@myserver.example.com
```

then SSH will create the control socket at */tmp/ubuntu@myserver.example.com:22* the first time you SSH to the server.

The `ControlPersist 10m` line tells SSH to close the master connection if there have been no SSH connections for 10 minutes.

You can check whether a master connection is open by using the `-O check` flag:

```
$ ssh -O check ubuntu@myserver.example.com
```

It will return output like this if the control master is running:

```
Master running (pid=4388)
```

Here's what the control master process looks like if you use ps 4388:

```
PID  TT  STAT     TIME COMMAND
4388  ??  Ss    0:00.00 ssh: /tmp/ubuntu@myserver.example.com:22 [mux]
```

You can also terminate the master connection by using the -O exit flag, like this:

```
$ ssh -O exit ubuntu@myserver.example.com
```

You can see more details about these settings on the *ssh_config* man page.

I tested out the speed of making an SSH connection like this:

```
$ time ssh ubuntu@myserver.example.com /bin/true
```

This times how long it takes to initiate an SSH connection to the server and run the */bin/true* program, which simply exits with a 0 return code.

The first time I ran it, the timing part of the output looked like this:[1]

```
0.01s user 0.01s system 2% cpu 0.913 total
```

The time we really care about is the total time: 0.913 total. This tells us it took 0.913 seconds to execute the whole command. (Total time is also sometimes called *wall-clock time*, since it's how much time elapsed if we were measuring the time on the clock on the wall.)

The second time, the output looked like this:

```
0.00s user 0.00s system 8% cpu 0.063 total
```

The total time went down to 0.063s, for a savings of about 0.85s for each SSH connection after the first one. Recall that Ansible uses at least two SSH sessions to execute each task: one session to copy the module file to the host, and another session to execute the module file.[2] This means that SSH multiplexing should save you on the order of one or two seconds for each task that runs in your playbook.

SSH Multiplexing Options in Ansible

Ansible uses the options for SSH multiplexing shown in Table 11-1.

---

1 The output format may look different, depending on your shell and OS. I'm running Zsh on macOS.

2 One of these steps can be optimized away by using pipelining, described later in this chapter.

Table 11-1. Ansible's SSH multiplexing options

Option	Value
ControlMaster	auto
ControlPath	$HOME/.ansible/cp/ansible-ssh-%h-%p-%r
ControlPersist	60s

I've never needed to change Ansible's default `ControlMaster` or `ControlPersist` values. However, I have needed to change the value for the `ControlPath` option. That's because the operating system sets a maximum length on the path of a Unix domain socket, and if the `ControlPath` string is too long, then multiplexing won't work. Unfortunately, Ansible won't tell you if the `ControlPath` string is too long; it will simply run without using SSH multiplexing.

You can test it out on your control machine by manually trying to SSH by using the same `ControlPath` that Ansible would use:

```
$ CP=~/.ansible/cp/ansible-ssh-%h-%p-%r
$ ssh -o ControlMaster=auto -o ControlPersist=60s \
-o ControlPath=$CP \
ubuntu@ec2-203-0-113-12.compute-1.amazonaws.com \
/bin/true
```

If the `ControlPath` is too long, you'll see an error that looks like Example 11-2.

Example 11-2. ControlPath too long

```
ControlPath
"/Users/lorin/.ansible/cp/ansible-ssh-ec2-203-0-113-12.compute-1.amazonaws.
com-22-ubuntu.KIwEKEsRzCKFABch"
too long for Unix domain socket
```

This is a common occurrence when connecting to Amazon EC2 instances, because EC2 uses long hostnames.

The workaround is to configure Ansible to use a shorter `ControlPath`. The official documentation (*http://bit.ly/2kKpsJI*) recommends setting this option in your *ansible.cfg* file:

```
[ssh_connection]
control_path = %(directory)s/%%h-%%r
```

Ansible sets `%(directory)s` to `$HOME/.ansible/cp`, and the double percent signs (`%%`) are needed to escape these characters because percent signs are special characters for files in *.ini* format.

If you have SSH multiplexing enabled, and you change a configuration of your SSH connection, say by modifying the `ssh_args` configuration option, this change won't take effect if the control socket is still open from a previous connection.

Pipelining

Recall how Ansible executes a task:

1. It generates a Python script based on the module being invoked.
2. It copies the Python script to the host.
3. It executes the Python script.

Ansible supports an optimization called *pipelining*, whereby it will execute the Python script by piping it to the SSH session instead of copying it. This saves time because it tells Ansible to use one SSH session instead of two.

Enabling Pipelining

Pipelining is off by default because it can require some configuration on your remote hosts, but I like to enable it because it speeds up execution. To enable it, modify your *ansible.cfg* file as shown in Example 11-3.

Example 11-3. ansible.cfg Enable pipelining

```
[defaults]
pipelining = True
```

Configuring Hosts for Pipelining

For pipelining to work, you need to make sure that `requiretty` is not enabled in your */etc/sudoers* file on your hosts. Otherwise, you'll get errors that look like Example 11-4 when you run your playbook.

Example 11-4. Error when requiretty is enabled

```
failed: [vagrant1] => {"failed": true, "parsed": false}
invalid output was: sudo: sorry, you must have a tty to run sudo
```

If `sudo` on your hosts is configured to read files from the */etc/sudoers.d*, then the simplest way to resolve this is to add a *sudoers* config file that disables the `requiretty` restriction for the user you use SSH with.

If the /etc/sudoers.d directory is present, your hosts should support adding *sudoers* config files in that directory. You can use the `ansible` command-line tool to check if the directory there:

```
$ ansible vagrant -a "file /etc/sudoers.d"
```

If the directory is present, the output will look like this:

```
vagrant1 | success | rc=0 >>
/etc/sudoers.d: directory

vagrant3 | success | rc=0 >>
/etc/sudoers.d: directory

vagrant2 | success | rc=0 >>
/etc/sudoers.d: directory
```

If the directory is not present, the output will look like this:

```
vagrant3 | FAILED | rc=1 >>
/etc/sudoers.d: ERROR: cannot open `/etc/sudoers.d' (No such file or
directory)

vagrant2 | FAILED | rc=1 >>
/etc/sudoers.d: ERROR: cannot open `/etc/sudoers.d' (No such file or
directory)

vagrant1 | FAILED | rc=1 >>
/etc/sudoers.d: ERROR: cannot open `/etc/sudoers.d' (No such file or
directory)
```

If the directory is present, create a template file that looks like Example 11-5.

Example 11-5. templates/disable-requiretty.j2

```
Defaults:{{ ansible_user }} !requiretty
```

Then run the playbook shown in Example 11-6, replacing `myhosts` with your hosts. Don't forget to disable pipelining before you do this, or the playbook will fail with an error.

Example 11-6. disable-requiretty.yml

```
- name: do not require tty for ssh-ing user
  hosts: myhosts
  sudo: True
  tasks:
    - name: Set a sudoers file to disable tty
      template: >
        src=templates/disable-requiretty.j2
        dest=/etc/sudoers.d/disable-requiretty
```

```
owner=root group=root mode=0440
validate="visudo -cf %s"
```

Note the use of `validate="visudo -cf %s"`. See "Validating Files" on page 367 for a discussion of why it's a good idea to use validation when modifying *sudoers* files.

Fact Caching

If your play doesn't reference any Ansible facts, you can turn off fact gathering for that play. Recall that you can disable fact gathering with the `gather_facts` clause in a play; for example:

```
- name: an example play that doesn't need facts
  hosts: myhosts
  gather_facts: False
  tasks:
    # tasks go here:
```

You can disable fact gathering by default by adding the following to your *ansible.cfg* file:

```
[defaults]
gathering = explicit
```

If you write plays that do reference facts, you can use fact caching so that Ansible gathers facts for a host only once, even if you rerun the playbook or run a different playbook that connects to the same host.

If fact caching is enabled, Ansible will store facts in a cache the first time it connects to hosts. For subsequent playbook runs, Ansible will look up the facts in the cache instead of fetching them from the remote host, until the cache expires.

Example 11-7 shows the lines you must add to your *ansible.cfg* file to enable fact caching. The `fact_caching_timeout` value is in seconds, and the example uses a 24-hour (86,400 second) timeout.

As with all caching-based solutions, there's always the danger of the cached data becoming stale. Some facts, such as the CPU architecture (stored in the `ansible_architecture` fact), are unlikely to change often. Others, such as the date and time reported by the machine (stored in the `ansible_date_time` fact), are guaranteed to change often.

If you decide to enable fact caching, make sure you know how quickly the facts used in your playbook are likely to change, and set an appropriate fact-caching timeout value. If you want to clear the fact cache before running a playbook, pass the `--flush-cache` flag to `ansible-playbook`.

Example 11-7. ansible.cfg enable fact caching

```
[defaults]
gathering = smart
# 24-hour timeout, adjust if needed
fact_caching_timeout = 86400

# You must specify a fact caching implementation
fact_caching = ...
```

Setting the `gathering` configuration option to `smart` in *ansible.cfg* tells Ansible to use *smart gathering*. This means that Ansible will gather facts only if they are not present in the cache or if the cache has expired.

 If you want to use fact caching, make sure your playbooks do *not* explicitly specify `gather_facts: True` or `gather_facts: False`. With smart gathering enabled in the configuration file, Ansible will gather facts only if they are not present in the cache.

You must explicitly specify a `fact_caching` implementation in *ansible.cfg*, or Ansible will not cache facts between playbook runs. As of this writing, there are three fact-caching implementations:

- JSON files
- Redis
- Memcached

JSON File Fact-Caching Backend

With the JSON file fact-caching backend, Ansible will write the facts it gathers to files on your control machine. If the files are present on your system, it will use those files instead of connecting to the host and gathering facts.

To enable the JSON file fact-caching backend, add the settings in Example 11-8 to your *ansible.cfg* file.

Example 11-8. ansible.cfg with JSON fact caching

```
[defaults]
gathering = smart

# 24-hour timeout, adjust if needed
fact_caching_timeout = 86400
```

```
# JSON file implementation
fact_caching = jsonfile
fact_caching_connection = /tmp/ansible_fact_cache
```

Use the `fact_caching_connection` configuration option to specify a directory where Ansible should write the JSON files that contain the facts. If the directory does not exist, Ansible will create it.

Ansible uses the file modification time to determine whether the fact-caching time-out has occurred yet.

Redis Fact-Caching Backend

Redis is a popular key-value data store that is often used as a cache. To enable fact caching by using the Redis backend, you need to do the following:

1. Install Redis on your control machine.
2. Ensure that the Redis service is running on the control machine.
3. Install the Python Redis package.
4. Modify *ansible.cfg* to enable fact caching with Redis.

Example 11-9 shows how to configure *ansible.cfg* to use Redis as the cache backend.

Example 11-9. ansible.cfg with Redis fact caching

```
[defaults]
gathering = smart

# 24-hour timeout, adjust if needed
fact_caching_timeout = 86400

fact_caching = redis
```

Ansible needs the Python Redis package on the control machine, which you can install using pip:[3]

```
    $ pip install redis
```

You must also install Redis and ensure that it is running on your control machine. If you are using macOS, you can install Redis by using Homebrew. If you are using Linux, install Redis by using your native package manager.

---

3 You may need to sudo or activate a virtualenv, depending on how you installed Ansible on your control machine.

Memcached Fact-Caching Backend

Memcached is another popular key-value data store that is often used as a cache. To enable fact caching by using the Memcached backend, you need to do the following:

1. Install Memcached on your control machine.
2. Ensure that the Memcached service is running on the control machine.
3. Install the Python Memcached Python package.
4. Modify *ansible.cfg* to enable fact caching with Memcached.

Example 11-10 shows how to configure *ansible.cfg* to use Memcached as the cache backend.

Example 11-10. ansible.cfg with Memcached fact caching

```
[defaults]
gathering = smart

# 24-hour timeout, adjust if needed
fact_caching_timeout = 86400

fact_caching = memcached
```

Ansible needs the Python Memcached package on the control machine, which you can install using pip. You might need to sudo or activate a virtualenv, depending on how you installed Ansible on your control machine.

```
$ pip install python-memcached
```

You must also install Memcached and ensure that it is running on your control machine. If you are using macOS, you can install Memcached by using Homebrew. If you are using Linux, install Memcached by using your native package manager.

For more information on fact caching, check out the official documentation (*http://bit.ly/1F6BHap*).

Parallelism

For each task, Ansible will connect to the hosts in parallel to execute the tasks. But Ansible doesn't necessarily connect to *all* of the hosts in parallel. Instead, the level of parallelism is controlled by a parameter, which defaults to 5. You can change this default parameter in one of two ways.

You can set the ANSIBLE_FORKS environment variable, as shown in Example 11-11.

Example 11-11. Setting ANSIBLE_FORKS

```
$ export ANSIBLE_FORKS=20
$ ansible-playbook playbook.yml
```

You also can modify the Ansible configuration file (*ansible.cfg*) by setting a `forks` option in the defaults section, as shown in Example 11-12.

Example 11-12. ansible.cfg configuring number of forks

```
[defaults]
forks = 20
```

Concurrent Tasks with Async

Ansible introduced support for asynchronous actions with the `async` clause to work around the problem of SSH timeouts. If the execution time for a task exceeds the SSH timeout, Ansible will lose its connection to the host and report an error. Marking a long-running task with the `async` clause eliminates the risk of an SSH timeout.

However, asynchronous actions can also be used for a different purpose: to start a second task before the first task has completed. This can be useful if you have two tasks that both take a long time to execute and are independent (i.e., you don't need the first to complete to execute the second).

Example 11-13 shows a list of tasks that use the `async` clause to clone a large Git repository. Because the task is marked as `async`, Ansible will not wait until the Git clone is complete before it begins to install the operating system packages.

Example 11-13. Using async to overlap tasks

```
- name: install git
  apt: name=git update_cache=yes
  become: yes
- name: clone Linus's git repo
  git:
    repo: git://git.kernel.org/pub/scm/linux/kernel/git/torvalds/linux.git
    dest: /home/vagrant/linux
  async: 3600   ❶
  poll: 0 ❷
  register: linux_clone ❸
- name: install several packages
  apt:
    name: "{{ item }}"
  with_items:
    - apt-transport-https
    - ca-certificates
    - linux-image-extra-virtual
```

```
      - software-properties-common
      - python-pip
  become: yes
- name: wait for linux clone to complete
  async_status: ❹
    jid: "{{ linux_clone.ansible_job_id }}" ❺
  register: result
  until: result.finished ❻
  retries: 3600
```

❶ We specify that this is an `async` task that should take less than 3,600 seconds. If the execution time exceeds this value, Ansible will automatically terminate the process associated with the task.

❷ We specify a poll argument of 0 to tell Ansible that it should immediately move on to the next task after it spawns this task asynchronously. If we had specified a nonzero value instead, Ansible would not move on to the next task. Instead, it would periodically poll the status of the `async` task to check whether it was complete, sleeping between checks for the amount of time in seconds specified by the poll argument.

❸ When we run `async`, we must use the `register` clause to capture the `async` result. The `result` object contains an `ansible_job_id` value that we will use later to poll for the job status.

❹ We use the `async_status` module to poll for the status of the `async` job we started earlier.

❺ We must specify a `jid` value that identifies the `async` job.

❻ The `async_status` module polls only a single time. We need to specify an `until` clause so that it will keep polling until the job completes, or until we exhaust the specified number of retries.

You should now know how to configure SSH multiplexing, pipelining, fact caching, parallelism, and async in order to get your playbooks to run more quickly. Next, we'll discuss writing your own Ansible modules.

## CHAPTER 12

Custom Modules

Sometimes you want to perform a task that is too complex for the command or shell modules, and there is no existing module that does what you want. In that case, you might want to write your own module.

In the past, I've written custom modules to retrieve my public IP address when I'm behind a network address translation (NAT) getaway, and to initialize the databases in an OpenStack deployment. I've thought about writing a custom module for generating self-signed TLS certificates, though I've never gotten around to it.

Another common use for custom modules is interacting with a third-party service over a REST API. For example, GitHub offers what it calls Releases, which let you attach binary assets to repositories, and these are exposed via GitHub's API. If your deployment requires you to download a binary asset attached to a private GitHub repository, this would be a good candidate for implementing inside a custom module.

Example: Checking That We Can Reach a Remote Server

Let's say we want to check that we can connect to a remote server on a particular port. If we can't, we want Ansible to treat that as an error and stop running the play.

> The custom module we will develop in this chapter is basically a simpler version of the wait_for module.

Using the Script Module Instead of Writing Your Own

Recall in Example 6-17 how we used the `script` module to execute custom scripts on remote hosts. Sometimes it's simpler to just use the `script` module rather than write a full-blown Ansible module.

I like putting these types of scripts in a *scripts* folder along with my playbooks. For example, we could create a script file called *playbooks/scripts/can_reach.sh* that accepts as arguments the name of a host, the port to connect to, and how long it should try to connect before timing out:

```
can_reach.sh www.example.com 80 1
```

We can create a script as shown in Example 12-1.

Example 12-1. can_reach.sh

```
#!/bin/bash
host=$1
port=$2
timeout=$3

nc -z -w $timeout $host $port
```

We can then invoke this:

```
- name: run my custom script
  script: scripts/can_reach.sh www.example.com 80 1
```

Keep in mind that your script will execute on the remote hosts, just like Ansible modules do. Therefore, any programs your script requires must have been installed previously on the remote hosts. For example, you can write your script in Ruby, as long as Ruby has been installed on the remote hosts, and the first line of the script invokes the Ruby interpreter, such as the following:

```
#!/usr/bin/ruby
```

can_reach as a Module

Next, let's implement `can_reach` as a proper Ansible module, which we will be able to invoke like this:

```
- name: check if host can reach the database server
  can_reach: host=db.example.com port=5432 timeout=1
```

This checks whether the host can make a TCP connection to *db.example.com* on port 5432. It will time out after one second if it fails to make a connection.

We'll use this example throughout the rest of this chapter.

Where to Put Custom Modules

Ansible will look in the *library* directory relative to the playbook. In our example, we put our playbooks in the *playbooks* directory, so we will put our custom module at *playbooks/library/can_reach*.

How Ansible Invokes Modules

Before we implement the module, let's go over how Ansible invokes them. Ansible will do the following:

1. Generate a standalone Python script with the arguments (Python modules only)
2. Copy the module to the host
3. Create an arguments file on the host (non-Python modules only)
4. Invoke the module on the host, passing the arguments file as an argument
5. Parse the standard output of the module

Let's look at each of these steps in more detail.

Generate a Standalone Python Script with the Arguments (Python Only)

If the module is written in Python and uses the helper code that Ansible provides (described later), then Ansible will generate a self-contained Python script that injects helper code, as well as the module arguments.

Copy the Module to the Host

Ansible will copy the generated Python script (for Python-based modules) or the local file *playbooks/library/can_reach* (for non-Python-based modules) to a temporary directory on the remote host. If you are accessing the remote host as the ubuntu user, Ansible will copy the file to a path that looks like the following:

/home/ubuntu/.ansible/tmp/ansible-tmp-1412459504.14-47728545618200/can_reach

Create an Arguments File on the Host (Non-Python Only)

If the module is not written in Python, Ansible will create a file on the remote host with a name like this:

/home/ubuntu/.ansible/tmp/ansible-tmp-1412459504.14-47728545618200/arguments

If we invoke the module like this:

```
- name: check if host can reach the database server
  can_reach: host=db.example.com port=5432 timeout=1
```

then the arguments file will have the following content:

```
host=db.example.com port=5432 timeout=1
```

We can tell Ansible to generate the arguments file for the module as JSON, by adding the following line to *playbooks/library/can_reach*:

```
# WANT_JSON
```

If our module is configured for JSON input, the arguments file will look like this:

```
{"host": "www.example.com", "port": "80", "timeout": "1"}
```

Invoke the Module

Ansible will call the module and pass the arguments file as arguments. If it's a Python-based module, Ansible executes the equivalent of the following (with */path/to/* replaced by the actual path):

```
/path/to/can_reach
```

If it's a non-Python-based module, Ansible will look at the first line of the module to determine the interpreter and execute the equivalent of this:

```
/path/to/interpreter /path/to/can_reach /path/to/arguments
```

Assuming the `can_reach` module is implemented as a Bash script and starts with this:

```
#!/bin/bash
```

then Ansible will do something like this:

```
/bin/bash /path/to/can_reach /path/to/arguments
```

But even this isn't strictly true. What Ansible actually does is the following:

```
/bin/sh -c 'LANG=en_US.UTF-8 LC_CTYPE=en_US.UTF-8 /bin/bash /path/to/can_reach \
/path/to/arguments; rm -rf /path/to/ >/dev/null 2>&1'
```

You can see the exact command that Ansible invokes by passing -vvv to `ansible-playbook`.

Expected Outputs

Ansible expects modules to output JSON. For example:

```
{'changed': false, 'failed': true, 'msg': 'could not reach the host'}
```

Prior to version 1.8, Ansible supported a shorthand output format, also known as *baby JSON*, that looked like key=value. Ansible dropped support for this format in 1.8. As you'll see later, if you write your modules in Python, Ansible provides helper methods that make it easy to generate JSON output.

Output Variables that Ansible Expects

Your module can return whatever variables you like, but Ansible has special treatment for certain returned variables.

changed

All Ansible modules should return a changed variable. The changed variable is a Boolean that indicates whether the module execution caused the host to change state. When Ansible runs, it will show in the output whether a state change has happened. If a task has a notify clause to notify a handler, the notification will fire only if changed is true.

failed

If the module fails to complete, it should return failed=true. Ansible will treat this task execution as a failure and will not run any further tasks against the host that failed, unless the task has an ignore_errors or failed_when clause.

If the module succeeds, you can either return failed=false or you can simply leave out the variable.

msg

Use the msg variable to add a descriptive message that describes the reason that a module failed.

If a task fails, and the module returns a msg variable, then Ansible will output that variable slightly differently than it does the other variables. For example, if a module returns the following:

```
{"failed": true, "msg": "could not reach www.example.com:81"}
```

then Ansible will output the following lines when executing this task:

```
failed: [vagrant1] => {"failed": true}
msg: could not reach www.example.com:81
```

Implementing Modules in Python

If you implement your custom module in Python, Ansible provides the `AnsibleMod`
`ule` Python class that makes it easier to do the following:

- Parse the inputs
- Return outputs in JSON format
- Invoke external programs

In fact, when writing a Python module, Ansible will inject the arguments directly into
the generated Python file rather than require you to parse a separate arguments file.
We'll discuss how that works later in this chapter.

We'll create our module in Python by creating a *can_reach* file. I'll start with the
implementation and then break it down (see Example 12-2).

Example 12-2. can_reach

```
#!/usr/bin/python
from ansible.module_utils.basic import AnsibleModule ❶

def can_reach(module, host, port, timeout):
    nc_path = module.get_bin_path('nc', required=True) ❷
    args = [nc_path, "-z", "-w", str(timeout),
            host, str(port)]
    (rc, stdout, stderr) = module.run_command(args) ❸
    return rc == 0

def main():
    module = AnsibleModule( ❹
        argument_spec=dict( ❺
            host=dict(required=True), ❻
            port=dict(required=True, type='int'),
            timeout=dict(required=False, type='int', default=3) ❼
        ),
        supports_check_mode=True ❽
    )

    # In check mode, we take no action
    # Since this module never changes system state, we just
    # return changed=False
    if module.check_mode: ❾
        module.exit_json(changed=False) ❿

    host = module.params['host'] ⓫
    port = module.params['port']
    timeout = module.params['timeout']
```

```
    if can_reach(module, host, port, timeout):
        module.exit_json(changed=False)
    else:
        msg = "Could not reach %s:%s" % (host, port)
        module.fail_json(msg=msg) ⓬

if __name__ == "__main__":
    main()
```

❶ Imports the `AnsibleModule` helper class

❷ Gets the path of an external program

❸ Invokes an external program

❹ Instantiates the `AnsibleModule` helper class

❺ Specifies the permitted set of arguments

❻ A required argument

❼ An optional argument with a default value

❽ Specifies that this module supports check mode

❾ Tests whether the module is running in check mode

❿ Exits successfully, passing a return value

⓫ Extracts an argument

⓬ Exits with failure, passing an error message

Parsing Arguments

It's easier to understand the way `AnsibleModule` handles argument parsing by looking at an example. Recall that our module is invoked like this:

```
- name: check if host can reach the database server
  can_reach: host=db.example.com port=5432 timeout=1
```

Let's assume that the `host` and `port` parameters are required, and `timeout` is an optional parameter with a default value of 3 seconds.

You instantiate an `AnsibleModule` object by passing it an `argument_spec`, which is a dictionary in which the keys are parameter names and the values are dictionaries that contain information about the parameters.

```
module = AnsibleModule(
    argument_spec=dict(
        ...
```

In our example, we declare a required argument named host. Ansible will report an error if this argument isn't passed to the module when we use it in a task:

```
host=dict(required=True),
```

The variable named timeout is optional. Ansible assumes that arguments are strings unless specified otherwise. Our timeout variable is an integer, so we specify the type as int so that Ansible will automatically convert it into a Python number. If timeout is not specified, the module will assume it has a value of 3:

```
timeout=dict(required=False, type='int', default=3)
```

The AnsibleModule constructor takes arguments other than argument_spec. In the preceding example, we added this argument:

```
supports_check_mode = True
```

This indicates that our module supports check mode. We'll explain that a little later in this chapter.

Accessing Parameters

Once you've declared an AnsibleModule object, you can access the values of the arguments through the params dictionary, like this:

```
module = AnsibleModule(...)

host = module.params["host"]
port = module.params["port"]
timeout = module.params["timeout"]
```

Importing the AnsibleModule Helper Class

Starting with Ansible 2.1.0, Ansible deploys a module to the host by sending a ZIP file containing the module file along with the imported helper files. One consequence of this it that you can now explicitly import classes, such as the following:

```
from ansible.module_utils.basic import AnsibleModule
```

Prior to Ansible 2.1.0, the import statement in an Ansible module was really a pseudo import statement. In these earlier versions, Ansible copied only a single Python file to the remote host to execute it. Ansible simulated the behavior of a traditional Python import by including the imported code directly into the generated Python file (similar to how an #include statement works in C or C+\+). Because these did not behave like a traditional Python import, if you explicitly imported a class, the Ansible module debugging scripts would not work properly. You had to use a wildcard import, and put the import at the end of the file, just before invoking the main function:

```
...
from ansible.module_utils.basic import *
if __name__ == "__main__":
    main()
```

Argument Options

For each argument to an Ansible module, you can specify several options, as listed in Table 12-1.

Table 12-1. Argument options

Option	Description
required	If `true`, argument is required
default	Default value if argument is not required
choices	A list of possible values for the argument
aliases	Other names you can use as an alias for this argument
type	Argument type. Allowed values: `'str'`, `'list'`, `'dict'`, `'bool'`, `'int'`, `'float'`

required

The `required` option is the only option that you should always specify. If it is `true`, Ansible will return an error if the user fails to specify the argument.

In our `can_reach` module example, `host` and `port` are required, and `timeout` is not required.

default

For arguments that have `required=False` set, you should generally specify a default value for that option. In our example:

```
timeout=dict(required=False, type='int', default=3)
```

If the user invokes the module like this:

```
can_reach: host=www.example.com port=443
```

then `module.params["timeout"]` will contain the value 3.

choices

The choices option allows you to restrict the allowed arguments to a predefined list.

Consider the distros argument in the following example:

```
distro=dict(required=True, choices=['ubuntu', 'centos', 'fedora'])
```

If the user were to pass an argument that was not in the list—for example:

```
distro=suse
```

this would cause Ansible to throw an error.

aliases

The aliases option allows you to use different names to refer to the same argument. For example, consider the package argument in the apt module:

```
module = AnsibleModule(
    argument_spec=dict(
        ...
        package = dict(default=None, aliases=['pkg', 'name'], type='list'),
    )
)
```

Since pkg and name are aliases for the package argument, these invocations are all equivalent:

```
- apt: package=vim
- apt: name=vim
- apt: pkg=vim
```

type

The type option enables you to specify the type of an argument. By default, Ansible assumes all arguments are strings.

However, you can specify a type for the argument, and Ansible will convert the argument to the desired type. The types supported are as follows:

- str
- list
- dict
- bool
- int
- float

In our example, we specified the `port` argument as `int`:

```
port=dict(required=True, type='int'),
```

When we access it from the `params` dictionary, like this:

```
port = module.params['port']
```

the value of the `port` variable will be an integer. If we had not specified the type as `int` when declaring the `port` variable, the `module.params['port']` value would have been a string instead of an integer.

Lists are comma-delimited. For example, if you have a module named `foo` with a list parameter named `colors`:

```
colors=dict(required=True, type='list')
```

then you pass a `list` like this:

```
foo: colors=red,green,blue
```

For dictionaries, you can either use `key=value` pairs, delimited by commas, or you can use JSON inline.

For example, if you have a module named `bar`, with a `dict` parameter named `tags`:

```
tags=dict(required=False, type='dict', default={})
```

then you can pass the argument like this:

```
- bar: tags=env=staging,function=web
```

Or you can pass the argument like this:

```
- bar: tags={"env": "staging", "function": "web"}
```

The official Ansible documentation uses the term *complex args* to refer to lists and dictionaries that are passed to modules as arguments. See "Complex Arguments in Tasks: A Brief Digression" on page 105 for how to pass these types of arguments in playbooks.

AnsibleModule Initializer Parameters

The `AnsibleModule` initializer method takes various arguments, listed in Table 12-2. The only required argument is `argument_spec`.

Table 12-2. AnsibleModule initializer arguments

Parameter	Default	Description
argument_spec	(*None*)	Dictionary that contains information about arguments
bypass_checks	False	If true, don't check any of the parameter constraints
no_log	False	If true, don't log the behavior of this module

Parameter	Default	Description
check_invalid_arguments	True	If true, return error if user passed an unknown argument
mutually_exclusive	(None)	List of mutually exclusive arguments
required_together	(None)	List of arguments that must appear together
required_one_of	(None)	List of arguments where at least one must be present
add_file_common_args	False	Supports the arguments of the file module
supports_check_mode	False	If true, indicates module supports check mode

argument_spec

This is a dictionary that contains the descriptions of the allowed arguments for the module, as described in the previous section.

no_log

When Ansible executes a module on a host, the module will log output to the syslog, which on Ubuntu is at */var/log/syslog*.

The logging output looks like this:

```
Sep 28 02:31:47 vagrant-ubuntu-trusty-64 ansible-ping: Invoked with data=None
Sep 28 02:32:18 vagrant-ubuntu-trusty-64 ansible-apt: Invoked with dpkg_options=
force-confdef,force-confold upgrade=None force=False name=nginx package=['nginx'
] purge=False state=installed update_cache=True default_release=None install_rec
ommends=True deb=None cache_valid_time=None Sep 28 02:33:01 vagrant-ubuntu-trust
y-64 ansible-file: Invoked with src=None
original_basename=None directory_mode=None force=False remote_src=None selevel=N
one seuser=None recurse=False serole=None content=None delimiter=None state=dire
ctory diff_peek=None mode=None regexp=None owner=None group=None path=/etc/nginx
/ssl backup=None validate=None setype=None
Sep 28 02:33:01 vagrant-ubuntu-trusty-64 ansible-copy: Invoked with src=/home/va
grant/.ansible/tmp/ansible-tmp-1411871581.19-43362494744716/source directory_mod
e=None force=True remote_src=None dest=/etc/nginx/ssl/nginx.key selevel=None seu
ser=None serole=None group=None content=NOT_LOGGING_PARAMETER setype=None origin
al_basename=nginx.key delimiter=None mode=0600 owner=root regexp=None validate=N
one backup=False
Sep 28 02:33:01 vagrant-ubuntu-trusty-64 ansible-copy: Invoked with src=/home/va
grant/.ansible/tmp/ansible-tmp-1411871581.31-95111161791436/source directory_mod
e=None force=True remote_src=None dest=/etc/nginx/ssl/nginx.crt selevel=None seu
ser=None serole=None group=None content=NOT_LOGGING_PARAMETER setype=None origin
al_basename=nginx.crt delimiter=None mode=None owner=None regexp=None validate=N
one backup=False
```

If a module accepts sensitive information as an argument, you might want to disable this logging. To configure a module so that it does not write to syslog, pass the no_log=True parameter to the AnsibleModule initializer.

check_invalid_arguments

By default, Ansible will verify that all of the arguments that a user passed to a module are legal arguments. You can disable this check by passing the `check_invalid_arguments=False` parameter to the `AnsibleModule` initializer.

mutually_exclusive

The `mutually_exclusive` parameter is a list of arguments that cannot be specified during the same module invocation. For example, the `lineinfile` module allows you to add a line to a file. You can use the `insertbefore` argument to specify which line it should appear before, or the `insertafter` argument to specify which line it should appear after, but you can't specify both.

Therefore, this module specifies that the two arguments are mutually exclusive, like this:

```
mutually_exclusive=[['insertbefore', 'insertafter']]
```

required_one_of

The `required_one_of` parameter expects a list of arguments with at least one that must be passed to the module. For example, the `pip` module, which is used for installing Python packages, can take either the name of a package or the name of a requirements file that contains a list of packages. The module specifies that one of these arguments is required like this:

```
required_one_of=[['name', 'requirements']]
```

add_file_common_args

Many modules create or modify a file. A user will often want to set some attributes on the resulting file, such as the owner, group, and file permissions.

You could invoke the `file` module to set these parameters, like this:

```
- name: download a file
  get_url: url=http://www.example.com/myfile.dat dest=/tmp/myfile.dat

- name: set the permissions
  file: path=/tmp/myfile.dat owner=ubuntu mode=0600
```

As a shortcut, Ansible allows you to specify that a module will accept all of the same arguments as the `file` module, so you can simply set the file attributes by passing the relevant arguments to the module that created or modified the file. For example:

```
- name: download a file
  get_url: url=http://www.example.com/myfile.dat dest=/tmp/myfile.dat \
  owner=ubuntu mode=0600
```

To specify that a module should support these arguments:

```
add_file_common_args=True
```

The `AnsibleModule` module provides helper methods for working with these arguments.

The `load_file_common_arguments` method takes the parameters dictionary as an argument and returns a parameters dictionary that contains all of the arguments that relate to setting file attributes.

The `set_fs_attributes_if_different` method takes a file parameters dictionary and a Boolean indicating whether a host state change has occurred yet. The method sets the file attributes as a side effect and returns `true` if there was a host state change (either the initial argument was true, or it made a change to the file as part of the side effect).

If you are using the common file arguments, do not specify the arguments explicitly. To get access to these attributes in your code, use the helper methods to extract the arguments and set the file attributes, like this:

```
module = AnsibleModule(
    argument_spec=dict(
        dest=dict(required=True),
        ...
    ),
    add_file_common_args=True
)

# "changed" is True if module caused host to change state
changed = do_module_stuff(param)

file_args = module.load_file_common_arguments(module.params)

changed = module.set_fs_attributes_if_different(file_args, changed)
module.exit_json(changed=changed, ...)
```

 Ansible assumes your module has an argument named `path` or `dest`, which contains the path to the file.

bypass_checks

Before an Ansible module executes, it first checks that all of the argument constraints are satisfied, and returns an error if they aren't. These include the following:

- No mutually exclusive arguments are present.
- Arguments marked with the `required` option are present.
- Arguments restricted by the `choices` option have the expected values.
- Arguments that specify a `type` have values that are consistent with the `type`.
- Arguments marked as `required_together` appear together.
- At least one argument in the list of `required_one_of` is present.

You can disable all of these checks by setting `bypass_checks=True`.

Returning Success or Failure

Use the `exit_json` method to return success. You should always return `changed` as an argument, and it's good practice to return `msg` with a meaningful message:

```
module = AnsibleModule(...)
...
module.exit_json(changed=False, msg="meaningful message goes here")
```

Use the `fail_json` method to indicate failure. You should always return a `msg` parameter to explain to the user the reason for the failure:

```
module = AnsibleModule(...)
...
module.fail_json(msg="Out of disk space")
```

Invoking External Commands

The `AnsibleModule` class provides the `run_command` convenience method for calling an external program, which wraps the native Python `subprocess` module. It accepts the arguments listed in Table 12-3.

Table 12-3. run_command arguments

Argument	Type	Default	Description
args (default)	String or list of strings	(*None*)	The command to be executed (see the following section)
check_rc	Boolean	False	If `true`, will call `fail_json` if command returns a nonzero value
close_fds	Boolean	True	Passes as `close_fds` argument to `subprocess.Popen`
executable	String (path to program)	(*None*)	Passes as `executable` argument to `subprocess.Popen`
data	String	(*None*)	Send to `stdin` if child process
binary_data	Boolean	False	If `false` and `data` is present, Ansible will send a newline to `stdin` after sending `data`

Argument	Type	Default	Description
path_prefix	String (list of paths)	(None)	Colon-delimited list of paths to prepend to PATH environment variable
cwd	String (directory path)	(None)	If specified, Ansible will change to this directory before executing
use_unsafe_shell	Boolean	False	See the following section

If `args` is passed as a list, as shown in Example 12-3, then Ansible will invoke `subprocess.Popen` with `shell=False`.

Example 12-3. Passing args as a list

```
module = AnsibleModule(...)
...
module.run_command(['/usr/local/bin/myprog', '-i', 'myarg'])
```

If `args` is passed as a string, as shown in Example 12-4, then the behavior depends on the value of `use_unsafe_shell`. If `use_unsafe_shell` is `false`, Ansible will split `args` into a list and invoke `subprocess.Popen` with `shell=False`. If `use_unsafe_shell` is `true`, Ansible will pass `args` as a string to `subprocess.Popen` with `shell=True`.[1]

Example 12-4. Passing args as a string

```
module = AnsibleModule(...)
...
module.run_command('/usr/local/bin/myprog -i myarg')
```

Check Mode (Dry Run)

Ansible supports something called *check mode*, which is enabled when passing the `-C` or `--check` flag to `ansible-playbook`. It is similar to the *dry run* mode supported by many other tools.

When Ansible runs a playbook in check mode, it will not make any changes to the hosts when it runs. Instead, it will simply report whether each task would have changed the host, returned successfully without making a change, or returned an error.

---

1 For more on the Python standard library `subprocess.Popen` class, see its online documentation (*http://bit.ly/1F72tiU*).

Modules must be explicitly configured to support check mode. If you're going to write your own module, I recommend you support check mode so that your module is a good Ansible citizen.

To tell Ansible that your module supports check mode, set `supports_check_mode` to `true` in the AnsibleModule initializer method, as shown in Example 12-5.

Example 12-5. Telling Ansible the module supports check mode

```
module = AnsibleModule(
    argument_spec=dict(...),
    supports_check_mode=True)
```

Your module should check that check mode has been enabled by checking the value of the `check_mode`[2] attribute of the `AnsibleModule` object, as shown in Example 12-6. Call the `exit_json` or `fail_json` methods as you would normally.

Example 12-6. Checking whether check mode is enabled

```
module = AnsibleModule(...)
...
if module.check_mode:
    # check if this module would make any changes
    would_change = would_executing_this_module_change_something()
    module.exit_json(changed=would_change)
```

It is up to you, the module author, to ensure that your module does not modify the state of the host when running in check mode.

Documenting Your Module

You should document your modules according to the Ansible project standards so that HTML documentation for your module will be correctly generated and the *ansible-doc* program will display documentation for your module. Ansible uses a special YAML-based syntax for documenting modules.

Near the top of your module, define a string variable called `DOCUMENTATION` that contains the documentation, and a string variable called `EXAMPLES` that contains example usage.

---

2 Phew! That was a lot of checks.

Example 12-7 shows an example for the documentation section for our `can_reach` module.

Example 12-7. Example of module documentation

```
DOCUMENTATION = '''
---
module: can_reach
short_description: Checks server reachability
description:
 - Checks if a remote server can be reached
version_added: "1.8"
options:
  host:
    description:
       - A DNS hostname or IP address
    required: true
  port:
    description:
     - The TCP port number
    required: true
  timeout:
    description:
     - The amount of time trying to connect before giving up, in seconds
    required: false
    default: 3
  flavor:
    description:
     - This is a made-up option to show how to specify choices.
    required: false
    choices: ["chocolate", "vanilla", "strawberry"]
    aliases: ["flavor"]
    default: chocolate
requirements: [netcat]
author: Lorin Hochstein
notes:
  - This is just an example to demonstrate how to write a module.
  - You probably want to use the native M(wait_for) module instead.
'''

EXAMPLES = '''
# Check that ssh is running, with the default timeout
- can_reach: host=myhost.example.com port=22

# Check if postgres is running, with a timeout
- can_reach: host=db.example.com port=5432 timeout=1
'''
```

Ansible supports limited markup in the documentation. Table 12-4 shows the markup syntax supported by the Ansible documentation tool, with recommendations about when you should use this markup.

Table 12-4. Documentation markup

Type	Syntax with example	When to use
URL	U(*http://www.example.com*)	URLs
Module	M(apt)	Module names
Italics	I(port)	Parameter names
Constant-width	C(/bin/bash)	File and option names

The existing Ansible modules are a great source of examples for documentation.

Debugging Your Module

The Ansible repository in GitHub contains a couple of scripts that allow you to invoke your module directly on your local machine, without having to run it by using the `ansible` or `ansible-playbook` commands.

Clone the Ansible repo:

```
$ git clone https://github.com/ansible/ansible.git --recursive
```

Set up your environment variables so that you can invoke the module:

```
$ source ansible/hacking/env-setup
```

Invoke your module:

```
$ ansible/hacking/test-module -m /path/to/can_reach -a "host=example.com port=81"
```

> You might get an import error, such as these:
> ```
> ImportError: No module named yaml
> ImportError: No module named jinja2.exceptions
> ```
> If so, you'll need to install these missing dependencies:
> ```
> pip install pyYAML jinja2
> ```

Since `example.com` doesn't have a service that listens on port 81, our module should fail with a meaningful error message. And it does:

```
* including generated source, if any, saving to:
/Users/lorin/.ansible_module_generated
* ansiballz module detected; extracted module source to:
/Users/lorin/debug_dir
**********************************
RAW OUTPUT
```

```
{"msg": "Could not reach example.com:81", "failed": true, "invocation":
{"module_args": {"host": "example.com", "port": 81, "timeout": 3}}}


**********************************
PARSED OUTPUT
{
    "failed": true,
    "invocation": {
        "module_args": {
            "host": "example.com",
            "port": 81,
            "timeout": 3
        }
    },
    "msg": "Could not reach example.com:81"
}
```

As the output suggests, when you run this `test-module`, Ansible will generate a Python script and copy it to *~/.ansible_module_generated*. This is a standalone Python script that you can execute directly if you like.

Starting with Ansible 2.1.0, this Python script contains a base64-encoded ZIP file with the actual source code from your module, as well as code to expand the ZIP file and execute the source code within it.

This file does not take any arguments; rather, Ansible inserts the arguments directly into the file in the `ANSIBALLZ_PARAMS` variable:

```
ANSIBALLZ_PARAMS = '{"ANSIBLE_MODULE_ARGS": {"host": "example.com", \
    "_ansible_selinux_special_fs": ["fuse", "nfs", "vboxsf", "ramfs"], \
    "port": "81"}}'
```

Implementing the Module in Bash

If you're going to write an Ansible module, I recommend writing it in Python because, as you saw earlier in this chapter, Ansible provides helper classes for writing your modules in Python. However, you can write modules in other languages as well. Perhaps you need to write in another language because your module depends on a third-party library that's not implemented in Python. Or maybe the module is so simple that it's easiest to write it in Bash. Or maybe you just prefer writing your scripts in Ruby.

In this section, we'll work through an example of implementing the module as a Bash script. It's going to look quite similar to the implementation in Example 12-1. The main difference is parsing the input arguments and generating the outputs that Ansible expects.

I'm going to use the JSON format for input and use a tool called jq (*http://stedo lan.github.io/jq/*) for parsing out JSON on the command line. This means that you'll need to install jq on the host before invoking this module. Example 12-8 shows the complete Bash implementation of our module.

Example 12-8. can_reach module in Bash

```bash
#!/bin/bash
# WANT_JSON

# Read the variables from the file
host=`jq -r .host < $1`
port=`jq -r .port < $1`
timeout=`jq -r .timeout < $1`

# Default timeout=3
if [[ $timeout = null ]]; then
    timeout=3
fi

# Check if we can reach the host
nc -z -w $timeout $host $port

# Output based on success or failure
if [ $? -eq 0 ]; then
    echo '{"changed": false}'
else
    echo "{\"failed\": true, \"msg\": \"could not reach $host:$port\"}"
fi
```

We added `WANT_JSON` in a comment to tell Ansible that we want the input to be in JSON syntax.

Bash Modules with Shorthand Input

It's possible to implement Bash modules by using the shorthand notation for input. I don't recommend doing it this way, since the simplest approach involves using the `source` built-in, which is a potential security risk. However, if you're really determined, check out the blog post "Shell scripts as Ansible modules" (*http://bit.ly/1F789tb*) by Jan-Piet Mens.

Specifying an Alternative Location for Bash

Note that our module assumes that Bash is located at */bin/bash*. However, not all systems will have the Bash executable in that location. You can tell Ansible to look elsewhere for the Bash interpreter by setting the `ansible_bash_interpreter` variable on hosts that install it elsewhere.

For example, let's say you have a FreeBSD host named *fileserver.example.com* that has Bash installed in */usr/local/bin/bash*. You can create a host variable by creating the file *host_vars/fileserver.example.com* that contains the following:

```
ansible_bash_interpreter: /usr/local/bin/bash
```

Then, when Ansible invokes this module on the FreeBSD host, it will use */usr/local/bin/bash* instead of */bin/bash*.

Ansible determines which interpreter to use by looking for the *shebang* (!) and then looking at the base name of the first element. In our example, Ansible will see this line:

```
#!/bin/bash
```

Ansible will then look for the base name of */bin/bash*, which is *bash*. It will then use the `ansible_bash_interpreter` if the user specified one.

> Because of how Ansible looks for the interpreter, if your shebang calls */usr/bin/env*, for example:
>
> ```
> #!/usr/bin/env bash
> ```
>
> Ansible will mistakenly identify the interpreter as `env` because it will call `basename` on */usr/bin/env* to identify the interpreter.
>
> The takeaway is: don't invoke `env` in shebang. Instead, explicitly specify the location of the interpreter and override with `ansible_bash_interpreter` (or equivalent) when needed.

Example Modules

The best way to learn how to write Ansible modules is to read the source code for the modules that ship with Ansible. Check them out on GitHub (*https://github.com/ansible/ansible/tree/devel/lib/ansible/modules*).

In this chapter, we covered how to write modules in Python, as well as other languages, and how to avoid writing your own full-blown modules by using the `script` module. If you do write a module, I encourage you to propose it for inclusion in the main Ansible project.

## CHAPTER 13

Vagrant

Vagrant is a great environment for testing Ansible playbooks, which is why I've been using it all along in this book, and why I often use Vagrant for testing my own Ansible playbooks. Vagrant isn't just for testing configuration management scripts; it was originally designed to create repeatable development environments. If you've ever joined a new software team and spent a couple of days discovering what software you had to install on your laptop so you could run a development version of an internal product, you've felt the pain that Vagrant was built to alleviate. Ansible playbooks are a great way to specify how to configure a Vagrant machine so newcomers on your team can get up and running on day one.

Vagrant has some built-in support for Ansible that we haven't been taking advantage of. This chapter covers Vagrant's support for using Ansible to configure Vagrant machines.

A full treatment of Vagrant is beyond the scope of this book. For more information, check out *Vagrant: Up and Running*, authored by Mitchell Hashimoto, the creator of Vagrant.

Convenient Vagrant Configuration Options

Vagrant exposes many configuration options for virtual machines, but there are two that I find particularly useful when using Vagrant for testing: setting a specific IP address and enabling agent forwarding.

Port Forwarding and Private IP Addresses

When you create a new Vagrantfile by using the `vagrant init` command, the default networking configuration allows you to reach the Vagrant box only via an SSH port that is forwarded from `localhost`. For the first Vagrant machine that you start, that's port 2222, and each subsequent Vagrant machine that you bring up will forward a different port. As a consequence, the only way to access your Vagrant machine in the default configuration is to SSH to `localhost` on port 2222. Vagrant forwards this to port 22 on the Vagrant machine.

This default configuration isn't very useful for testing web-based applications, since the web application will be listening on a port that we can't access.

There are two ways around this. One way is to tell Vagrant to set up another forwarded port. For example, if your web application listens on port 80 inside your Vagrant machine, you can configure Vagrant to forward port 8000 on your local machine to port 80 on the Vagrant machine. Example 13-1 shows how to configure port forwarding by editing the Vagrantfile.

Example 13-1. Forwarding local port 8000 to Vagrant machine port 80

```
# Vagrantfile
VAGRANTFILE_API_VERSION = "2"

Vagrant.configure(VAGRANTFILE_API_VERSION) do |config|
  # Other config options not shown

  config.vm.network :forwarded_port, host: 8000, guest: 80
end
```

Port forwarding works, but I find it more useful to assign the Vagrant machine its own IP address. That way, interacting with it is more like interacting with a real remote server: I can connect directly to port 80 on the machine's IP rather than connecting to port 8000 on localhost.

A simpler approach is to assign the machine a private IP. Example 13-2 shows how to assign the IP address *192.168.33.10* to the machine by editing the Vagrantfile.

Example 13-2. Assign a private IP to a Vagrant machine

```
# Vagrantfile
VAGRANTFILE_API_VERSION = "2"

Vagrant.configure(VAGRANTFILE_API_VERSION) do |config|
  # Other config options not shown

  config.vm.network "private_network", ip: "192.168.33.10"

end
```

If we run a web server on port 80 of our Vagrant machine, we can access it at *http://192.168.33.10*.

This configuration uses a Vagrant *private network*. The machine will be accessible only from the machine that runs Vagrant. You won't be able to connect to this IP address from another physical machine, even if it's on the same network as the machine running Vagrant. However, different Vagrant machines can connect to each other.

Check out the Vagrant documentation for more details on the different networking configuration options.

Enabling Agent Forwarding

If you are checking out a remote Git repository over SSH, and you need to use agent forwarding, then you must configure your Vagrant machine so that Vagrant enables agent forwarding when it connects to the agent via SSH. See Example 13-3 for how to enable this. For more on agent forwarding, see Appendix A.

Example 13-3. Enabling agent forwarding

```
# Vagrantfile
VAGRANTFILE_API_VERSION = "2"

Vagrant.configure(VAGRANTFILE_API_VERSION) do |config|
  # Other config options not shown

  config.ssh.forward_agent = true

end
```

The Ansible Provisioner

Vagrant has a notion of *provisioners*. A provisioner is an external tool that Vagrant uses to configure a virtual machine after it has started up. In addition to Ansible, Vagrant can also provision with shell scripts, Chef, Puppet, Salt, CFEngine, and even Docker.

Example 13-4 shows a Vagrantfile that has been configured to use Ansible as a provisioner, specifically using the *playbook.yml* playbook.

Example 13-4. Vagrantfile

```
VAGRANTFILE_API_VERSION = "2"

Vagrant.configure(VAGRANTFILE_API_VERSION) do |config|
  config.vm.box = "ubuntu/trusty64"
```

```
  config.vm.provision "ansible" do |ansible|
    ansible.playbook = "playbook.yml"
  end
end
```

When the Provisioner Runs

The first time you run `vagrant up`, Vagrant will execute the provisioner and will
record that the provisioner was run. If you halt the virtual machine and then start it
up, Vagrant remembers that it has already run the provisioner and will not run it a
second time.

You can force Vagrant to run the provisioner against a running virtual machine as
follows:

```
$ vagrant provision
```

You can reboot a virtual machine and run the provisioner after reboot:

```
$ vagrant reload --provision
```

Similarly, you can start up a halted virtual machine and have Vagrant run the provisioner:

```
$ vagrant up --provision
```

Inventory Generated by Vagrant

When Vagrant runs, it generates an Ansible inventory file named *.vagrant/provision-
ers/ansible/inventory/vagrant_ansible_inventory*. Example 13-5 shows what this file
looks like for our example.

Example 13-5. vagrant_ansible_inventory

```
# Generated by Vagrant

default ansible_host=127.0.0.1 ansible_port=2202
```

Note that it uses `default` as the inventory hostname. When writing playbooks for the
Vagrant provisioner, specify `hosts: default` or `hosts: all`.

More interesting is the case where you have a multimachine Vagrant environment,
where the Vagrantfile specifies multiple virtual machines. For example, see
Example 13-6.

Example 13-6. Vagrantfile (multimachine)

```
VAGRANTFILE_API_VERSION = "2"

Vagrant.configure(VAGRANTFILE_API_VERSION) do |config|
  config.vm.define "vagrant1" do |vagrant1|
    vagrant1.vm.box = "ubuntu/trusty64"
    vagrant1.vm.provision "ansible" do |ansible|
      ansible.playbook = "playbook.yml"
    end
  end
  config.vm.define "vagrant2" do |vagrant2|
    vagrant2.vm.box = "ubuntu/trusty64"
    vagrant2.vm.provision "ansible" do |ansible|
      ansible.playbook = "playbook.yml"
    end
  end
  config.vm.define "vagrant3" do |vagrant3|
    vagrant3.vm.box = "ubuntu/trusty64"
    vagrant3.vm.provision "ansible" do |ansible|
      ansible.playbook = "playbook.yml"
    end
  end
end
```

The generated inventory file will look like Example 13-7. Note that the Ansible aliases (vagrant1, vagrant2, vagrant3) match the names assigned to the machines in the Vagrantfile.

Example 13-7. vagrant_ansible_inventory (multimachine)

```
# Generated by Vagrant

vagrant1 ansible_host=127.0.0.1 ansible_port=2222
vagrant2 ansible_host=127.0.0.1 ansible_port=2200
vagrant3 ansible_host=127.0.0.1 ansible_port=2201
```

Provisioning in Parallel

In Example 13-6, Vagrant is shown running ansible-playbook once for each virtual machine, and it uses the --limit flag so that the provisioner runs against only a single virtual machine at a time.

Alas, running Ansible this way doesn't take advantage of Ansible's capability to execute tasks in parallel across the hosts. We can work around this by configuring our Vagrantfile to run the provisioner only when the last virtual machine is brought up, and to tell Vagrant not to pass the --limit flag to Ansible. See Example 13-8 for the modified playbook.

Example 13-8. Vagrantfile (multimachine with parallel provisioning)

```
VAGRANTFILE_API_VERSION = "2"

Vagrant.configure(VAGRANTFILE_API_VERSION) do |config|
  # Use the same key for each machine
  config.ssh.insert_key = false

  config.vm.define "vagrant1" do |vagrant1|
    vagrant1.vm.box = "ubuntu/trusty64"
  end
  config.vm.define "vagrant2" do |vagrant2|
    vagrant2.vm.box = "ubuntu/trusty64"
  end
  config.vm.define "vagrant3" do |vagrant3|
    vagrant3.vm.box = "ubuntu/trusty64"
    vagrant3.vm.provision "ansible" do |ansible|
      ansible.limit = 'all'
      ansible.playbook = "playbook.yml"
    end
  end
end
```

Now, when you run `vagrant up` the first time, it will run the Ansible provisioner only after all three virtual machines have started up.

From Vagrant's perspective, only the last virtual machine, `vagrant3`, has a provisioner, so using `vagrant provision vagrant1` or `vagrant provision vagrant2` will have no effect.

As we discussed in "Preliminaries: Multiple Vagrant Machines" on page 46, Vagrant 1.7+ defaults to using a different SSH key for each host. If we want to provision in parallel, we need to configure the Vagrant machines so that they all use the same SSH key, which is why Example 13-8 includes this line:

```
config.ssh.insert_key = false
```

Specifying Groups

It can be useful to assign groups to Vagrant virtual machines, especially if you are reusing playbooks that reference existing groups. Example 13-9 shows how to assign `vagrant1` to the `web` group, `vagrant2` to the `task` group, and `vagrant3` to the `redis` group.

Example 13-9. Vagrantfile (multimachine with groups)

```
VAGRANTFILE_API_VERSION = "2"

Vagrant.configure(VAGRANTFILE_API_VERSION) do |config|
```

```
# Use the same key for each machine
config.ssh.insert_key = false

config.vm.define "vagrant1" do |vagrant1|
  vagrant1.vm.box = "ubuntu/trusty64"
end
config.vm.define "vagrant2" do |vagrant2|
  vagrant2.vm.box = "ubuntu/trusty64"
end
config.vm.define "vagrant3" do |vagrant3|
  vagrant3.vm.box = "ubuntu/trusty64"
  vagrant3.vm.provision "ansible" do |ansible|
    ansible.limit = 'all'
    ansible.playbook = "playbook.yml"
    ansible.groups = {
      "web"   => ["vagrant1"],
      "task"  => ["vagrant2"],
      "redis" => ["vagrant3"]
    }
  end
end
end
```

Example 13-10 shows the resulting inventory file generated by Vagrant.

Example 13-10. vagrant_ansible_inventory (multimachine, with groups)

```
# Generated by Vagrant

vagrant1 ansible_host=127.0.0.1 ansible_port=2222
vagrant2 ansible_host=127.0.0.1 ansible_port=2200
vagrant3 ansible_host=127.0.0.1 ansible_port=2201

[web]
vagrant1

[task]
vagrant2

[redis]
vagrant3
```

Ansible Local Provisioner

Starting from version 1.8, Vagrant can also be configured to run Ansible from the guest instead of the host. This mode is useful if you don't want to install Ansible on the host machine. If Ansible is not installed on the guest, Vagrant will attempt to install using pip, although this behavior is configurable.

Vagrant looks in the guest's */vagrant* directory for playbooks. The default behavior of Vagrant is to mount the directory on the host that contains the Vagrantfile to */vagrant*, so Vagrant effectively looks in the same place as when you use the ordinary Ansible provisioner.

To use the Ansible local provisioner, specify `ansible_local` as the provisioner, as shown in Example 13-11.

Example 13-11. Vagrantfile (Ansible local provisioner)

```
Vagrant.configure("2") do |config|
  config.vm.box = "ubuntu/trusty64"
  config.vm.provision "ansible_local" do |ansible|
      ansible.playbook = "playbook.yml"
  end
end
```

This chapter was a quick—but I hope useful—overview on how to get the most out of combining Vagrant and Ansible. Vagrant's Ansible provisioner supports many other options to Ansible that aren't covered in this chapter. For more details, see the official Vagrant documentation on the Ansible provisioner (*http://bit.ly/1F7ekxp*).

## CHAPTER 14

Amazon EC2

Ansible has several features that make working with infrastructure-as-a-service (IaaS) clouds much easier. This chapter focuses on Amazon Elastic Compute Cloud (EC2) because it's the most popular IaaS cloud and the one I know best. However, many of the concepts should transfer to other clouds supported by Ansible.

Ansible supports EC2 in two ways:

- A dynamic inventory plugin for automatically populating your Ansible inventory instead of manually specifying your servers
- Modules that perform actions on EC2 such as creating new servers

This chapter covers both the EC2 dynamic inventory plugin and the EC2 modules.

 As of this writing, Ansible has nearly one hundred modules that relate to EC2 as well as other features offered by Amazon Web Services (AWS). We have space to cover only a few of them here, so we focus on the basics.

What Is an IaaS Cloud?

You've probably heard so many references to *the cloud* in the technical press that you're suffering from buzzword overload.[1] I'll be precise about what I mean by an infrastructure-as-a-service (IaaS) cloud.

To start, here's a typical user interaction with an IaaS cloud:

User

> I want five new servers, each one with two CPUs, 4 GB of memory, and 100 GB of storage, running Ubuntu 16.04.

Service

> Request received. Your request number is 432789.

User

> What's the current status of request 432789?

Service

> Your servers are ready to go, at IP addresses *203.0.113.5*, *203.0.113.13*, *203.0.113.49*, *203.0.113.124*, *203.0.113.209*.

User

> I'm done with the servers associated with request 432789.

Service

> Request received. The servers will be terminated.

An IaaS cloud is a service that enables a user to *provision* (create) new servers. All IaaS clouds are *self-serve*, meaning that the user interacts directly with a software service rather than, say, filing a ticket with the IT department. Most IaaS clouds offer three types of interfaces to allow users to interact with the system:

- Web interface
- Command-line interface
- REST API

In the case of EC2, the web interface is called the AWS Management Console (*https://console.aws.amazon.com*), and the command-line interface is called (unimaginatively) the AWS Command-Line Interface (*http://aws.amazon.com/cli/*). The REST API is documented at Amazon (*http://amzn.to/1F7g6yA*).

IaaS clouds typically use virtual machines to implement the servers, although you can build an IaaS cloud by using bare-metal servers (i.e., users run directly on the

---

1 The National Institute of Standards and Technology (NIST) has a pretty good definition of cloud computing in *The NIST Definition of Cloud Computing*.

hardware rather than inside a virtual machine) or containers. For example, SoftLayer and Rackspace have bare-metal offerings, and Amazon EC2, Google Compute Engine, and Azure clouds offer containers.

Most IaaS clouds let you do more than just start up and tear down servers. In particular, they typically let you provision storage so you can attach and detach disks to your servers. This type of storage is commonly referred to as *block storage*. They also provide networking features, so you can define network topologies that describe how your servers are interconnected, and you can define firewall rules that restrict networking access to your servers.

Amazon EC2 is the most popular public IaaS cloud provider, but there are other IaaS clouds out there. In addition to EC2, Ansible ships with modules for many other clouds, including Microsoft Azure, Digital Ocean, Google Compute Engine, SoftLayer, and Rackspace, as well as clouds built using oVirt, OpenStack, CloudStack and VMWare vSphere.

Terminology

EC2 exposes many concepts. I'll explain these concepts as they come up in this chapter, but there are three terms I'd like to cover up front.

Instance

EC2's documentation uses the term *instance* to refer to a virtual machine, and I use that terminology in this chapter. Keep in mind that an EC2 instance is a *host* from Ansible's perspective.

EC2 documentation (*http://amzn.to/1Fw5S8l*) interchangeably uses the terms *creating instances*, *launching instances*, and *running instances* to describe the process of bringing up a new instance. However, *starting instances* means something different—starting up an instance that had previously been put in the stopped state.

Amazon Machine Image

An *Amazon Machine Image* (*AMI*) is a virtual machine image, which contains a filesystem with an installed operating system on it. When you create an instance on EC2, you choose which operating system you want your instance to run by specifying the AMI that EC2 will use to create the instance.

Each AMI has an associated identifier string, called an *AMI ID*, which starts with ami- and then contains eight hexadecimal characters; for example, ami-12345abc.

Tags

EC2 lets you annotate your instances[2] with custom metadata that it calls *tags*. Tags are just key-value pairs of strings. For example, we could annotate an instance with the following tags:

```
Name=Staging database
env=staging
type=database
```

If you've ever given your EC2 instance a name in the AWS Management Console, you've used tags without even knowing it. EC2 implements instance names as tags; the key is Name, and the value is whatever name you gave the instance. Other than that, there's nothing special about the Name tag, and you can configure the management console to show the value of other tags in addition to the Name tag.

Tags don't have to be unique, so you can have 100 instances that all have the same tag. Because Ansible's EC2 modules often use tags to identify resources and implement idempotence, they will come up several times in this chapter.

 It's good practice to add meaningful tags to all of your EC2 resources, since they act as a form of documentation.

Specifying Credentials

When you make requests against Amazon EC2, you need to specify credentials. If you've used the Amazon web console, you've used your username and password to log in. However, all the bits of Ansible that interact with EC2 talk to the EC2 API. The API does not use a username and password for credentials. Instead, it uses two strings: an *access key ID* and a *secret access key*.

These strings typically look like this:

- Sample EC2 access key ID: AKIAIOSFODNN7EXAMPLE
- Sample EC2 secret access key: wJalrXUtnFEMI/K7MDENG/bPxRfiCYEXAMPLEKEY

You can obtain these credentials through the *Identity and Access Management* (IAM) service. Using this service, you can create different IAM users with different permissions. Once you have created an IAM user, you can generate the access key ID and secret access key for that user.

---

2 You can add tags to entities other than instances, such as AMIs, volumes, and security groups.

When you are calling EC2-related modules, you can pass these strings as module arguments. For the dynamic inventory plugin, you can specify the credentials in the *ec2.ini* file (discussed in the next section). However, both the EC2 modules and the dynamic inventory plugin also allow you to specify these credentials as environment variables. You can also use something called IAM roles if your control machine is itself an Amazon EC2 instance, which is covered in Appendix B.

Environment Variables

Although Ansible does allow you to pass credentials explicitly as arguments to modules, it also supports setting EC2 credentials as environment variables. Example 14-1 shows how to set these environment variables.

Example 14-1. Setting EC2 environment variables

```
# Don't forget to replace these values with your actual credentials!
export AWS_ACCESS_KEY_ID=AKIAIOSFODNN7EXAMPLE
export AWS_SECRET_ACCESS_KEY=wJalrXUtnFEMI/K7MDENG/bPxRfiCYEXAMPLEKEY
```

> While you can set your default AWS region by environment variable, I recommend that you always explicitly pass the EC2 region as an argument when invoking your modules. All of the examples in this chapter explicitly pass the region as an argument.

I recommend using environment variables for `AWS_ACCESS_KEY_ID` and `AWS_SECRET_ACCESS_KEY` because this allows you to use EC2-related modules and inventory plugins without putting your credentials in any of your Ansible-related files. I put these in a dotfile that runs when my session starts. I use Zsh, so in my case that file is *~/.zshrc*. If you're running Bash, you might want to put it in your *~/.profile* file.[3] If you're using a shell other than Bash or Zsh, you're probably knowledgeable enough to know which dotfile to modify to set these environment variables.

Once you have set these credentials in your environment variables, you can invoke the Ansible EC2 modules on your control machine, as well as use the dynamic inventory.

Configuration Files

An alternative to using environment variables is to place your EC2 credentials in a configuration file. As discussed in the next section, Ansible uses the Python Boto library, so it supports Boto's conventions for maintaining credentials in a Boto config-

---

3 Or maybe it's *~/.bashrc*? I've never figured out the difference between the various Bash dotfiles.

uration file. I don't cover the format here; for more information, check out the Boto config documentation (*http://bit.ly/1Fw66MM*).

Prerequisite: Boto Python Library

All of the Ansible EC2 functionality requires you to install the Python Boto library as a Python system package on the control machine. To do so, use this command:[4]

```
$ pip install boto
```

If you already have instances running on EC2, you can verify that Boto is installed properly and that your credentials are correct by interacting with the Python command line, as shown in Example 14-2.

Example 14-2. Testing out Boto and credentials

```
$ python
Python 2.7.12 (default, Nov  6 2016, 20:41:56)
[GCC 4.2.1 Compatible Apple LLVM 8.0.0 (clang-800.0.42.1)] on darwin
Type "help", "copyright", "credits" or "license" for more information.
>>> import boto.ec2
>>> conn = boto.ec2.connect_to_region("us-east-1")
>>> statuses = conn.get_all_instance_status()
>>> statuses
[]
```

Dynamic Inventory

If your servers live on EC2, you don't want to keep a separate copy of these servers in an Ansible inventory file, because that file is going to go stale as you spin up new servers and tear down old ones. It's much simpler to track your EC2 servers by taking advantage of Ansible's support for dynamic inventory to pull information about hosts directly from EC2. Ansible ships with a dynamic inventory script for EC2, although I recommend you just grab the latest one from the Ansible GitHub repository.[5]

You need two files:

ec2.py
> The actual inventory script (*http://bit.ly/2lAsfV8*)

ec2.ini
> The configuration file for the inventory script (*http://bit.ly/2l168KP*)

---

4 You might need to use sudo or activate a virtualenv to install this package, depending on how you installed Ansible.

5 And, to be honest, I have no idea where the package managers install this file.

Previously, we had a *playbooks/hosts* file, which served as our inventory. Now, we're going to use a *playbooks/inventory* directory. We'll place *ec2.py* and *ec2.ini* into that directory, and set *ec2.py* as executable. Example 14-3 shows one way to do that.

Example 14-3. Installing the EC2 dynamic inventory script

```
$ cd playbooks/inventory
$ wget https://raw.githubusercontent.com/ansible/ansible/devel/contrib/inventory\
/ec2.py
$ wget https://raw.githubusercontent.com/ansible/ansible/devel/contrib/inventory\
/ec2.ini
$ chmod +x ec2.py
```

If you are running Ansible on a Linux distribution that uses Python 3.*x* as the default Python (e.g., Arch Linux), then *ec2.py* will not work unmodified because it is a Python 2.*x* script.

Make sure your system has Python 2.*x* installed and then modify the first line of *ec2.py* from this:

```
#!/usr/bin/env python
```

to this:

```
#!/usr/bin/env python2
```

If you've set up your environment variables as described in the previous section, you should be able to confirm that the script is working by running the following:

```
$ ./ec2.py --list
```

The script should output information about your various EC2 instances. The structure should look something like this:

```
{
  "_meta": {
    "hostvars": {
      "ec2-203-0-113-75.compute-1.amazonaws.com": {
        "ec2_id": "i-1234567890abcdef0",
        "ec2_instance_type": "c3.large",
        ...
      }
    }
  },
  "ec2": [
    "ec2-203-0-113-75.compute-1.amazonaws.com",
    ...
  ],
  "us-east-1": [
    "ec2-203-0-113-75.compute-1.amazonaws.com",
    ...
  ],
```

```
    "us-east-1a": [
      "ec2-203-0-113-75.compute-1.amazonaws.com",
      ...
    ],
    "i-12345678": [
      "ec2-203-0-113-75.compute-1.amazonaws.com",
    ],
    "key_mysshkeyname": [
      "ec2-203-0-113-75.compute-1.amazonaws.com",
      ...
    ],
    "security_group_ssh": [
      "ec2-203-0-113-75.compute-1.amazonaws.com",
      ...
    ],
    "tag_Name_my_cool_server": [
      "ec2-203-0-113-75.compute-1.amazonaws.com",
      ...
    ],
    "type_c3_large": [
      "ec2-203-0-113-75.compute-1.amazonaws.com",
      ...
    ]
}
```

 If you have not explicitly enabled both RDS and ElastiCache on your AWS account, the *ec2.py* script will fail with an error. To enable RDS and ElastiCache, you must log in to the Relational Database Service (RDS) and ElastiCache services via the AWS console, and then wait for Amazon to activate these services for you.

If you are not using these services, edit your *ec2.ini* to prevent the inventory script from trying to connect to them:

```
[ec2]
...
rds = False

elasticache = False
```

Those lines are present but commented out by default, so make sure to uncomment them!

Inventory Caching

When Ansible executes the EC2 dynamic inventory script, the script has to make requests against one or more EC2 endpoints to retrieve this information. Because this can take time, the script will cache the information the first time it is invoked by writing to the following files:

- *$HOME/.ansible/tmp/ansible-ec2.cache*
- *$HOME/.ansible/tmp/ansible-ec2.index*

On subsequent calls, the dynamic inventory script will use the cached information until the cache expires.

You can modify the behavior by editing the *cache_max_age* configuration option in the *ec2.ini* configuration file. It defaults to 300 seconds (5 minutes). If you don't want caching at all, you can set it to 0:

```
[ec2]
...
cache_max_age = 0
```

You can also force the inventory script to refresh the cache by invoking it with the `--refresh-cache` flag:

```
$ ./ec2.py --refresh-cache
```

If you create or destroy instances, the EC2 dynamic inventory script will not reflect these changes unless the cache expires, or you manually refresh the cache.

Other Configuration Options

The *ec2.ini* file includes configuration options that control the behavior of the dynamic inventory script. Because the file itself is well-documented with comments, I won't cover those options in detail here.

Autogenerated Groups

The EC2 dynamic inventory script will create the groups listed in Table 14-1.

Table 14-1. Generated EC2 groups

Type	Example	Ansible group name
Instance	i-1234567890abcdef0	i-1234567890abcdef0
AMI	ami-79df8219	ami_79df8219
Instance type	c1.medium	type_c1_medium
Security group	ssh	security_group_ssh
Key pair	foo	key_foo
Region	us-east-1	us-east-1
Tag	env=staging	tag_env_staging
Availability zone	us-east-1b	us-east-1b

Type	Example	Ansible group name
VPC	vpc-14dd1b70	vpc_id_vpc-14dd1b70
All ec2 instances	N/A	ec2

The only legal characters in a group name are alphanumeric, hyphen, and underscore. The dynamic inventory script will convert any other character into underscore.

For example, say you have an instance with a tag:

```
Name=My cool server!
```

Ansible will generate the group name `tag_Name_my_cool_server_`.

Defining Dynamic Groups with Tags

Recall that the dynamic inventory script automatically creates groups based on things such as instance type, security group, key pair, and tags. EC2 tags are the most convenient way of creating Ansible groups because you can define them however you like.

For example, you could tag all of your web servers with this:

```
type=web
```

Ansible will automatically create a group called `tag_type_web` that contains all of the servers tagged with a name of `type` and a value of `web`.

EC2 allows you to apply multiple tags to an instance. For example, if you have separate staging and production environments, you can tag your production web servers like this:

```
env=production
type=web
```

Now you can refer to production machines as `tag_env_production` and your webservers as `tag_type_web`. If you want to refer to your production web servers, use the Ansible intersection syntax, like this:

```
hosts: tag_env_production:&tag_type_web
```

Applying Tags to Existing Resources

Ideally, you tag your EC2 instances as soon as you create them. However, if you're using Ansible to manage existing EC2 instances, you will likely already have instances running that you need to tag. Ansible has an `ec2_tag` module that allows you to add tags to your instances.

For example, if you want to tag an instance with `env=production` and `type=web`, you could do it in a simple playbook as shown in Example 14-4.

Example 14-4. Adding EC2 tags to instances

```
- name: Add tags to existing instances
  hosts: localhost
  vars:
    web_production:
      - i-1234567890abcdef0
      - i-1234567890abcdef1
    web_staging:
      - i-abcdef01234567890
      - i-33333333333333333
  tasks:
    - name: Tag production webservers
      ec2_tag: resource={{ item }} region=us-west-1
      args:
        tags: { type: web, env: production }
      with_items: "{{ web_production }}"

    - name: Tag staging webservers
      ec2_tag: resource={{ item }} region=us-west-1
      args:
        tags: { type: web, env: staging }
      with_items: "{{ web_staging }}"
```

This example uses the inline syntax for YAML dictionaries when specifying the tags ({ type: web, env: production}) in order to make the playbook more compact, but the regular YAML dictionary syntax would work as well:

```
tags:
  type: web
  env: production
```

Nicer Group Names

Personally, I don't like the name tag_type_web for a group. I prefer to just call it web.

To do this, we need to add a new file to the *playbooks/inventory* directory that will have information about groups. This is just a traditional Ansible inventory file, which we'll call *playbooks/inventory/hosts* (see Example 14-5).

Example 14-5. playbooks/inventory/hosts

```
[web:children]
tag_type_web

[tag_type_web]
```

Once you do this, you can refer to web as a group in your Ansible plays.

If you don't define the empty `tag_type_web` group in your static inventory file, and the group doesn't exist in the dynamic inventory script, Ansible will fail with an error:

```
ERROR! Attempted to read "/Users/lorin/dev/ansiblebook
/ch12/playbooks/inventory/hosts" as YAML:
'AnsibleUnicode' object has no attribute 'keys'
Attempted to read "/Users/lorin/dev/ansiblebook
/ch12/playbooks/inventory/hosts" as ini file:
/Users/lorin/dev/ansiblebook/ch12
/playbooks/inventory/hosts:4:
Section [web:children] includes undefined group:
tag_type_web
```

EC2 Virtual Private Cloud and EC2 Classic

When Amazon first launched EC2 back in 2006, all of the EC2 instances were effectively connected to the same flat network.[6] Every EC2 instance had a private IP address and a public IP address.

In 2009, Amazon introduced a new feature called *Virtual Private Cloud* (VPC). VPC allows users to control how their instances are networked together, and whether they will be publicly accessible from the internet or isolated. Amazon uses the term *VPC* to describe the virtual networks that users can create inside EC2. Amazon uses the term *EC2-VPC* to refer to instances that are launched inside VPCs, and *EC2-Classic* to refer to instances that are not launched inside VPCs.

Amazon actively encourages users to use EC2-VPC. For example, some instance types, such as *t2.micro*, are available only on EC2-VPC. Depending on when your AWS account was created and which EC2 regions you've previously launched instances in, you might not have access to EC2-Classic at all. Table 14-2 describes which accounts have access to EC2-Classic.[7]

Table 14-2. Do I have access to EC2-Classic?

My account was created	Access to EC2-Classic
Before March 18, 2013	Yes, but only in regions you've used before
Between March 18, 2013, and December 4, 2013	Maybe, but only in regions you've used before
After December 4, 2013	No

---

6 Amazon's internal network is divided into subnets, but users do not have any control over how instances are allocated to subnets.

7 Go to Amazon (*http://amzn.to/1Fw6v1D*) for more details on VPC and whether you have access to EC2-Classic (*http://amzn.to/1Fw6w5M*) in a region.

The main difference between having support for EC2-Classic versus having access to only EC2-VPC is what happens when you create a new EC2 instance and do not explicitly associate a VPC ID with that instance. If your account has EC2-Classic enabled, the new instance is not associated with a VPC. If your account does not have EC2-Classic enabled, the new instance is associated with the default VPC.

Here's one reason that you should care about the distinction: in EC2-Classic, all instances are permitted to make outbound network connections to any host on the internet. In EC2-VPC, instances are not permitted to make outbound network connections by default. If a VPC instance needs to make outbound connections, it must be associated with a security group that permits outbound connections.

For the purposes of this chapter, I'm going to assume EC2-VPC only, so I will associate instances with a security group that enables outbound connections.

Configuring ansible.cfg for Use with ec2

When I'm using Ansible to configure EC2 instances, I add the following lines in my *ansible.cfg*:

```
[defaults]
remote_user = ubuntu
host_key_checking = False
```

I always use Ubuntu images, and on those images you are supposed to SSH as the ubuntu user. I also turn off host-key checking, since I don't know in advance what the host keys are for new instances.[8]

Launching New Instances

The ec2 module allows you to launch new instances on EC2. It's one of the most complex Ansible modules because it supports so many arguments.

Example 14-6 shows a simple playbook for launching an Ubuntu 16.04 EC2 instance.

Example 14-6. Simple playbook for creating an EC2 instance

```
- name: Create an ubuntu instance on Amazon EC2
  hosts: localhost
  tasks:
  - name: start the instance
    ec2:
```

---

8 It's possible to retrieve the host key by querying EC2 for the instance console output, but I must admit that I never bother to doing this because I've never gotten around to writing a proper script that parses out the host key from the console output.

```
image: ami-79df8219
region: us-west-1
instance_type: m3.medium
key_name: mykey
group: [web, ssh, outbound]
instance_tags: { Name: ansiblebook, type: web, env: production }
```

Let's go over what these parameters mean.

The `image` parameter refers to the AMI ID, which you must always specify. As described earlier in the chapter, an image is basically a filesystem that contains an installed operating system. The example just used, `ami-79df8219`, refers to an image that has the 64-bit version of Ubuntu 16.04 installed on it.

The `region` parameter specifies the geographical region where the instance will be launched.[9]

The `instance_type` parameter describes the number of CPU cores and the amount of memory and storage your instance will have. EC2 doesn't let you choose arbitrary combinations of cores, memory, and storage. Instead, Amazon defines a collection of instance types.[10] Example 14-6 uses the *m3.medium* instance type. This is a 64-bit instance type with one core, 3.75 GB of RAM, and 4 GB of SSD-based storage.

 Not all images are compatible with all instance types. I haven't actually tested whether `ami-8caa1ce4` works with *m3.medium*. Caveat lector!

The `key_name` parameter refers to an SSH key pair. Amazon uses SSH key pairs to provide users with access to their servers. Before you start your first server, you must either create a new SSH key pair, or upload the public key of a key pair that you have previously created. Regardless of whether you create a new key pair or you upload an existing one, you must give a name to your SSH key pair.

The `group` parameter refers to a list of security groups associated with an instance. These groups determine the kinds of inbound and outbound network connections that are permitted.

The `instance_tags` parameter associates metadata with the instance in the form of EC2 tags, which are key-value pairs. In the preceding example, we set the following tags:

---

9 Visit Amazon (*http://amzn.to/1Fw6OcE*) for a list of supported regions.

10 There's also a handy (unofficial) website (*http://www.ec2instances.info*) that provides a single table with all of the available EC2 instance types.

```
Name=ansiblebook
type=web
env=production
```

 Invoking the `ec2` module from the command line is a simple way to terminate an instance, assuming you know the instance ID:

```
$ ansible localhost -m ec2 -a \
    'instance_id=i-01176c6682556a360 \
    state=absent'
```

EC2 Key Pairs

In Example 14-6, we assumed that Amazon already knew about an SSH key pair named mykey. Let's see how we can use Ansible to create new key pairs.

Creating a New Key

When you create a new key pair, Amazon generates a private key and the corresponding public key; then it sends you the private key. Amazon does not keep a copy of the private key, so you need to make sure that you save it after you generate it. Example 14-7 shows how to create a new key with Ansible.

Example 14-7. Create a new SSH key pair

```
- name: create a new keypair
  hosts: localhost
  tasks:
  - name: create mykey
    ec2_key: name=mykey region=us-west-1
    register: keypair

  - name: write the key to a file
    copy:
      dest: files/mykey.pem
      content: "{{ keypair.key.private_key }}"
      mode: 0600
    when: keypair.changed
```

In Example 14-7, we invoke the `ec2_key` to create a new key pair. We then use the copy module with the `content` parameter in order to save the SSH private key to a file.

If the module creates a new key pair, the variable `keypair` that is registered will contain a value that looks like this:

```json
"keypair": {
  "changed": true,
  "key": {
    "fingerprint": "c5:33:74:84:63:2b:01:29:6f:14:a6:1c:7b:27:65:69:61:f0:e8:b9",
    "name": "mykey",
    "private_key": "-----BEGIN RSA PRIVATE KEY-----\nMIIEowIBAAKCAQEAjAJpvhY3QGKh
...
0PkCRPl8ZHKtShKESIsG3WC\n-----END RSA PRIVATE KEY-----"
  }
}
```

If the key pair already exists, the variable `keypair` that is registered will contain a value that looks like this:

```json
"keypair": {
  "changed": false,
  "key": {
    "fingerprint": "c5:33:74:84:63:2b:01:29:6f:14:a6:1c:7b:27:65:69:61:f0:e8:b9",
    "name": "mykey"
  }
}
```

Because the `private_key` value will not be present if the key already exists, we need to add a `when` clause to the `copy` invocation to make sure that we write a private key file to disk only if there is a private-key file to write.

We add this line:

```
when: keypair.changed
```

to write the file to disk only if there was a change of state when `ec2_key` was invoked (i.e., that a new key was created). Another way we could have done it is to check for the existence of the `private_key` value, like this:

```
- name: write the key to a file
  copy:
    dest: files/mykey.pem
    content: "{{ keypair.key.private_key }}"
    mode: 0600
  when: keypair.key.private_key is defined
```

We use the Jinja2 `defined` test[11] to check whether `private_key` is present.

Uploading an Existing Key

If you already have an SSH public key, you can upload that to Amazon and associate it with a key pair:

---

11 For more information on Jinja2 tests, see the Jinja2 documentation page on built-in tests (*http://bit.ly/1Fw77nO*).

```
- name: create a keypair based on my ssh key
  hosts: localhost
  tasks:
  - name: upload public key
    ec2_key: name=mykey key_material="{{ item }}"
    with_file: ~/.ssh/id_rsa.pub
```

Security Groups

Example 14-6 assumes that the web, ssh, and outbound security groups already exist.
We can use the ec2_group module to ensure that these security groups have been cre‐
ated before we use them.

Security groups are similar to firewall rules: you specify rules about who is allowed to
connect to the machine and how.

In Example 14-8, we specify the web group as allowing anybody on the internet to
connect to ports 80 and 443. For the ssh group, we allow anybody on the internet to
connect on port 22. For the outbound group, we allow outbound connections to any‐
where on the internet. We need outbound connections enabled in order to download
packages from the internet.

Example 14-8. Security groups

```
- name: web security group
  ec2_group:
    name: web
    description: allow http and https access
    region: "{{ region }}"
    rules:
      - proto: tcp
        from_port: 80
        to_port: 80
        cidr_ip: 0.0.0.0/0
      - proto: tcp
        from_port: 443
        to_port: 443
        cidr_ip: 0.0.0.0/0

- name: ssh security group
  ec2_group:
    name: ssh
    description: allow ssh access
    region: "{{ region }}"
    rules:
      - proto: tcp
        from_port: 22
        to_port: 22
        cidr_ip: 0.0.0.0/0
```

```
- name: outbound group
  ec2_group:
    name: outbound
    description: allow outbound connections to the internet
    region: "{{ region }}"
    rules_egress:
      - proto: all
        cidr_ip: 0.0.0.0/0
```

 If you are using EC2-Classic, you don't need to specify the out
bound group, since EC2-Classic does not restrict outbound connections on instances.

If you haven't used security groups before, the parameters to the rules dictionary bear
some explanation. Table 14-3 provides a quick summary of the parameters for security group connection rules.

Table 14-3. Security group rule parameters

Parameter	Description
proto	IP protocol (tcp, udp, icmp) or all to allow all protocols and ports
cidr_ip	Subnet of IP addresses that are allowed to connect, using CIDR notation
from_port	The first port in the range of permitted ports
to_port	The last port in the range of permitted ports

Permitted IP Addresses

Security groups allow you to restrict which IP addresses are permitted to connect to
an instance. You specify a subnet by using classless interdomain routing (CIDR)
notation. An example of a subnet specified with CIDR notation is *203.0.113.0/24*,[12]
which means that the first 24 bits of the IP address must match the first 24 bits of
203.0.113.0. People sometimes just say "/24" to refer to the size of a CIDR that ends
in */24*.

A */24* is a nice value because it corresponds to the first three octets of the address,
namely *203.0.113*.[13] What this means is that any IP address that starts with *203.0.113*
is in the subnet, meaning any IP address in the range *203.0.113.0* to *203.0.113.255*.

---

12 This example happens to correspond to a special IP address range named TEST-NET-3, which is reserved for
examples. It's the example.com of IP subnets.

13 Subnets that are /8, /16, and /24 make great examples because the math is much easier than, say, /17 or /23.

If you specify *0.0.0.0/0*, any IP address is permitted to connect.

Security Group Ports

One of the things that I find confusing about EC2 security groups is the `from port` and `to port` notation. EC2 allows you to specify a range of ports that you are allowed to access. For example, you could indicate that you are allowing TCP connections on any port from 5900 to 5999 by specifying the following:

```
- proto: tcp
  from_port: 5900
  to_port: 5999
  cidr_ip: 0.0.0.0/0
```

However, I often find the from/to notation confusing, because I almost never specify a range of ports.[14] Instead, I usually want to enable nonconsecutive ports, such as 80 and 443. Therefore, in almost every case, the `from_port` and `to_port` parameters are going to be the same.

The `ec2_group` module has other parameters, including specifying inbound rules by using security group IDs, as well as specifying outbound connection rules. Check out the module's documentation for more details.

Getting the Latest AMI

In Example 14-6, we explicitly specified the AMI like this:

```
image: ami-79df8219
```

However, if you want to launch the latest Ubuntu 16.04 image, you don't want to hardcode the AMI like this. That's because Canonical[15] frequently makes minor updates to Ubuntu, and every time it makes a minor update, it generates a new AMI. Just because `ami-79df8219` corresponds to the latest release of Ubuntu 16.04 yesterday doesn't mean it will correspond to the latest release of Ubuntu 16.04 tomorrow.

Ansible ships with a module called `ec2_ami_find` that will retrieve a list of AMIs based on search criteria, such as the name of the image or by tags. Example 14-9 shows how to use this to launch an AMI for the latest version of 64-bit Ubuntu Xenial Xerus 16.04 running for an EBS-backed instance that uses SSDs.

---

14 Astute observers might have noticed that ports 5900–5999 are commonly used by the VNC remote desktop protocol, one of the few applications where specifying a range of ports makes sense.

15 Canonical is the company that runs the Ubuntu project.

Example 14-9. Retrieving the latest Ubuntu AMI

```
- name: Create an ubuntu instance on Amazon EC2
  hosts: localhost
  tasks:
  - name: Get the ubuntu xenial ebs ssd AMI
    ec2_ami_find:
      name: "ubuntu/images/ebs-ssd/ubuntu-xenial-16.04-amd64-server-*"
      region: "{{ region }}"
      sort: name
      sort_order: descending
      sort_end: 1
          no_result_action: fail
    register: ubuntu_image

  - name: start the instance
    ec2:
      region: "{{ region }}"
      image: "{{ ubuntu_image.results[0].ami_id }}"
      instance_type: m3.medium
      key_name: mykey
      group: [web, ssh, outbound]
      instance_tags: { type: web, env: production }
```

Here we needed to know the naming convention that Ubuntu uses for their images. In Ubuntu's case, the image name always ends with a date stamp, for example: *ubuntu/images/ebs-ssd/ubuntu-xenial-16.04-amd64-server-20170202*.

The name option for the ec2_ami_find module permits specifying * as a glob, so the way we get the most recent image is to sort, descending by name, and limit our search to just one item.

By default, the ec2_ami_find module will return success even if no AMIs match the search. Since this is almost never what you want, I recommend adding the no_result_action: fail option in order to force the module to fail if the AMI search yields no results.

> Each distribution uses its own naming strategy for AMIs, so if you want to deploy an AMI from a distribution other than Ubuntu, you'll need to do some research to figure out the appropriate search string.

Adding a New Instance to a Group

Sometimes I like to write a single playbook that launches an instance and then runs a playbook against that instance.

Unfortunately, before you've run the playbook, the host doesn't exist yet. Disabling caching on the dynamic inventory script won't help here, because Ansible invokes the dynamic inventory script only at the beginning of playbook execution, which is before the host exists.

You can add a task that uses the add_host module to add the instance to a group, as shown in Example 14-10.

Example 14-10. Adding an instance to groups

```
- name: Create an ubuntu instance on Amazon EC2
  hosts: localhost
  tasks:
  - name: start the instance
    ec2:
      image: ami-8caa1ce4
      instance_type: m3.medium
      key_name: mykey
      group: [web, ssh, outbound]
      instance_tags: { type: web, env: production }
    register: ec2

  - name: add the instance to web and production groups
    add_host: hostname={{ item.public_dns_name }} groups=web,production
    with_items: "{{ ec2.instances }}"

- name: do something to production webservers
  hosts: web:&production
  tasks:
  - ...
```

Return Type of the ec2 Module

The ec2 module returns a dictionary with three fields, shown in Table 14-4.

Table 14-4. Return value of ec2 module

Parameter	Description
instance_ids	List of instance IDs
instances	List of instance dicts
tagged_instances	List of instance dicts

If the user passes the exact_count parameter to the ec2 module, the module might not create new instances, as described in "Creating Instances the Idempotent Way" on page 268. In this case, the instance_ids and instances fields will be populated only if the module creates new instances. However, the tagged_instances field will contain instance `dicts` for all of the instances that match the tags, whether they were just created or already existed.

An instance `dict` contains the fields shown in Table 14-5.

Table 14-5. Contents of instance dicts

Parameter	Description
id	Instance ID
ami_launch_index	Instance index within a reservation (between 0 and $N - 1$) if N launched
private_ip	Internal IP address (not routable outside EC2)
private_dns_name	Internal DNS name (not routable outside EC2)
public_ip	Public IP address
public_dns_name	Public DNS name
state_code	Reason code for the state change
architecture	CPU architecture
image_id	AMI
key_name	Key pair name
placement	Location where the instance was launched
kernel	AKI (Amazon kernel image)
ramdisk	ARI (Amazon ramdisk image)
launch_time	Time instance was launched
instance_type	Instance type
root_device_type	Type of root device (ephemeral, EBS)
root_device_name	Name of root device
state	State of instance
hypervisor	Hypervisor type

For more details on what these fields mean, check out the Boto documentation for the `boto.ec2.instance.Instance` (*http://bit.ly/1Fw7HSO*) class or the documentation for the output of the `run-instances` command of Amazon's command-line tool (*http://amzn.to/1Fw7Jd9*).

Waiting for the Server to Come Up

While IaaS clouds like EC2 are remarkable feats of technology, they still require a finite amount of time to create new instances. You can't run a playbook against an EC2 instance immediately after you've submitted a request to create it. Instead, you need to wait for the EC2 instance to come up.

The ec2 module supports a `wait` parameter. If it's set to `yes`, the ec2 task will not return until the instance has transitioned to the running state:

```
- name: start the instance
  ec2:
    image: ami-8caa1ce4
    instance_type: m3.medium
    key_name: mykey
    group: [web, ssh, outbound]
    instance_tags: { type: web, env: production }
    wait: yes
  register: ec2
```

Unfortunately, waiting for the instance to be in the running state isn't enough to ensure that you can execute a playbook against a host. You still need to wait until the instance has advanced far enough in the boot process that the SSH server has started and is accepting incoming connections.

The `wait_for` module is designed for this kind of scenario. Here's how you would use the ec2 and `wait_for` modules in concert to start an instance and then wait until the instance is ready to receive SSH connections:

```
- name: start the instance
  ec2:
    image: ami-8caa1ce4
    instance_type: m3.medium
    key_name: mykey
    group: [web, ssh, outbound]
    instance_tags: { type: web, env: production }
    wait: yes
  register: ec2

- name: wait for ssh server to be running
  wait_for: host={{ item.public_dns_name }} port=22 search_regex=OpenSSH
  with_items: "{{ ec2.instances }}"
```

This invocation of `wait_for` uses the `search_regex` argument to look for the string `OpenSSH` after connecting to the host. This `regex` takes advantage of the fact that a fully functioning SSH server will return a string that looks something like Example 14-11 when an SSH client first connects.

Example 14-11. Initial response of an SSH server running on Ubuntu

```
SSH-2.0-OpenSSH_5.9p1 Debian-5ubuntu1.4
```

We could invoke the `wait_for` module to just check if port 22 is listening for incoming connections. However, sometimes an SSH server has gotten far enough along in the startup process that it is listening on port 22, but is not fully functional yet.

Waiting for the initial response ensures that the `wait_for` module will return only when the SSH server has fully started up.

Creating Instances the Idempotent Way

Playbooks that invoke the `ec2` module are not generally idempotent. If you were to execute Example 14-6 multiple times, EC2 would create multiple instances.

You can write idempotent playbooks with the `ec2` module by using the `count_tag` and `exact_count` parameters. Let's say we want to write a playbook that starts three instances. We want this playbook to be idempotent, so if three instances are already running, we want the playbook to do nothing. Example 14-12 shows what it would look like.

Example 14-12. Idempotent instance creation

```
- name: start the instance
  ec2:
    image: ami-8caa1ce4
    instance_type: m3.medium
    key_name: mykey
    group: [web, ssh, outbound]
    instance_tags: { type: web, env: production }
    exact_count: 3
    count_tag: { type: web }
```

The `exact_count: 3` parameter tells Ansible to ensure that exactly three instances are running that match the tags specified in `count_tag`. In our example, I specified only one tag for `count_tag`, but it does support multiple tags.

When running this playbook for the first time, Ansible will check how many instances are currently running that are tagged with `type=web`. Assuming there are no such instances, Ansible will create three new instances and tag them with `type=web` and `env=production`.

When running this playbook the next time, Ansible will check how many instances are currently running that are tagged with `type=web`. It will see that there are three instances running and will not start any new instances.

Putting It All Together

Example 14-13 shows the playbook that creates three EC2 instances and configures them as web servers. The playbook is idempotent, so you can safely run it multiple times, and it will create new instances only if they haven't been created yet.

Note that we use the `tagged_instances` return value of the `ec2` module, instead of the `instances` return value, for reasons described in "Return Type of the ec2 Module" on page 265. This example uses the Ubuntu Xenial AMI, which doesn't come pre-installed with Python 2. Therefore, we install Python 2.7 by using the `pre_tasks` clause.

Example 14-13. ec2-example.yml: complete EC2 playbook

```
---
- name: launch webservers
  hosts: localhost
  vars:
    region: us-west-1
    instance_type: t2.micro
    count: 1
  tasks:
  - name: ec2 keypair
    ec2_key: "name=mykey key_material={{ item }} region={{ region }}"
    with_file: ~/.ssh/id_rsa.pub
  - name: web security group
    ec2_group:
      name: web
      description: allow http and https access
      region: "{{ region }}"
      rules:
        - proto: tcp
          from_port: 80
          to_port: 80
          cidr_ip: 0.0.0.0/0
        - proto: tcp
          from_port: 443
          to_port: 443
          cidr_ip: 0.0.0.0/0
  - name: ssh security group
    ec2_group:
      name: ssh
      description: allow ssh access
      region: "{{ region }}"
      rules:
        - proto: tcp
          from_port: 22
          to_port: 22
          cidr_ip: 0.0.0.0/0
  - name: outbound security group
    ec2_group:
      name: outbound
      description: allow outbound connections to the internet
      region: "{{ region }}"
      rules_egress:
        - proto: all
```

```
          cidr_ip: 0.0.0.0/0
  - name: Get the ubuntu xenial ebs ssd AMI
    ec2_ami_find:
      name: "ubuntu/images/hvm-ssd/ubuntu-xenial-16.04-amd64-server-*"
      region: "{{ region }}"
      sort: name
      sort_order: descending
      sort_end: 1
      no_result_action: fail
    register: ubuntu_image
  - set_fact: "ami={{ ubuntu_image.results[0].ami_id }}"
  - name: start the instances
    ec2:
      region: "{{ region }}"
      image: "{{ ami }}"
      instance_type: "{{ instance_type }}"
      key_name: mykey
      group: [web, ssh, outbound]
      instance_tags: { Name: ansiblebook, type: web, env: production }
      exact_count: "{{ count }}"
      count_tag: { type: web }
      wait: yes
    register: ec2
  - name: add the instance to web and production groups
    add_host: hostname={{ item.public_dns_name }} groups=web,production
    with_items: "{{ ec2.tagged_instances }}"
    when: item.public_dns_name is defined
  - name: wait for ssh server to be running
    wait_for: host={{ item.public_dns_name }} port=22 search_regex=OpenSSH
    with_items: "{{  ec2.tagged_instances }}"
    when: item.public_dns_name is defined

- name: configure webservers
  hosts: web:&production
  become: True
  gather_facts: False
  pre_tasks:
    - name: install python
      raw: apt-get install -y python-minimal
  roles:
    - web
```

Specifying a Virtual Private Cloud

So far, we've been launching our instances into the default Virtual Private Cloud
(VPC). Ansible also allows us to create new VPCs and launch instances into them.

What Is a VPC?

Think of a VPC as an isolated network. When you create a VPC, you specify an IP address range. It must be a subset of one of the private address ranges (*10.0.0.0/8*, *172.16.0.0/12*, or *192.168.0.0/16*).

You carve your VPC into subnets, which have IP ranges that are subsets of the IP range of your entire VPC. In Example 14-14, the VPC has the IP range *10.0.0.0/16*, and we associate two subnets: *10.0.0.0/24* and *10.0.10/24*.

When you launch an instance, you assign it to a subnet in a VPC. You can configure your subnets so that your instances get either public or private IP addresses. EC2 also allows you to define routing tables for routing traffic between your subnets and to create internet gateways for routing traffic from your subnets to the internet.

Configuring networking is a complex topic that's (way) outside the scope of this book. For more info, check out Amazon's EC2 documentation on VPC (*http://amzn.to/1Fw89Af*).

Example 14-14 shows how to create a VPC with an internet gateway, two subnets, and a routing table that routes outbound connections using the internet gateway.

Example 14-14. create-vpc.yml: creating a VPC

```
- name: create a vpc
  ec2_vpc_net:
    region: "{{ region }}"
    name: "Book example"
    cidr_block: 10.0.0.0/16
    tags:
      env: production
  register: result
- set_fact: "vpc_id={{ result.vpc.id }}"
- name: add gateway
  ec2_vpc_igw:
    region: "{{ region }}"
    vpc_id: "{{ vpc_id }}"
- name:  create web subnet
  ec2_vpc_subnet:
    region: "{{ region }}"
    vpc_id: "{{ vpc_id }}"
    cidr: 10.0.0.0/24
    tags:
      env: production
      tier: web
- name: create db subnet
  ec2_vpc_subnet:
    region: "{{ region }}"
```

```
    vpc_id: "{{ vpc_id }}"
    cidr: 10.0.1.0/24
    tags:
      env: production
      tier: db
- name: set routes
  ec2_vpc_route_table:
    region: "{{ region }}"
    vpc_id: "{{ vpc_id }}"
    tags:
      purpose: permit-outbound
    subnets:
      - 10.0.0.0/24
      - 10.0.1.0/24
    routes:
      - dest: 0.0.0.0/0
        gateway_id: igw
```

Each of these commands is idempotent, but the idempotence-checking mechanism differs slightly per module, as shown in Table 14-6.

Table 14-6. Idempotence-checking logic for some VPC modules

Module	Idempotence check
ec2_vpc_net	Name and CIDR options
ec2_vpc_igw	An internet gateway exists
ec2_vpc_subnet	vpc_id and CIDR options
ec2_vpc_route_table	vpc_id and tags [a]

[a] If the lookup option is set to id, the route_table_id option will be used instead of tags for idempotence check

If multiple entities match the idempotent check, Ansible will fail the module.

If you don't specify tags to the ec2_vpc_route_table, it will create a new route table each time you execute the module.

Admittedly, Example 14-14 is a simple example from a networking perspective, as we've just defined two subnets that both can connect out to the internet. A more realistic example would have one subnet that's routable to the internet, and another subnet that's not routable to the internet, and we'd have some rules for routing traffic between the two subnets.

Example 14-15 shows a complete example of creating a VPC and launching instances into it.

Example 14-15. ec2-vpc-example.yml: complete EC2 playbook that specifies a VPC

```
---
- name: launch webservers into a specific vpc
  hosts: localhost
  vars:
    region: us-west-1
    instance_type: t2.micro
    count: 1
    cidrs:
      web: 10.0.0.0/24
      db: 10.0.1.0/24
  tasks:
  - name: create a vpc
    ec2_vpc_net:
      region: "{{ region }}"
      name: book
      cidr_block: 10.0.0.0/16
      tags: {env: production }
    register: result
  - set_fact: "vpc_id={{ result.vpc.id }}"
  - name: add gateway
    ec2_vpc_igw:
      region: "{{ region }}"
      vpc_id: "{{ vpc_id }}"
  - name: create web subnet
    ec2_vpc_subnet:
      region: "{{ region }}"
      vpc_id: "{{ vpc_id }}"
      cidr: "{{ cidrs.web }}"
      tags: { env: production, tier: web}
    register: web_subnet
  - set_fact: "web_subnet_id={{ web_subnet.subnet.id }}"
  - name: create db subnet
    ec2_vpc_subnet:
      region: "{{ region }}"
      vpc_id: "{{ vpc_id }}"
      cidr: "{{ cidrs.db }}"
      tags: { env: production, tier: db}
  - name: add routing table
    ec2_vpc_route_table:
      region: "{{ region }}"
      vpc_id: "{{ vpc_id }}"
      tags:
        purpose: permit-outbound
      subnets:
        - "{{ cidrs.web }}"
        - "{{ cidrs.db }}"
      routes:
        - dest: 0.0.0.0/0
          gateway_id: igw
  - name: set ec2 keypair
```

```
    ec2_key: "name=mykey key_material={{ item }}"
    with_file: ~/.ssh/id_rsa.pub
- name: web security group
  ec2_group:
    name: web
    region: "{{ region }}"
    description: allow http and https access
    vpc_id: "{{ vpc_id }}"
    rules:
      - proto: tcp
        from_port: 80
        to_port: 80
        cidr_ip: 0.0.0.0/0
      - proto: tcp
        from_port: 443
        to_port: 443
        cidr_ip: 0.0.0.0/0
- name: ssh security group
  ec2_group:
    name: ssh
    region: "{{ region }}"
    description: allow ssh access
    vpc_id: "{{ vpc_id }}"
    rules:
      - proto: tcp
        from_port: 22
        to_port: 22
        cidr_ip: 0.0.0.0/0
- name: outbound security group
  ec2_group:
    name: outbound
    description: allow outbound connections to the internet
    region: "{{ region }}"
    vpc_id: "{{ vpc_id }}"
    rules_egress:
      - proto: all
        cidr_ip: 0.0.0.0/0
- name: Get the ubuntu xenial ebs ssd AMI
  ec2_ami_find:
    name: "ubuntu/images/hvm-ssd/ubuntu-xenial-16.04-amd64-server-*"
    region: "{{ region }}"
    sort: name
    sort_order: descending
    sort_end: 1
    no_result_action: fail
  register: ubuntu_image
- set_fact: "ami={{ ubuntu_image.results[0].ami_id }}"
- name: start the instances
  ec2:
    image: "{{ ami }}"
    region: "{{ region }}"
    instance_type: "{{ instance_type }}"
```

```
      assign_public_ip: True
      key_name: mykey
      group: [web, ssh, outbound]
      instance_tags: { Name: book, type: web, env: production }
      exact_count: "{{ count }}"
      count_tag: { type: web }
      vpc_subnet_id: "{{ web_subnet_id }}"
      wait: yes
    register: ec2
  - name: add the instance to web and production groups
    add_host: hostname={{ item.public_dns_name }} groups=web,production
    with_items: "{{ ec2.tagged_instances }}"
    when: item.public_dns_name is defined
  - name: wait for ssh server to be running
    wait_for: host={{ item.public_dns_name }} port=22 search_regex=OpenSSH
    with_items: "{{ ec2.tagged_instances }}"
    when: item.public_dns_name is defined

- name: configure webservers
  hosts: web:&production
  become: True
  gather_facts: False
  pre_tasks:
    - name: install python
      raw: apt-get install -y python-minimal
  roles:
    - web
```

Dynamic Inventory and VPC

When using a VPC, you often will place some instances inside a private subnet that is not routable from the internet. When you do this, no public IP address is associated with the instance.

In this case, you might want to run Ansible from an instance inside your VPC. The Ansible dynamic inventory script is smart enough that it will return internal IP addresses for VPC instances that don't have public IP addresses.

See Appendix B for details on how to use IAM roles to run Ansible inside a VPC without needing to copy EC2 credentials to the instance.

Building AMIs

There are two approaches you can take to creating custom Amazon Machine Images (AMIs) with Ansible. You can use the `ec2_ami` module, or you can use a third-party tool called Packer that has support for Ansible.

With the ec2_ami Module

The `ec2_ami` module will take a running instance and snapshot it into an AMI. Example 14-16 shows this module in action.

Example 14-16. Creating an AMI with the ec2_ami module

```
- name: create an AMI
  hosts: localhost
  vars:
    instance_id: i-e5bfc266641f1b918
  tasks:
    - name: create the AMI
      ec2_ami:
        name: web-nginx
        description: Ubuntu 16.04 with nginx installed
        instance_id: "{{ instance_id }}"
        wait: yes
      register: ami

    - name: output AMI details
      debug: var=ami
```

With Packer

The `ec2_ami` module works just fine, but you have to write additional code to create and terminate the instance. There's an open source tool called Packer (*https://www.packer.io*) that will automate the creation and termination of an instance for you. Packer also happens to be written by Mitchell Hashimoto, the creator of Vagrant.

Packer can create different types of images and works with different configuration management tools. This section focuses on using Packer to create AMIs using Ansible, but you can also use Packer to create images for other IaaS clouds, such as Google Compute Engine, DigitalOcean, or OpenStack. It can even be used to create Vagrant boxes and Docker containers. It also supports other configuration management tools, such as Chef, Puppet, and Salt.

To use Packer, you create a configuration file in JSON format (called a *template*) and then use the `packer` command-line tool to create the image using the configuration file.

Packer provides two mechanisms (called *provisioners*) for using Ansible to create an AMI: the newer Ansible Remote provisioner (called `ansible`) and the older Ansible Local provisioner (called `ansible-local`). To understand the difference, you first need to understand how Packer works.

When you use Packer to build an AMI, Packer executes the following steps:

1. Launches a new EC2 instance based on the AMI specified in your template

2. Creates a temporary key pair and security group

3. Uses SSH to log into the new instance and executes any provisioners specified in the template

4. Stops the instance

5. Creates a new AMI

6. Deletes the instance, security group, and key pair

7. Outputs the AMI ID to the terminal

Ansible Remote Provisioner

When using the Ansible Remote provisioner, Packer will run Ansible on your local machine. When using the Ansible Local provisioner, Packer will copy the playbook files over to the instance and run Ansible from the instance. I prefer the Ansible Remote provisioner because the template is simpler, as you'll see.

We'll start with the Ansible Remote provisioner. Example 14-17 shows the *web-ami.yml* playbook we will use for configuring the instance that will be used to create the image. It's a simple playbook that applies the web role to a machine named default. Packer creates the default alias by, well, default. If you like, you can change the alias name by specifying a host_alias parameter in the Ansible section of the Packer template.

Example 14-17. web-ami.yml

```
- name: configure a webserver as an ami
  hosts: default
  become: True
  roles:
    - web
```

Example 14-18 shows a sample Packer template that uses the Ansible Remote provisioner to create an AMI using our playbook.

Example 14-18. web.json using Remote Ansible provisioner

```
{
  "builders": [
    {
      "type": "amazon-ebs",
      "region": "us-west-1",
      "source_ami": "ami-79df8219",
      "instance_type": "t2.micro",
```

```
        "ssh_username": "ubuntu",
        "ami_name": "web-nginx-{{timestamp}}",
        "tags": {
          "Name": "web-nginx"
        }
      }
    ],
    "provisioners": [
      {
        "type": "shell",
        "inline": [
          "sleep 30",
          "sudo apt-get update",
          "sudo apt-get install -y python-minimal"
        ]
      },
      {
        "type": "ansible",
        "playbook_file": "web-ami.yml"
      }
    ]
}
```

Use the `packer build` command to create the AMI:

```
$ packer build web.json
```

The output looks like this:

```
==> amazon-ebs: Prevalidating AMI Name...
    amazon-ebs: Found Image ID: ami-79df8219
==> amazon-ebs: Creating temporary keypair:
packer_58a0d118-b798-62ca-50d3-18d0e270e423
==> amazon-ebs: Creating temporary security group for this instance...
==> amazon-ebs: Authorizing access to port 22 the temporary security group...
==> amazon-ebs: Launching a source AWS instance...
    amazon-ebs: Instance ID: i-0f4b09dc0cd806248
==> amazon-ebs: Waiting for instance (i-0f4b09dc0cd806248) to become ready...
==> amazon-ebs: Adding tags to source instance
==> amazon-ebs: Waiting for SSH to become available...
==> amazon-ebs: Connected to SSH!
==> amazon-ebs: Provisioning with shell script: /var/folders/g_/523vq6g1037d1
0231mmbx1780000gp/T/packer-shell574734910
...

==> amazon-ebs: Stopping the source instance...
==> amazon-ebs: Waiting for the instance to stop...
==> amazon-ebs: Creating the AMI: web-nginx-1486934296
    amazon-ebs: AMI: ami-42ffa322
==> amazon-ebs: Waiting for AMI to become ready...
==> amazon-ebs: Adding tags to AMI (ami-42ffa322)...
==> amazon-ebs: Tagging snapshot: snap-01b570285183a1d35
==> amazon-ebs: Creating AMI tags
```

```
==> amazon-ebs: Creating snapshot tags
==> amazon-ebs: Terminating the source AWS instance...
==> amazon-ebs: Cleaning up any extra volumes...
==> amazon-ebs: No volumes to clean up, skipping
==> amazon-ebs: Deleting temporary security group...
==> amazon-ebs: Deleting temporary keypair...

Build 'amazon-ebs' finished.

==> Builds finished. The artifacts of successful builds are:
--> amazon-ebs: AMIs were created:

us-west-1: ami-42ffa322
```

Example 14-18 has two sections: builders and provisioners. The builders section refers to the type of image being created. In our case, we are creating an Elastic Block Store–backed (EBS) AMI, so we use the amazon-ebs builder.

Because Packer needs to start a new instance to create an AMI, you need to configure Packer with all of the information typically needed when creating an instance: EC2 region, AMI, and instance type. Packer doesn't need to be configured with a security group because, as mentioned earlier, it will create a temporary security group automatically, and then delete that security group when it is finished. Like Ansible, Packer needs to be able to SSH to the created instance. Therefore, you need to specify the SSH username in the Packer configuration file.

You also need to tell Packer what to name your instance, as well as any tags you want to apply to your instance. Because AMI names must be unique, we use the {{timestamp}} function to insert a Unix timestamp. A Unix timestamp encodes the date and time as the number of seconds since Jan. 1, 1970, UTC. See the Packer documentation (*http://bit.ly/1Fw9hEc*) for more information about the functions that Packer supports.

Because Packer needs to interact with EC2 to create the AMI, it needs access to your EC2 credentials. Like Ansible, Packer can read your EC2 credentials from environment variables, so you don't need to specify them explicitly in the configuration file, although you can if you prefer.

The provisioners section refers to the tools used to configure the instance before it is captured as an image. Packer supports a shell provisioner that lets you run arbitrary commands on the instance. Example 14-18 uses this provisioner to install Python 2. To avoid a race situation with trying to install packages before the operating system is fully booted up, the shell provisioner in our example is configured to wait for 30 seconds before installing Ansible.

Ansible Local Provisioner

Using the Ansible Local Provisioner is similar to using the remote version, but there are some differences to be aware of.

By default, the Ansible local provisioner copies only the playbook file itself to the remote host: any files that the playbook depends on are not automatically copied. To address the need for accessing multiple files, Packer allows you to specify a directory to be recursively copied into a staging directory on the instance, using the play book_dir option. Here's an example of section of a Packer template that specifies a directory:

```
{
  "type": "ansible-local",
  "playbook_file": "web-ami-local.yml",
  "playbook_dir": "../playbooks"
}
```

If all of the files to be copied up are part of roles, you can explicitly specify a list of role directories, using the role_paths option:

```
{
  "type": "ansible-local",
  "playbook_file": "web-ami-local.yml",
  "role_paths": [
    "../playbooks/roles/web"
  ]
}
```

Another important difference is that you need to use localhost instead of default in the hosts clause of your playbook.

Packer has a lot more functionality than we can cover here, including numerous options for both types of Ansible provisioners. Check out its documentation (*https://www.packer.io/docs/*) for more details.

Other Modules

Ansible supports even more of EC2, as well as other AWS services. For example, you can use Ansible to launch CloudFormation stacks with the cloudformation module, put files into S3 with the s3 module, modify DNS records with the route53 module, create autoscaling groups with the ec2_asg module, create autoscaling configuration with the ec2_lc module, and much more.

Using Ansible with EC2 is a large enough topic that you could write a whole book about it. In fact, Yan Kurniawan wrote a book on Ansible and AWS. After digesting this chapter, you should have enough knowledge under your belt to pick up these additional modules without difficulty.

## CHAPTER 15

Docker

The Docker project has taken the IT world by storm. I can't think of another technology that was so quickly embraced by the community. This chapter covers how to use Ansible to create Docker images and deploy Docker containers.

What Is a Container?

A *container* is a form of virtualization. When you use virtualization to run processes in a guest operating system, these guest processes have no visibility into the host operating system that runs on the physical hardware. In particular, processes running in the guest are not able to directly access physical resources, even if these guest processes are provided with the illusion that they have root access.

Containers are sometimes referred to as *operating system virtualization* to distinguish them from *hardware virtualization* technologies. In hardware virtualization, a program called the *hypervisor* virtualizes an entire physical machine, including a virtualized CPU, memory, and devices such as disks and network interfaces. Because the entire machine is virtualized, hardware virtualization is flexible. In particular, you can run an entirely different operating system in the guest than in the host (e.g., running a Windows Server 2012 guest inside a Red Hat Enterprise Linux host), and you can suspend and resume a virtual machine just as you can a physical machine. This flexibility brings with it additional overhead needed to virtualize the hardware.

With operating system virtualization (containers), the guest processes are isolated from the host by the operating system. The guest processes run on the same kernel as the host. The host operating system is responsible for ensuring that the guest processes are fully isolated from the host. When running a Linux-based container program such as Docker, the guest processes also must be Linux programs. However, the overhead is much lower than that of hardware virtualization, because you are running

---

only a single operating system. In particular, processes start up much more quickly inside containers than inside virtual machines.

Docker is more than just containers. Think of Docker as being a platform where containers are a building block. To use an analogy, containers are to Docker what virtual machines are to IaaS clouds. The other two major pieces that make up Docker are its image format and the Docker API.

You can think of Docker images as similar to virtual machine images. A Docker image contains a filesystem with an installed operating system, along with some metadata. One important difference is that Docker images are layered. You create a new Docker image by taking an existing Docker image and customizing it by adding, modifying, and deleting files. The representation for the new Docker image contains a reference to the original Docker image, as well as the filesystem differences between the original Docker image and the new Docker image. As an example, the official Nginx docker image (*http://bit.ly/2ktXbqS*) is built as layers on top of the official Debian Jessie image. The layered approach means that Docker images are smaller than traditional virtual machine images, so it's faster to transfer Docker images over the internet than it would be to transfer a traditional virtual machine image. The Docker project maintains a registry of publicly available images (*https://regis try.hub.docker.com*).

Docker also supports a remote API, which enables third-party tools to interact with it. In particular, Ansible's docker module uses the Docker remote API.

The Case for Pairing Docker with Ansible

Docker containers make it easier to package your application into a single image that's easy to deploy in different places, which is why the Docker project has embraced the metaphor of the shipping container. Docker's remote API simplifies the automation of software systems that run on top of Docker.

Ansible simplifies working with Docker in two areas. One is in the orchestration of Docker containers. When you deploy a "Dockerized" software app, you're typically creating multiple Docker containers that contain different services. These services need to communicate with each other, so you need to connect the appropriate containers correctly and ensure they start up in the right order. Initially, the Docker project did not provide orchestration tools, so third-party tools emerged to fill in the gap. Ansible was built for doing orchestration, so it's a natural fit for deploying your Docker-based application.

The other area is the creation of Docker images. The official way to create your own Docker images is by writing special text files called *Dockerfiles*, which resemble shell scripts. For simpler images, Dockerfiles work just fine. However, when you start to create more-complex images, you'll quickly miss the power that Ansible provides. Fortunately, you can use Ansible to create playbooks.

 A new project called *Ansible Container* is the official approach for using Ansible playbooks to build Docker container images. At the time this book was written, the latest release of Ansible Container is 0.2. On January 29, 2017, the project maintainers announced on the Ansible Container mailing list that the next release of the project, dubbed *Ansible Container Mk. II*, will be substantially different.

Because Ansible Container is still in flux, we chose not to cover it here. However, we do recommend that you take a look at this project once it has stabilized.

Docker Application Life Cycle

Here's what the typical life cycle of a Docker-based application looks like:

1. Create Docker images on your local machine.
2. Push Docker images up from your local machine to the registry.
3. Pull Docker images down to your remote hosts from the registry.
4. Start up Docker containers on the remote hosts, passing in any configuration information to the containers on startup.

You typically create your Docker image on your local machine, or on a continuous integration system that supports creating Docker images, such as Jenkins or CircleCI. Once you've created your image, you need to store it somewhere that will be convenient for downloading onto your remote hosts.

Docker images typically reside in a repository called a *registry*. The Docker project runs a registry called *Docker Hub*, which can host both public and private Docker images, and where the Docker command-line tools have built-in support for pushing images up to a registry and for pulling images down from a registry.

Once your Docker image is in the registry, you connect to a remote host, pull down the container image, and then run the container. Note that if you try to run a container whose image isn't on the host, Docker will automatically pull down the image from the registry, so you do not need to explicitly issue a command to download an image from the registry.

When you use Ansible to create the Docker images and start the containers on the remote hosts, the application life cycle looks like this:

1. Write Ansible playbooks for creating Docker images.
2. Run the playbooks to create Docker images on your local machine.
3. Push Docker images up from your local machine to the registry.
4. Write Ansible playbooks to pull Docker images down to remote hosts and start up Docker containers on remote hosts, passing in configuration information.
5. Run Ansible playbooks to start up the containers.

Example Application: Ghost

In this chapter, we're going to switch from Mezzanine to Ghost as our example application. Ghost is an open source blogging platform, similar to WordPress. The Ghost project has an official Docker container that we'll be using.

What we'll cover in this chapter:

- Running a Ghost container on your local machine
- Running a Ghost container fronted by an Nginx container with SSL configured
- Pushing a custom Nginx image to a registry
- Deploying our Ghost and Nginx containers to a remote machine

Connecting to the Docker Daemon

All of the Ansible Docker modules communicate with the Docker daemon. If you are running on Linux, or if you are running on macOS using Docker for Mac, all of the modules should just work without passing additional arguments.

If you are running on macOS using Boot2Docker or Docker Machine, or for other cases where the machine that executes the module is not the same as the machine that is running the Docker daemon, you may need to pass extra information to the Docker modules so they can reach the Docker daemon. Table 15-1 lists these options, which can be passed as either module arguments or environment variables. See the `docker_container` module documentation for more details about what these options do.

Table 15-1. Docker connection options

Module argument	Environment variable	Default
docker_host	DOCKER_HOST	unix://var/run/docker.sock
tls_hostname	DOCKER_TLS_HOSTNAME	localhost
api_version	DOCKER_API_VERSION	auto

Module argument	Environment variable	Default
cert_path	DOCKER_CERT_PATH	*(None)*
ssl_version	DOCKER_SSL_VERSION	*(None)*
tls	DOCKER_TLS	no
tls_verify	DOCKER_TLS_VERIFY	no
timeout	DOCKER_TIMEOUT	60 (seconds)

Running a Container on Our Local Machine

The `docker_container` module starts and stops Docker containers, implementing some of the functionality of the `docker` command-line tool such as the `run`, `kill`, and `rm` commands.

Assuming you have Docker installed locally, the following invocation will download the ghost image from the Docker registry and execute it locally. It will map port 2368 inside the container to 8000 on your machine, so you can access Ghost at *http://local-host:8000*.

```
$ ansible localhost -m docker_container -a "name=test-ghost image=ghost \
    ports=8000:2368"
```

The first time you run this, it may take some time for Docker to download the image. If it succeeds, the `docker ps` command will show the running container:

```
$ docker ps
CONTAINER ID   IMAGE          COMMAND               CREATED
48e69da90023   ghost          "/entrypoint.sh np..." 37 seconds ago
               STATUS         PORTS                 NAMES
               Up 36 seconds  0.0.0.0:8000->2368/tcp  test-ghost
```

To stop and remove the container:

```
$ ansible localhost -m docker_container -a "name=test-ghost state=absent"
```

The `docker_container` module supports many options: if you can pass an argument by using the `docker` command-line tool, you're likely to find an equivalent option on the module.

Building an Image from a Dockerfile

The stock Ghost image works great on its own, but if we want to ensure that access is secure, we'll need to front it with a web server configured for TLS.

The Nginx project puts out a stock Nginx image, but we'll need to configure it to act as a frontend for Ghost and to enable TLS, similar to the way we did it in Chapter 6 for Mezzanine. Example 15-1 shows the Dockerfile for this.

Example 15-1. Dockerfile

```
FROM nginx
RUN rm /etc/nginx/conf.d/default.conf
COPY ghost.conf /etc/nginx/conf.d/ghost.conf
```

Example 15-2 shows the Nginx configuration for being a frontend for Ghost. The main difference between this one and the one for Mezzanine is that in this case Nginx is communicating with Ghost by using a TCP socket (port 2368), whereas in the Mezzanine case the communication was over a Unix domain socket.

The other difference is that the path containing the TLS files is */certs*.

Example 15-2. ghost.conf

```
upstream ghost {
    server ghost:2368;
}

server {

    listen 80;

    listen 443 ssl;

    client_max_body_size 10M;
    keepalive_timeout    15;

    ssl_certificate      /certs/nginx.crt;
    ssl_certificate_key  /certs/nginx.key;
    ssl_session_cache    shared:SSL:10m;
    ssl_session_timeout  10m;
    # # ssl_ciphers entry is too long to show in this book
    ssl_prefer_server_ciphers on;

    location / {
        proxy_redirect      off;
        proxy_set_header    Host                 $host;
        proxy_set_header    X-Real-IP            $remote_addr;
        proxy_set_header    X-Forwarded-For      $proxy_add_x_forwarded_for;
        proxy_set_header    X-Forwarded-Protocol $scheme;
        proxy_pass          http://ghost;
    }
}
```

This configuration assumes that Nginx can reach the Ghost server via the hostname ghost. When we deploy these containers, we must ensure that this is the case; otherwise, the Nginx container will not be able to reach the Ghost container.

Assuming we put the Dockerfile and *nginx.conf* file in a directory named *nginx*, this task will create an image named *lorin/nginx-ghost*. We use the prefix *ansiblebook/* since this will eventually be pushed to the *ansiblebook/nginx-ghost* Docker Hub repository:

```
- name: create Nginx image
  docker_image:
    name: ansiblebook/nginx-ghost
    path: nginx
```

We can confirm this with the `docker images` command:

```
$ docker images
REPOSITORY                 TAG          IMAGE ID          CREATED
ansiblebook/nginx-ghost    latest       23fd848947a7      37 seconds ago
ghost                      latest       066a22d980f4      3 days ago
nginx                      latest       cc1b61406712      11 days ago
                           SIZE
                           182 MB
                           326 MB
                           182 MB
```

Note that invoking the `docker_image` module to build an image will have no effect if an image with that name already exists, even if you've made changes to the Docker-file. If you've made changes to the Dockerfile and want to rebuild, you need to add the `force: yes` option.

In general, though, it's a good idea to add a `tag` option with a version number, and increment this each time you do a new build. The `docker_image` module would then build the new image without needing to be forced.

Orchestrating Multiple Containers on Our Local Machine

It's common to run multiple Docker containers and wire them up together. During development, you typically run all of these containers together on your local machine. In production, these containers are commonly hosted on different machines.

For local development where all of the containers are running on the same machine, the Docker project has a tool called *Docker Compose* that makes it simpler to bring the containers up and wire them together. The `docker_service` module can be used to control Docker Compose to bring the services up or down.

Example 15-3 shows a *docker-compose.yml* file that will start up Nginx and Ghost. The file assumes there's a *./certs* directory that contains the TLS certificate files.

Example 15-3. docker-compose.yml

```
version: '2'
services:
  nginx:
    image: ansiblebook/nginx-ghost
    ports:
      - "8000:80"
      - "8443:443"
    volumes:
      - ${PWD}/certs:/certs
    links:
      - ghost
  ghost:
    image: ghost
```

Example 15-4 shows a playback that creates the custom Nginx image file, creates self-signed certificates, and then starts up the services specified by Example 15-3.

Example 15-4. ghost.yml

```
---
- name: Run Ghost locally
  hosts: localhost
  gather_facts: False
  tasks:
    - name: create Nginx image
      docker_image:
        name: ansiblebook/nginx-ghost
        path: nginx
    - name: create certs
      command: >
        openssl req -new -x509 -nodes
        -out certs/nginx.crt -keyout certs/nginx.key
        -subj '/CN=localhost' -days 3650
        creates=certs/nginx.crt
    - name: bring up services
      docker_service:
        project_src: .
        state: present
```

Pushing Our Image to the Docker Registry

We'll use a separate playbook to publish our image to Docker Hub; it's shown as Example 15-5. Note that the docker_login module must be invoked first to log in to the registry before the image is to be pushed. The docker_login and docker_image modules both default to Docker Hub as the registry.

Example 15-5. publish.yml

```
- name: publish images to docker hub
  hosts: localhost
  gather_facts: False
  vars_prompt:
    - name: username
      prompt: Enter Docker Registry username
    - name: email
      prompt: Enter Docker Registry email
    - name: password
      prompt: Enter Docker Registry password
      private: yes
  tasks:
    - name: authenticate with repository
      docker_login:
        username: "{{ username }}"
        email: "{{ email }}"
        password: "{{ password }}"
    - name: push image up
      docker_image:
        name: ansiblebook/nginx-ghost
        push: yes
```

If you wish to use a different registry, specify a `registry_url` option to `docker_login` and prefix the image name with the hostname and port (if not using the standard HTTP/HTTPS port) of the registry. Example 15-6 shows how the tasks would change when using a registry at *http://reg.example.com*. The playbook for creating the image would also need to change to reflect the new name of the image: *reg.example.com/ansiblebook/nginx-ghost*.

Example 15-6. publish.yml with custom registry

```
  tasks:
    - name: authenticate with repository
      docker_login:
        username: "{{ username }}"
        email: "{{ email }}"
        password: "{{ password }}"
        registry_url: http://reg.example.com
    - name: push image up
      docker_image:
        name: reg.example.com/ansiblebook/nginx-ghost
        push: yes
```

We can test pushing to Docker registries by using a local registry. Example 15-7 starts a registry inside a Docker container, tags the *ansiblebook/nginx-ghost* image as *localhost:5000/ansiblebook/nginx-ghost*, and pushes it to the registry. Note that the local registry doesn't require authentication by default, so there's no task that involves `docker_login` in this playbook.

Example 15-7. publish.yml with a local registry

```
- name: publish images to local docker registry
  hosts: localhost
  gather_facts: False
  vars:
    repo_port: 5000
    repo: "localhost:{{repo_port}}"
    image: ansiblebook/nginx-ghost
  tasks:
    - name: start a registry locally
      docker_container:
        name: registry
        image: registry:2
        ports: "{{ repo_port }}:5000"
    - debug:
        msg: name={{ image }} repo={{ repo }}/{{ image }}
    - name: tag the nginx-ghost image to the repository
      docker_image:
        name: "{{ image }}"
        repository: "{{ repo }}/{{ image }}"
        push: yes
```

We can verify the upload worked by downloading the manifest:

```
$ curl http://localhost:5000/v2/ansiblebook/nginx-ghost/manifests/latest
{
    "schemaVersion": 1,
    "name": "ansiblebook/nginx-ghost",
    "tag": "latest",
    ...
}
```

Querying Local Images

The `docker_image_facts` module allows you to query the metadata on a locally stored image. Example 15-8 shows an example of a playbook that uses this module to query the ghost image for the exposed port and volumes.

Example 15-8. image-facts.yml

```
---
- name: get exposed ports and volumes
  hosts: localhost
  gather_facts: False
  vars:
```

```
    image: ghost
  tasks:
    - name: get image info
      docker_image_facts: name=ghost
      register: ghost
    - name: extract ports
      set_fact:
        ports: "{{ ghost.images[0].Config.ExposedPorts.keys() }}"
    - name: we expect only one port to be exposed
      assert:
        that: "ports|length == 1"
    - name: output exposed port
      debug:
        msg: "Exposed port: {{ ports[0] }}"
    - name: extract volumes
      set_fact:
        volumes: "{{ ghost.images[0].Config.Volumes.keys() }}"
    - name: output volumes
      debug:
        msg: "Volume: {{ item }}"
      with_items: "{{ volumes }}"
```

The output looks like this:

```
$ ansible-playbook image-facts.yml

PLAY [get exposed ports and volumes] *****************************************

TASK [get image info] ********************************************************
ok: [localhost]

TASK [extract ports] *********************************************************
ok: [localhost]

TASK [we expect only one port to be exposed] ********************************
ok: [localhost] => {
    "changed": false,
    "msg": "All assertions passed"
}

TASK [output exposed port] **************************************************
ok: [localhost] => {
    "msg": "Exposed port: 2368/tcp"
}

TASK [extract volumes] *******************************************************
ok: [localhost]

TASK [output volumes] ********************************************************
ok: [localhost] => (item=/var/lib/ghost) => {
    "item": "/var/lib/ghost",
    "msg": "Volume: /var/lib/ghost"
}
```

```
PLAY RECAP ******************************************************************
localhost                  : ok=6    changed=0    unreachable=0    failed=0
```

Deploying the Dockerized Application

By default, Ghost uses SQLite as its database backend. For deployment, we're going to use Postgres as the database backend, for the reasons we discussed in Chapter 5.

We're going to deploy onto two separate machines. One machine (ghost) will run the Ghost container and the Nginx container. The other machine (postgres) will run a Postgres container that will serve as a persistent store for the Ghost data.

This example assumes the following variables are defined somewhere such as *group_vars/all*, where they are in scope for the frontend and backend machines:

- database_name
- database_user
- database_password

Backend: Postgres

To configure the Postgres container, we need to pass the database user, database password, and database name as environment variables that the container expects. We also want to mount a directory from a host machine as a volume for storing the persistent data, because we don't want our persistent data to disappear if the container stops and gets removed.

Example 15-9 shows the playbook for deploying the Postgres container. It has only two tasks: one to create the directory that will hold the data, and the other to start the Postgres container. Note that this playbook assumes that Docker Engine is already installed on the postgres host.

Example 15-9. postgres.yml

```
- name: deploy postgres
  hosts: postgres
  become: True
  gather_facts: False
  vars:
    data_dir: /data/pgdata
  tasks:
    - name: create data dir with correct ownership
      file:
        path: "{{ data_dir }}"
```

```
        state: directory
  - name: start postgres container
    docker_container:
      name: postgres_ghost
      image: postgres:9.6
      ports:
        - "0.0.0.0:5432:5432"
      volumes:
        - "{{ data_dir }}:/var/lib/postgresql/data"
      env:
        POSTGRES_USER: "{{ database_user }}"
        POSTGRES_PASSWORD: "{{ database_password }}"
        POSTGRES_DB: "{{ database_name }}"
```

Frontend

The frontend deployment is more complex, since we have two containers to deploy:
Ghost and Nginx. We also need to wire them up, and we need to pass configuration
information to the Ghost container so it can access the Postgres database.

We're going to use Docker networks to enable the Nginx container to connect to the
Ghost container. Networks replace the legacy links functionality that was previously
used for connecting containers. Using Docker networks, you create a custom Docker
network, attach containers to that network, and the containers can access each other
by using the container names as hostnames.

Creating a Docker network is simple:

```
  - name: create network
    docker_network: name=ghostnet
```

It makes more sense to use a variable for the network name, since we'll need to reference it for each container we bring up. This is how our playbook will start:

```
- name: deploy ghost
  hosts: ghost
  become: True
  gather_facts: False
  vars:
    url: "https://{{ ansible_host }}"
    database_host: "{{ groups['postgres'][0] }}"
    data_dir: /data/ghostdata
    certs_dir: /data/certs
    net_name: ghostnet
  tasks:
    - name: create network
      docker_network: "name={{ net_name }}"
```

Note that this playbook assumes there's a group named postgres that contains a single host; it uses this information to populate the database_host variable.

Frontend: Ghost

We need to configure Ghost to connect to the Postgres database, as well as to run in production mode by passing the `--production` flag to the `npm start` command.

We also want to ensure that the persistent files that it generates are written to a volume mount.

Here's the part of the playbook that creates the directory that will hold the persistent data, generates a Ghost config file from a template, and starts up the container, connected to the `ghostnet` network:

```
- name: create ghostdata directory
  file:
    path: "{{ data_dir }}"
    state: directory
- name: generate the config file
  template: src=templates/config.js.j2 dest={{ data_dir }}/config.js
- name: start ghost container
  docker_container:
    name: ghost
    image: ghost
    command: npm start --production
    volumes:
      - "{{ data_dir }}:/var/lib/ghost"
    networks:
      - name: "{{ net_name }}"
```

Note that we don't need to publish any ports here, since only the Nginx container will communicate with the Ghost container.

Frontend: Nginx

The Nginx container had its configuration hardwired into it when we created the *ansiblebook/nginx-ghost* image: it is configured to connect to `ghost:2368`.

However, we do need to copy the TLS certificates. As in previous examples, we'll just generate self-signed certificates:

```
- name: create certs directory
  file:
    path: "{{ certs_dir }}"
    state: directory
- name: generate tls certs
  command: >
    openssl req -new -x509 -nodes
    -out "{{ certs_dir }}/nginx.crt" -keyout "{{ certs_dir }}/nginx.key"
    -subj "/CN={{ ansible_host}}" -days 3650
    creates=certs/nginx.crt
- name: start nginx container
  docker_container:
```

```
name: nginx_ghost
image: ansiblebook/nginx-ghost
pull: yes
networks:
  - name: "{{ net_name }}"
ports:
  - "0.0.0.0:80:80"
  - "0.0.0.0:443:443"
volumes:
  - "{{ certs_dir }}:/certs"
```

Cleaning Out Containers

Ansible makes it easy to stop and remove containers, which is useful when you're developing and testing deployment scripts. Here is a playbook that cleans up the ghost host.

```
- name: remove all ghost containers and networks
  hosts: ghost
  become: True
  gather_facts: False
  tasks:
    - name: remove containers
      docker_container:
        name: "{{ item }}"
        state: absent
      with_items:
        - nginx_ghost
        - ghost
    - name: remove network
      docker_network:
        name: ghostnet
        state: absent
```

Connecting Directly to Containers

Ansible has support for interacting directly with running containers. Ansible's Docker inventory plugin will automatically generate an inventory of accessible running hosts, and its Docker connection plugin does the equivalent of docker exec to execute processes in the context of a running container.

The Docker inventory plugin is available in the GitHub *ansible/ansible* repo at *contrib/inventory/docker.py*. By default, this plugin accesses the Docker daemon running on your local machine. It can be configured to connect to Docker daemons on remote machines using Docker's REST API, or to connect to running Docker containers that have an SSH server running inside them. Both of these require additional setup work. To access the Docker API remotely, the host running Docker must be configured to bind to a TCP port. To connect to a container via SSH, the container must be configured to start up an SSH server. We don't cover those scenarios here, but you can check out the example configuration file in the repo at *contrib/inventory/docker.yml*.

Assuming we have the following containers running locally:

```
CONTAINER ID      IMAGE                           NAMES
63b6767de77f      ansiblebook/nginx-ghost  ch14_nginx_1
057d72a95016      ghost                           ch14_ghost_1
```

the *docker.py* inventory script creates a host per name. In this case:

- ch14_nginx_1

- ch14_ghost_1

It also creates groups for short ID, long ID, Docker image, and a group for all running containers. Continuing on with our example, the created groups are as follows:

- 63b6767de77fe (ch14_nginx_1)

- 63b6767de77fe01aa6d840dd897329766bbd3dc60409001cc36e900f8d501d6d (ch14_nginx_1)

- 057d72a950163 (ch14_ghost_1)

- 057d72a950163769c2bcc1ecc81ba377d03c39b1d19f8f4a9f0c748230b42c5c (ch14_ghost_1)

- image_ansiblebook/nginx-ghost (ch14_nginx_1)

- image_ghost (ch14_ghost_1)

- running (ch14_nginx_1, ch14_ghost_1)

Here's how we combine the Docker dynamic inventory script with the Docker connection plugin (enabled by passing -c docker as an argument) to list all of the processes running inside each container:

```
$ ansible -c docker running -m raw -a 'ps aux'

ch14_ghost_1 | SUCCESS | rc=0 >>
USER        PID %CPU %MEM     VSZ    RSS TTY      STAT START    TIME COMMAND
user          1  0.0  2.2 1077892  45040 ?        Ssl  05:19   0:00 npm
user         34  0.0  0.0    4340    804 ?        S    05:19   0:00 sh -c node ind
user         35  0.0  5.9 1255292 121728 ?        Sl   05:19   0:02 node index
root        108  0.0  0.0    4336    724 ?        Ss   06:20   0:00 /bin/sh -c ps
root        114  0.0  0.1   17500   2076 ?        R    06:20   0:00 ps aux


ch14_nginx_1 | SUCCESS | rc=0 >>
USER        PID %CPU %MEM     VSZ    RSS TTY      STAT START    TIME COMMAND
root          1  0.0  0.2   46320   5668 ?        Ss   05:19   0:00 nginx: master
nginx         6  0.0  0.1   46736   3020 ?        S    05:19   0:00 nginx: worker
```

```
root          71  0.0  0.0   4336    752 ?        Ss   06:20   0:00 /bin/sh -c ps
root          77  0.0  0.0  17500   2028 ?        R    06:20   0:00 ps aux
```

Ansible Container

Coinciding with the release of Ansible 2.1, the Ansible project released a new tool called *Ansible Container* to simplify working with Docker images and containers. We cover Ansible Container 0.9, which coincided with the release of Ansible 2.3.

Ansible Container does quite a few things. In particular, you can use it to do the following:

- Create new images (replaces Dockerfiles)
- Publish Docker images to registries (replaces docker push)
- Run Docker containers in development mode (replaces Docker Compose)
- Deploy to a production cloud (alternative to Docker Swarm)

As of this writing, Ansible Container supports deploying to Kubernetes and Open-Shift, although this list is likely to grow. If you don't run on one of these environments, don't worry: you can write a playbook by using the docker_container module (described later in this chapter) to pull down and start your containers on whatever production environment you like.

The Conductor

Ansible Container enables you to configure Docker images by using Ansible roles instead of Dockerfiles. When using Ansible to configure hosts, Python must be installed on the host. However, this requirement is generally considered undesirable for Docker containers because users typically want minimal containers; users don't want to have Python installed in a container if that container won't actually need Python.

Ansible Container eliminates the need to have Python installed inside the container by using a special container called the *Conductor*, and taking advantage of Docker's ability to mount volumes from one container to another.

When you run Ansible Container, it creates a local directory named *ansible-deployment*, copies all the files that the Conductor needs, and mounts the directory from your local machine into the Conductor.

Ansible Container mounts directories containing the Python runtime and any needed library dependencies from the Conductor container into the containers that are being configured. It does this by mounting */usr* from the Conductor container instance to */_usr* inside the container being configured, and configures Ansible to use the Python interpreter under */_usr*. For this to work properly, the Linux distribution of the Docker container you use for the Conductor should match the Linux distribution of the base image of the Docker containers that you are configuring.

If your Conductor base image is an official image from one of the supported Linux distributions, Ansible Container will automatically add some required packages to the container. As of 0.9.0, the supported distributions are Fedora, CentOS, Debian, Ubuntu, and Alpine. You can use an unsupported base image, but you must ensure that it has the required packages installed.

See the *container/docker/templates/conductor-dockerfile.j2* file in the Ansible Container GitHub repository (*https://github.com/ansible/ansible-container*) for information on which packages are installed into the Conductor image.

If you don't want Ansible Container to mount the runtime from the Conductor into the container being configured, you can disable this behavior by passing the `--use-local-python` flag to the `ansible-container` command. Ansible Container will then use the native Python interpreter of the container image being configured.

Creating Docker Images

Let's use Ansible Container to build that simple Nginx image from Example 15-1.

Creating the initial files

The first thing we must do is run the initialize command:

```
$ ansible-container init
```

This command creates a set of files in the current directory:

```
.
├── ansible-requirements.txt
├── ansible.cfg
├── container.yml
├── meta.yml
└── requirements.yml
```

Creating the roles

Next, we need a role that will configure our container. We'll call our role `ghost-nginx`, since it configures an Nginx image for fronting Ghost.

This role will be very simple; it just needs the *ghost.conf* configuration file from Example 15-2 and a task file that implements the functionality of Example 15-1. Here's the directory structure for the role:

```
.
└── roles
    └── ghost-nginx
        ├── files
        │   └── ghost.conf
        └── tasks
            └── main.yml
```

Here's the *tasks/main.yml* file:

```
---
- name: remove default config
  file:
    path: /etc/nginx/conf.d/default.conf
    state: absent
- name: add ghost config
  copy:
    src: ghost.conf
    dest: /etc/nginx/conf.d/ghost.conf
```

Configuring container.yml

Next, we'll configure *container.yml* to use our role to build the container, as shown in Example 15-10. This file is similar to a Docker Compose file, with additional fields that are Ansible-specific, and support for Jinja2-style variable substitution and filters.

Example 15-10. container.yml

```
version: "2" ❶
settings:
  conductor_base: debian:jessie ❷
services: ❸
  ac-nginx: ❹
    from: nginx ❺
    command: [nginx, -g, daemon off;] ❻
    roles:
      - ghost-nginx ❼
registries: {} ❽
```

❶ This tells Ansible Container to support Docker Compose version 2 schemas. The default is version 1, but you probably always want version 2.

❷ We are using debian:jessie as the base image for our Conductor container, because we will be customizing the official Nginx image, which uses debian:jes sie as its base image.

❸ The services field is a map whose keys are the names of the containers we are going to create. In this example, there is only a single container.

❹ We call the container we are going to create `ac-nginx` for *Ansible Conductor Nginx*.

❺ We specify `nginx` as the base image.

❻ We need to specify the command that will be run when the container starts up.

❼ We specify the roles to be used to configure this image. For this case, there's only one role, `ghost-nginx`.

❽ The `registries` field is used to specify the external registries we will push our containers to. We haven't configured this yet, so it's blank.

Ansible Container does not automatically pull base images to your local machine. You must do that yourself before building the containers. For example, before you run Example 15-10, you would need to pull the `nginx` base image that is required to build `ac-nginx`:

```
$ docker pull nginx
```

Building the containers

Finally, we're ready to build:

```
$ ansible-container build
```

The output should look like this:

```
Building Docker Engine context...
Starting Docker build of Ansible Container Conductor image (please be patient)...
Parsing conductor CLI args.
Docker™ daemon integration engine loaded. Build starting.        project=ans-con
Building service...      project=ans-con service=ac-nginx

PLAY [ac-nginx] *****************************************************************

TASK [Gathering Facts] *********************************************************
ok: [ac-nginx]

TASK [ghost-nginx : remove default config] *************************************
changed: [ac-nginx]

TASK [ghost-nginx : add ghost config] ******************************************
changed: [ac-nginx]

PLAY RECAP *********************************************************************
ac-nginx                   : ok=3    changed=2    unreachable=0    failed=0

Applied role to service role=ghost-nginx service=ac-nginx
```

```
Committed layer as image    image=sha256:5eb75981fc5117b3fca3207b194f3fa6c9ccb85
7718f91d674ec53d86323ffe3 service=ac-nginx
Build complete. service=ac-nginx
All images successfully built.
Conductor terminated. Cleaning up.  command_rc=0 conductor_id=8c68ca4720beae5d9c
7ca10ed70a3c08b207cd3f68868b3670dcc853abf9b62b save_container=False
```

Ansible Container uses a `{project}-{service}` convention for naming Docker images; the project name is determined by the directory where you run `ansible-container init`. In my case, the directory is named *ans-con*, so the image that will be created will be named *ans-con-ac-nginx*.

Ansible will also always create a conductor image, named `{project}-conductor`.

If you don't want Ansible Container to use the directory name as the project name, you can specify a custom project name by passing the `--project-name` flag.

If we run the following:

```
$ docker images
```

we'll see the following new container images:

```
REPOSITORY          TAG              IMAGE ID      CREATED        SIZE
ans-con-ac-nginx    20170424035545   5eb75981fc51  2 minutes ago  182 MB
ans-con-ac-nginx    latest           5eb75981fc51  2 minutes ago  182 MB
ans-con-conductor   latest           742cf2e046a3  2 minutes ago  622 MB
```

Troubleshooting builds

If the build command fails with an error, you can learn more by viewing the logs generated by the Conductor container. There are two ways to see the log.

One way is to use the `--debug` flag when invoking `ansible-container`.

If you don't want to rerun with the `--debug` flag, you can get the log output from Docker. To get it, you need to get the ID of the Conductor container. Because the container will no longer be running, use the `ps -a` Docker command to find the ID of the exited container:

```
$ docker ps -a
CONTAINER ID  IMAGE         COMMAND             CREATED         STATUS
78e78b9a1863  0c238eaf1819  "/bin/sh -c 'cd /_..."  21 minutes ago  Exited (1)
```

Once you have the ID, you can view the log output like this:

```
$ docker logs 78e78b9a1863
```

Running Locally

Ansible Container allows you to run multiple containers locally, just like Docker Compose. The *container.yml* file is similar to the format of *docker-compose.yml*. We'll extend our *container.yml* so that it behaves the same way as Example 15-3. This is shown in Example 15-11.

Example 15-11. container.yml, configured for local execution

```
version: "2"
settings:
  conductor_base: debian:jessie
services:
  ac-nginx:
    from: nginx
    command: [nginx, -g, daemon off;]
    roles:
      - ghost-nginx
    ports:
      - "8443:443"
      - "8000:80"
    dev_overrides:    ❶
      volumes:
        - $PWD/certs:/certs
      links:
        - ghost
  ghost: ❷
    from: ghost
    dev_overrides:
      volumes:
        - $PWD/ghostdata:/var/lib/ghost
registries: {}
```

Note the changes from Example 15-10 to Example 15-11:

❶ We've added a dev_overrides section to the ac-nginx service that contains data that is specific for running locally (i.e., not used for creating images or for deploying to production). For this service, that involves mounting the TLS certificates from the local filesystem and linking the container to the ghost container.

❷ We've added a ghost service that contains the Ghost app. We didn't need this previously because we aren't creating a custom Ghost container; we're just running the official one unmodified.

Note that while the syntax is similar to Docker Compose, it isn't identical. For example, Ansible Container uses from, whereas Docker Compose uses image, and Docker Compose does not have a dev_overrides section.

You can start the containers on your local machine by doing this:

```
$ ansible-container run
```

You can stop them as follows:

```
$ ansible-container stop
```

If you want to stop all containers and delete all images that you've created, use the following:

```
$ ansible-container destroy
```

Publishing Images to Registries

Once you are satisfied with your images, you'll want to publish them to a registry so that you can deploy them.

You'll need to configure the registries section of Example 15-10 to specify a registry. For example, Example 15-12 shows how to configure *container.yml* to push images to the *ansiblebook* organization in the Docker registry.

Example 15-12. registries section of container.yml

```
registries:
  docker:
    url: https://index.docker.io/v1/
    namespace: ansiblebook
```

Authenticating

The first time you push your image, you need to pass your username as a command-line argument:

```
$ ansible-container push --username $YOUR_USERNAME
```

You'll be prompted to enter your password. The first time you push an image, Ansible Container stores your credentials in *~/.docker/config.json*, and on subsequent pushes you don't need to specify a username or password anymore.

The output looks like this:

```
Parsing conductor CLI args.
Engine integration loaded. Preparing push.      engine=Docker™ daemon
Tagging ansiblebook/ans-con-ac-nginx
Pushing ansiblebook/ans-con-ac-nginx:20170430055647...
The push refers to a repository [docker.io/ansiblebook/ans-con-ac-nginx]
Preparing
Pushing
Mounted from library/nginx
Pushed
20170430055647: digest: sha256:50507495a9538e9865fe3038d56793a1620b9b372482667a
Conductor terminated. Cleaning up.  command_rc=0 conductor_id=1d4cfa04a055c1040
```

Multiple registries

Ansible Container allows you to specify multiple registries. For example, here is a
`registries` section that has two registries, Docker Hub and Quay:

```
registries:
  docker:
    namespace: ansiblebook
    url: https://index.docker.io/v1/
  quay:
    namespace: ansiblebook
    url: https://quay.io
```

To push images to only one of the registries, use the `--push-to` flag. For example, this
pushes to the Quay registry:

```
$ ansible-container push --push-to quay
```

Deploying Containers to Production

Although we don't cover it here, Ansible Container also has support for deploying
your containers to a production environment, using the `ansible-container deploy`
command. As of this writing, Ansible Container has support for deploying to two
container management platforms: OpenShift and Kubernetes.

If you are looking for an Ansible Container-supported public cloud for running your
containers, Red Hat operates an OpenShift-based cloud platform called OpenShift
Online, and Google provides Kubernetes as part of its Google Compute Engine cloud
platform. Both platforms are also open source, so if you manage your own hardware,
you can deploy either OpenShift or Kubernetes on them for free. If you want to
deploy on another platform (e.g., EC2 Container Service or Azure Container Service),
you won't be able to use Ansible Container for the deployment.

Docker as a technology has clearly demonstrated that it has staying power. In this
chapter, we covered how to manage Docker images, containers, and networks. While
we weren't able to cover the creation of Docker images with Ansible playbooks, by the
time you read this, you'll likely be able to use Ansible playbooks for creating images
as well.

## CHAPTER 16

Debugging Ansible Playbooks

Let's face it: mistakes happen. Whether it's a bug in a playbook, or a config file on your control machine with the wrong configuration value, eventually something's going to go wrong. In this chapter, I'll review some techniques you can use to help track down those errors.

Humane Error Messages

When an Ansible task fails, the output format isn't very friendly to any human reader trying to debug the problem. Here's an example of an error message generated while working on this book:

```
TASK [check out the repository on the host] ****************************************
fatal: [web]: FAILED! => {"changed": false, "cmd": "/usr/bin/git clone --origin o
rigin '' /home/vagrant/mezzanine/mezzanine_example", "failed": true, "msg": "Clon
ing into '/home/vagrant/mezzanine/mezzanine_example'...\nPermission denied (publi
ckey).\r\nfatal: Could not read from remote repository.\n\nPlease make sure you h
ave the correct access rights\nand the repository exists.", "rc": 128, "stderr":
"Cloning into '/home/vagrant/mezzanine/mezzanine_example'...\nPermission denied (
publickey).\r\nfatal: Could not read from remote repository.\n\nPlease make sure
you have the correct access rights\nand the repository exists.\n", "stderr_lines"
: ["Cloning into '/home/vagrant/mezzanine/mezzanine_example'...", "Permission den
ied (publickey).", "fatal: Could not read from remote repository.", "", "Please m
ake sure you have the correct access rights", "and the repository exists."], "std
out": "", "stdout_lines": []}
```

As mentioned in Chapter 10, the debug callback plugin makes this output much easier for a human to read:

```
TASK [check out the repository on the host] **************************************
fatal: [web]: FAILED! => {
    "changed": false,
    "cmd": "/usr/bin/git clone --origin origin '' /home/vagrant/mezzanine/mezzani
    ne_example",
    "failed": true,
    "rc": 128
}

STDERR:

Cloning into '/home/vagrant/mezzanine/mezzanine_example'...
Permission denied (publickey).
fatal: Could not read from remote repository.

Please make sure you have the correct access rights
and the repository exists.


MSG:

Cloning into '/home/vagrant/mezzanine/mezzanine_example'...
Permission denied (publickey).
fatal: Could not read from remote repository.

Please make sure you have the correct access rights
and the repository exists.
```

Enable the plugin by adding the following to the `defaults` section of *ansible.cfg*:

```
[defaults]
stdout_callback = debug
```

Debugging SSH Issues

Sometimes Ansible fails to make a successful SSH connection with the host. When this happens, it's helpful to see exactly what arguments Ansible is passing to the underlying SSH client so you can reproduce the problem manually on the command line.

If you invoke `ansible-playbook` with the -vvv argument, you can see the exact SSH commands that Ansible invokes. This can be handy for debugging.

Example 16-1 shows some sample Ansible output for executing a module that copies a file.

Example 16-1. Example output when verbose flags are enabled

```
TASK: [copy TLS key] ***********************************************************
task path: /Users/lorin/dev/ansiblebook/ch15/playbooks/playbook.yml:5
Using module file /usr/local/lib/python2.7/site-packages/ansible/modules/core/
files/stat.py
<127.0.0.1> SSH: EXEC ssh -C -o ControlMaster=auto -o ControlPersist=60s -o
StrictHostKeyChecking=no -o Port=2222 -o 'IdentityFile=".vagrant/machines/default/
virtualbox/private_key"' -o KbdInteractiveAuthentication=no -o
PreferredAuthentications=gssapi-with-mic,gssapi-keyex,hostbased,publickey -o
PasswordAuthentication=no -o User=vagrant -o ConnectTimeout=10 -o ControlPath=
/Users/lorin/.ansible/cp/ansible-ssh-%h-%p-%r 127.0.0.1 '/bin/sh -c '"'"'( umask
77 && mkdir -p "` echo ~/.ansible/tmp/ansible-tmp-1487128449.23-168248620529755 `"
&& echo ansible-tmp-1487128449.23-168248620529755="` echo ~/.ansible/tmp/ansible-
tmp-1487128449.23-168248620529755 `" ) && sleep 0'"'"''
<127.0.0.1> PUT /var/folders/g_/523vq6g1037d10231mmbx1780000gp/T/tmpyOxLAA TO
/home/vagrant/.ansible/tmp/ansible-tmp-1487128449.23-168248620529755/stat.py
<127.0.0.1> SSH: EXEC sftp -b - -C -o ControlMaster=auto -o ControlPersist=60s -o
StrictHostKeyChecking=no -o Port=2222 -o 'IdentityFile=".vagrant/machines/default/
virtualbox/private_key"' -o KbdInteractiveAuthentication=no -o
PreferredAuthentications=gssapi-with-mic,gssapi-keyex,hostbased,publickey -o
PasswordAuthentication=no -o User=vagrant -o ConnectTimeout=10 -o ControlPath=
/Users/lorin/.ansible/cp/ansible-ssh-%h-%p-%r '[127.0.0.1]'
```

Sometimes you might need to use -vvvv when debugging a connection issue, in order
to see an error message that the SSH client is throwing. For example, if the host
doesn't have SSH running, you'll see an error that looks like this:

```
testserver | FAILED => SSH encountered an unknown error. The output was:
OpenSSH_6.2p2, OSSLShim 0.9.8r 8 Dec 2011
debug1: Reading configuration data /etc/ssh_config
debug1: /etc/ssh_config line 20: Applying options for *
debug1: /etc/ssh_config line 102: Applying options for *
debug1: auto-mux: Trying existing master
debug1: Control socket "/Users/lorin/.ansible/cp/ansible-ssh-127.0.0.1-
2222-vagrant" does not exist
debug2: ssh_connect: needpriv 0
debug1: Connecting to 127.0.0.1 [127.0.0.1] port 2222.
debug2: fd 3 setting O_NONBLOCK
debug1: connect to address 127.0.0.1 port 2222: Connection refused
ssh: connect to host 127.0.0.1 port 2222: Connection refused
```

If you have host-key verification enabled, and the host key in *~/.ssh/known_hosts*
doesn't match the host key of the server, then using -vvvv will output an error that
looks like this:

```
@@@@@@@@@@@@@@@@@@@@@@@@@@@@@@@@@@@@@@@@@@@@@@@@@@@@@@@@@@@@@@
@    WARNING: REMOTE HOST IDENTIFICATION HAS CHANGED!     @
@@@@@@@@@@@@@@@@@@@@@@@@@@@@@@@@@@@@@@@@@@@@@@@@@@@@@@@@@@@@@@
IT IS POSSIBLE THAT SOMEONE IS DOING SOMETHING NASTY!
Someone could be eavesdropping on you right now (man-in-the-middle attack)!
It is also possible that a host key has just been changed.
```

```
The fingerprint for the RSA key sent by the remote host is
c3:99:c2:8f:18:ef:68:fe:ca:86:a9:f5:95:9e:a7:23.
Please contact your system administrator.
Add correct host key in /Users/lorin/.ssh/known_hosts to get rid of this
message.
Offending RSA key in /Users/lorin/.ssh/known_hosts:1
RSA host key for [127.0.0.1]:2222 has changed and you have requested strict
checking.
Host key verification failed.
```

If that's the case, you should delete the offending entry from your *~/.ssh/known_hosts*
file.

The Debug Module

We've used the `debug` module several times in this book. It's Ansible's version of a
`print` statement. As shown in Example 16-2, you can use it to print out either the
value of a variable or an arbitrary string.

Example 16-2. The debug module in action

```
- debug: var=myvariable
- debug: msg="The value of myvariable is {{ var }}"
```

As we discussed in Chapter 4, you can print out the values of all the variables associated with the current host by invoking the following:

```
- debug: var=hostvars[inventory_hostname]
```

Playbook Debugger

Ansible 2.1 added support for an interactive debugger. To enable debugging, add
`strategy: debug` to your play; for example:

```
- name: an example play
  strategy: debug
  tasks:
    ...
```

If debugging is enabled, Ansible drops into the debugger when a task fails:

```
TASK [try to apt install a package] *********************************************
fatal: [localhost]: FAILED! => {"changed": false, "cmd": "apt-get update",
"failed": true, "msg": "[Errno 2] No such file or directory", "rc": 2}
Debugger invoked
(debug)
```

Table 16-1 shows the commands supported by the debugger.

Table 16-1. Debugger commands

Command	Description
p var	Print out the value of a supported variable
task.args[key]=value	Modify an argument for the failed task
vars[key]=value	Modify the value of a variable
r	Rerun the failed task
c	Continue executing the play
q	Abort the play and execute the debugger
help	Show help message

Table 16-2 shows the variables supported by the debugger.

Table 16-2. Variables supported by the debugger

Command	Description
p task	The name of the task that failed
p task.args	The module arguments
p result	The result returned by the failed task
p vars	Value of all known variables
p vars[key]	Value of one variable

Here's an example interaction with the debugger:

```
(debug) p task
TASK: try to apt install a package
(debug) p task.args
{u'name': u'foo'}
(debug) p result
{'_ansible_no_log': False,
 '_ansible_parsed': True,
 'changed': False,
 u'cmd': u'apt-get update',
 u'failed': True,
 'invocation': {u'module_args': {u'allow_unauthenticated': False,
                                 u'autoremove': False,
                                 u'cache_valid_time': 0,
                                 u'deb': None,
                                 u'default_release': None,
                                 u'dpkg_options': u'force-confdef,force-confold',
                                 u'force': False,
                                 u'install_recommends': None,
                                 u'name': u'foo',
                                 u'only_upgrade': False,
                                 u'package': [u'foo'],
                                 u'purge': False,
                                 u'state': u'present',
```

```
                                    u'update_cache': False,
                                    u'upgrade': None},
                        'module_name': u'apt'},
    u'msg': u'[Errno 2] No such file or directory',
    u'rc': 2}
(debug) p vars['inventory_hostname']
u'localhost'
(debug) p vars
{u'ansible_all_ipv4_addresses': [u'192.168.86.113'],
 u'ansible_all_ipv6_addresses': [u'fe80::f89b:ffff:fe32:5e5%awdl0',
                                 u'fe80::3e60:8f83:34b5:fc17%utun0',
                                 u'fe80::9679:241b:e93:8b7f%utun2'],
 u'ansible_architecture': u'x86_64',
 ...
```

While you'll probably find printing out variables to be the most useful feature of the
debugger, you can also use it to modify variables and modify arguments to the failed
task. See the Ansible playbook debugger docs (*http://bit.ly/2lvAm8B*) for more details.

The Assert Module

The `assert` module will fail with an error if a specified condition is not met. For
example, to fail the playbook if there's no `eth1` interface:

```
- name: assert that eth1 interface exists
  assert:
    that: ansible_eth1 is defined
```

When debugging a playbook, it can be helpful to insert assertions so that a failure
happens as soon as any assumption you've made has been violated.

Keep in mind that the code in an `assert` statement is Jinja2, not
Python. For example, if you want to assert the length of a list, you
might be tempted to do this:

```
# Invalid Jinja2, this won't work!
assert:
    that: "len(ports) == 1"
```

Unfortunately, Jinja2 does not support Python's built-in `len` function. Instead, you need to use the Jinja2 `length` filter:

```
assert:
  that: "ports|length == 1"
```

If you want to check on the status of a file on the host's filesystem, it's useful to call the
`stat` module first and make an assertion based on the return value of that module:

```
- name: stat /opt/foo
  stat: path=/opt/foo
  register: st
```

```
- name: assert that /opt/foo is a directory
  assert:
    that: st.stat.isdir
```

The stat module collects information about the state of a file path. It returns a dictionary that contains a stat field with the values shown in Table 16-3.

Table 16-3. stat module return values

Field	Description
atime	Last access time of path, in Unix timestamp format
ctime	Creation time of path, in Unix timestamp format
dev	Numerical ID of the device that the inode resides on
exists	True if path exists
gid	Numerical group ID of path owner
inode	Inode number
isblk	True if path is block special device file
ischr	True if path is character special device file
isdir	True if path is a directory
isfifo	True if path is a FIFO (named pipe)
isgid	True if set-group-ID bit is set on file
islnk	True if path is a symbolic link
isreg	True if path is a regular file
issock	True if path is a Unix domain socket
isuid	True if set-user-ID bit is set on file
mode	File mode as a string, in octal (e.g., "1777")
mtime	Last modification time of path, in Unix timestamp format
nlink	Number of hard links to the file
pw_name	Login name of file owner
rgrp	True if group read permission enabled
roth	True if other read permission enabled
rusr	True if user read permission enabled
size	File size in bytes, if regular file
uid	Numerical user ID of path owner
wgrp	True if group write permission enabled
woth	True if other write permission enabled
wusr	True if user write permission enabled
xgrp	True if group execute permission enabled
xoth	True if other execute permission enabled
xusr	True if user execute permission enabled

Checking Your Playbook Before Execution

The `ansible-playbook` command supports several flags that allow you to sanity check your playbook before you execute it.

Syntax Check

The `--syntax-check` flag, shown in Example 16-3, checks that your playbook's syntax is valid, but it does not execute it.

Example 16-3. syntax check

```
$ ansible-playbook --syntax-check playbook.yml
```

List Hosts

The `--list-hosts` flag, shown in Example 16-4, outputs the hosts that the playbook will run against, but it does not execute the playbook.

Example 16-4. list hosts

```
$ ansible-playbook --list-hosts playbook.yml
```

Sometimes you get the dreaded error:

```
ERROR: provided hosts list is empty
```

There must be one host explicitly specified in your inventory, or you'll get this error, even if your playbook runs against only the `localhost`. If your inventory is initially empty (perhaps because you're using a dynamic inventory script and haven't launched any hosts yet), you can work around this by explicitly adding the following line to your inventory:

```
localhost ansible_connection=local
```

List Tasks

The `--list-tasks` flag, shown in Example 16-5, outputs the tasks that the playbook will run against. It does not execute the playbook.

Example 16-5. list tasks

```
$ ansible-playbook --list-tasks playbook.yml
```

Recall that we used this flag in Example 6-1 to list the tasks in our first Mezzanine playbook.

Check Mode

The -C and --check flags run Ansible in check mode (sometimes known as *dry-run*), which tells you whether each task in the playbook will modify the host, but does not make any changes to the server.

```
$ ansible-playbook -C playbook.yml
$ ansible-playbook --check playbook.yml
```

One of the challenges with using check mode is that later parts of a playbook might succeed only if earlier parts of the playbook were executed. Running check mode on Example 6-28 yields the error shown in Example 16-6 because the task depended on an earlier task (installing the Git program on the host).

Example 16-6. Check mode failing on a correct playbook

```
PLAY [Deploy mezzanine] *********************************************************

GATHERING FACTS ****************************************************************
ok: [web]

TASK: [install apt packages] ***************************************************
changed: [web] => (item=git,libjpeg-dev,libpq-dev,memcached,nginx,postgresql,py
thon-dev,python-pip,python-psycopg2,python-setuptools,python-virtualenv,supervi
sor)

TASK: [check out the repository on the host] ***********************************
failed: [web] => {"failed": true}
msg: Failed to find required executable git

FATAL: all hosts have already failed -- aborting
```

See Chapter 12 for more details on how modules implement check mode.

Diff (Show File Changes)

The -D and -diff flags output differences for any files that are changed on the remote machine. It's a helpful option to use in conjunction with --check to show how Ansible would change the file if it were run normally:

```
$ ansible-playbook -D --check playbook.yml
$ ansible-playbook --diff --check playbook.yml
```

If Ansible would modify any files (e.g., using modules such as copy, template, and lineinfile), it will show the changes in *.diff* format, like this:

```
TASK: [set the gunicorn config file] *******************************************
--- before: /home/vagrant/mezzanine-example/project/gunicorn.conf.py
+++ after: /Users/lorin/dev/ansiblebook/ch06/playbooks/templates/gunicor
n.conf.py.j2
```

```
@@ -1,7 +1,7 @@
 from __future__ import unicode_literals
 import multiprocessing

 bind = "127.0.0.1:8000"
 workers = multiprocessing.cpu_count() * 2 + 1
-loglevel = "error"
+loglevel = "warning"
 proc_name = "mezzanine-example"
```

Limiting Which Tasks Run

Sometimes you don't want Ansible to run every single task in your playbook, particularly when you're first writing and debugging the playbook. Ansible provides several command-line options that let you control which tasks run.

Step

The `--step` flag, shown in Example 16-7, has Ansible prompt you before running each task, like this:

```
Perform task: install packages (y/n/c):
```

You can choose to execute the task (y), skip it (n), or tell Ansible to continue running the rest of the playbook without prompting you (c).

Example 16-7. step

```
$ ansible-playbook --step playbook.yml
```

Start-at-Task

The `--start-at-task taskname` flag, shown in Example 16-8, tells Ansible to start running the playbook at the specified task, instead of at the beginning. This can be handy if one of your tasks failed because there was a bug in one of your tasks, and you want to rerun your playbook starting at the task you just fixed.

Example 16-8. start-at-task

```
$ ansible-playbook --start-at-task="install packages" playbook.yml
```

Tags

Ansible allows you to add one or more tags to a task or a play. For example, here's a play that's tagged with foo and a task that's tagged with bar and quux:

```
- hosts: myservers
  tags:
    - foo
  tasks:
    - name: install editors
      apt: name={{ item }}
      with_items:
        - vim
        - emacs
        - nano

    - name: run arbitrary command
      command: /opt/myprog
      tags:
        - bar
        - quux
```

Use the -t tagnames or --tags tagnames flag to tell Ansible to run only plays and tasks that have certain tags. Use the --skip-tags tagnames flag to tell Ansible to skip plays and tasks that have certain tags. See Example 16-9.

Example 16-9. Running or skipping tags

```
$ ansible-playbook -t foo,bar playbook.yml
$ ansible-playbook --tags=foo,bar playbook.yml
$ ansible-playbook --skip-tags=baz,quux playbook.yml
```

## CHAPTER 17

Managing Windows Hosts

Ansible is also known as SSH configuration management on steroids. Historically, Ansible has had a strong association with Unix and Linux, and we often see evidence of this in things like variable naming (e.g., `ansible_ssh_host`, `ansible_ssh_connec tion`, and `sudo`). However, Ansible has had built-in support for various connection mechanisms since the early days of the project.

Supporting an alien in terms of operating systems—as Windows is to Linux—was not only a matter of figuring out how to connect to Windows, but also making internal naming more operating-system generic (e.g., renaming variables `ansible_ssh_host` to `ansible_host`, and `sudo` to `become`).

Ansible introduced beta support of Microsoft Windows in version 1.7, but support has been out of beta only since version 2.1. In addition, the only way to run Ansible from a Windows host (i.e., to use a Windows-based control machine) is to run Ansible within the Windows Subsystem for Linux (WSL).

In terms of module contributions, Windows module contributions have been lagging behind a bit compared to the Linux community contributions.

Connection to Windows

To add Windows support, Ansible did not depart from its path by adding an agent on Windows—and in my opinion, this was a great decision. Ansible uses the integrated Windows Remote Management (WinRM) functionality, a SOAP-based protocol.

WinRM is our first dependency, and we need to get it covered in Python by installing the appropriate package on the managing host:

```
$ sudo pip install pywinrm
```

By default, Ansible will try to connect by SSH to a remote machine, which is why we have to tell Ansible in advance to change the connection mechanism. Usually, it is a good idea to put all of our Windows hosts into an inventory group. The particular group name you choose doesn't matter, but we will use the same group name later in our playbooks for referencing the hosts:

```
[windows]
win01.example.com
win02.example.com
```

After this, we add the connection configuration into *group_var/windows* so all hosts of this group will inherit this configuration.

> In 2015, Microsoft announced in its blog (*https://blogs.msdn.micro soft.com/powershell/2015/06/03/looking-forward-microsoft-support-for-secure-shell-ssh/*) work on native Secure Shell (SSH) integration. This means that Ansible most certainly won't need a different connection configuration for Windows hosts in the future.

As mentioned earlier, the protocol is SOAP based and relies on HTTP in this case. By default, Ansible attempts to establish a secured HTTP (HTTPS) connection on port 5986 unless the `ansible_port` is configured to 5985.

```
ansible_user: Administrator
ansible_password: 2XLL43hDpQ1z
ansible_connection: winrm
```

To use a custom port, for HTTPS or HTTP, configure the port *and* the scheme to use:

```
ansible_winrm_scheme: https
ansible_port: 5999
```

PowerShell

PowerShell on Microsoft Windows is a powerful command-line interface and scripting language built on top of the .NET framework and provides full management access not only from the local environment but also by using remote access.

Ansible modules for Windows are all written in PowerShell as PowerShell scripts.

> In 2016, Microsoft open sourced PowerShell under the MIT license. The source and binary packages for recent versions of macOS, Ubuntu, and CentOS can be found on GitHub (*https://github.com/PowerShell/PowerShell*). At the time of writing, the stable version of PowerShell is 5.1.

Ansible expects at least PowerShell version 3 to be installed on the remote machine. PowerShell 3 is available for Microsoft Windows 7 SP1, Microsoft Windows Server 2008 SP1, and later.

There is no requirement on the control machine, the machine we run Ansible from, to have PowerShell installed!

However, there were bugs in version 3, and it is necessary to use the latest patches from Microsoft if you have to stick with version 3 for any reason.

To simplify the process of installation, upgrade, setup, and configuring PowerShell and Windows, Ansible provides a script (*https://github.com/ansible/ansible/blob/devel/examples/scripts/ConfigureRemotingForAnsible.ps1*).

To get started quickly, run the few shell commands as in Example 17-1, and you are ready to go. The script does not break anything if we run it multiple times.

Example 17-1. Setting up Windows for Ansible

```
wget http://bit.ly/1rHMn7b -OutFile .\ansible-setup.ps1
.\ansible-setup.ps1
```

`wget` is an alias for *Invoke-WebRequest*, which is a built-in of PowerShell.

To see the version of PowerShell installed, run the following command in a PowerShell console:

```
$PSVersionTable
```

You should see the output as in Figure 17-1.

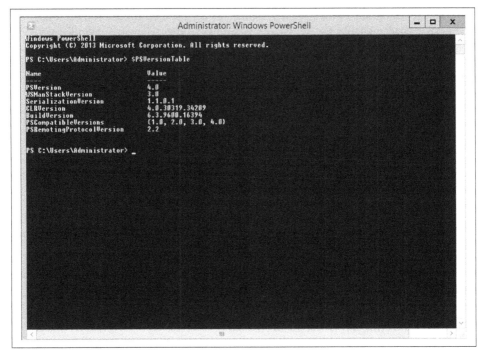

Figure 17-1. PowerShell version determination

We have made the connection configuration, so let's get started with a simple ping via `win_ping` to our Windows host. Similar to the `ping` on GNU/Linux or Unix, this is not an ICMP ping; it is a test for establishing a connection by Ansible:

```
$ ansible windows -i hosts -m win_ping
```

If we get an error like the following in Example 17-2, we must either get a valid public TLS/SSL certificate or add a trust chain for an existing internal certificate authority (CA).

Example 17-2. Error resulting from an invalid certificate

```
$ ansible -m win_ping -i hosts windows
win01.example.com | UNREACHABLE! => {
    "changed": false,
    "msg": "ssl: (\"bad handshake: Error([('SSL routines', 'tls_process_server_certi
ficate', 'certificate verify failed')],)\",)",
    "unreachable": true
}
```

To disable TLS/SSL certificate validation at our own risk:

```
ansible_winrm_server_cert_validation: ignore
```

If we see output similar to Example 17-3, we have successfully tested the connection.

Example 17-3. Result of a working connection

```
$ ansible -m win_ping -i hosts windows
win01.example.com | SUCCESS => {
    "changed": false,
    "ping": "pong"
}
```

Windows Modules

Ansible modules for Windows are prefixed with `win_`. At the time of writing, there are over 40 Windows modules, of which 19 are core modules. The online documentation (*http://docs.ansible.com/ansible/list_of_windows_modules.html*) has an overview of all available Windows modules.

> One exception regarding the module naming: to get Ansible facts from Windows, the module must not be run as `win_setup` but as setup: `ansible -m setup -i hosts windows`.

Our First Playbook

Now that we have a new Windows host, we should add it to our monitoring system. Let's create a playbook in which we will use some Windows modules.

Our monitoring of choice is the well-known open source Zabbix (*http://www.zabbix.com*) monitoring software, for which we need to install *zabbix-agentd* on our Windows host.

Let's create a simple playbook, as in Example 17-4, in which we install the *Zabbix Agent*.

Example 17-4. Playbook for installing Zabbix Agent on Windows

```
---
- hosts: windows
  gather_facts: yes
  tasks:
    - name: install zabbix-agent
      win_chocolatey: ❶
        name: zabbix-agent

    - name: configure zabbix-agent
      win_template:
```

```
      src: zabbix_agentd.conf.j2
      dest: "C:\ProgramData\zabbix\zabbix_agentd.conf"
    notify: zabbix-agent restart

  - name: zabbix-agent restart
    win_service:
      name: Zabbix Agent
      state: started
handlers:
  - name: zabbix-agent restart
    win_service:
      name: Zabbix Agent
      state: restarted
```

❶ win_chocolatey uses chocolatey, an open source package manager for Windows under the Apache License 2.0.

The corresponding playbook in Example 17-4 doesn't look much different from what we would have implemented for Linux, except the modules used.

For installing the software, we used the *chocolatey* package (*https://chocolatey.org/*). As an alternative module, win_package, could have been used.] For configuration, we used the win_template module, in which we were able to use the facts gathered (e.g., ansible_hostname) for configuration.

Of course, *zabbix_agentd.conf* must be copied from a Windows host in advance, before we can create a template of it. The template language is identical to the tem plate module: Jinja2.

The last module used, win_service, does not require further explanation.

Updating Windows

One of an administrator's daily hassles is to install software security updates. It is one of these tasks no administrator really likes, mainly because it is boring even though it is important and necessary, but also because it can cause a lot of trouble if the update goes wrong. This is why it can make sense to disable automated installation of security updates in our operating system settings and test the updates before we run the updates in production environments.

Ansible helps to automate software installation with one simple playbook, shown in Example 17-5. The playbook not only installs security updates but also reboots the machine afterward if necessary. Last but not least, it informs all users to log out before the system goes down.

Example 17-5. Playbook for installing security updates

```
---
- hosts: windows
  gather_facts: yes
  serial: 1 ❶
  tasks:
    - name: install software security updates
      win_updates:
        category_names:
          - SecurityUpdates
          - CriticalUpdates
      register: update_result

    - name: reboot windows if needed
      win_reboot:
        shutdown_timeout_sec: 1200 ❷
        msg: "Due to security updates this host will be rebooted in 20 minutes." ❸
      when: update_result.reboot_required
```

❶   Use `serial` for a rolling update.

❷   Allow some time to let the OS install all updates properly.

❸   Inform users on the system that it will be rebooted.

Let's give it a shot, as shown in Example 17-6.

Example 17-6. Playbook for installing security updates

```
$ ansible-playbook security-updates.yml -i hosts -v
No config file found; using defaults

PLAY [windows] ***********************************************************

TASK [Gathering Facts] ***************************************************
ok: [win01.example.com]

TASK [install software security updates] *********************************
ok: [win01.example.com] => {"changed": false, "found_update_count": 0, "install
ed_update_count": 0, "reboot_required": false, "updates": {}} ❶

TASK [reboot windows if needed] ******************************************
skipping: [win01.example.com] => {"changed": false, "skip_reason": "Conditional
result was False", "skipped": true} ❷

PLAY RECAP ***************************************************************
win01.example.com          : ok=2    changed=0    unreachable=0    failed=0
```

❶ `win_updates` returns `false` for `reboot_required`.

❷ Tasks are skipped because the condition `when:` `update_result` `.reboot_required` returns *false*.

That worked! Unfortunately, for once we do not have any pending security updates, and as a result the `reboot` task was skipped.

Adding Local Users

In this part of the chapter, we are going to create users and groups on Windows. You might think that this is a solved problem: just use Microsoft Active Directory. However, being able to run Windows anywhere in the cloud and not rely on a directory service can be advantageous for some use cases.

In Example 17-7, we are going to create two user groups and two users based on a list of dictionaries. In a more production-like Ansible project, the user dictionary would be defined in `group_vars` or `host_vars`, but for better readability we keep it in the playbook.

Example 17-7. Manage local groups and users on Windows

```
- hosts: windows
  gather_facts: no
  tasks:
    - name: create user groups
      win_group:
        name: "{{ item }}"
      with_items:
        - application
        - deployments

    - name: create users
      win_user:
        name: "{{ item.name }}"
        password: "{{ item.password }}"
        groups: "{{ item.groups }}"
        password_expired: "{{ item.password_expired | default(false) }}" ❶
        groups_action: "{{ item.groups_action | default('add') }}" ❷
      with_items:
        - name: gil
          password: t3lCj1hU2Tnr
          groups:
            - Users
            - deployments
        - name: sarina
          password: S3cr3t!
          password_expired: true ❸
```

```
groups:
  - Users
  - application
```

❶ The optional password expiration is defaulted to unexpired if not set in the user dictionary.

❷ The `win_user`'s default behavior of groups is `replace`: the user will be removed from any other group they are already a member of. We change the default to `add` to prevent any removal. However, we can overwrite the behavior per user.

❸ We expire Sarina's password. She needs to define a new password next time she logs on.

Let's run it:

```
$ ansible-playbook users.yml -i hosts

PLAY [windows] ****************************************************************

TASK [create user groups] ****************************************************
changed: [win01.example.com] => (item=application)
changed: [win01.example.com] => (item=deployments)

TASK [create users] **********************************************************
changed: [win01.example.com] => (item={u'password': u't3lCj1hU2Tnr', u'name':
u'gil', u'groups': [u'Users', u'deployments']})
changed: [win01.example.com] => (item={u'password_expired': True, u'password':
u'S3cr3t!', u'name': u'sarina', u'groups': [u'Users', u'application']})

PLAY RECAP *******************************************************************
win01.example.com          : ok=2    changed=2    unreachable=0    failed=0
```

OK, that seems to have worked, but let's verify it.

As we can see in Figure 17-2, the groups are there. Great!

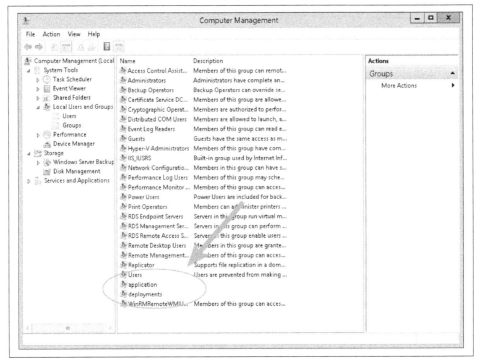

Figure 17-2. New groups have been created

Let's check the users as well, and whether all settings have been applied. In Figure 17-3, we see that Ansible has created our users, and `sarina` has to change her password at next logon—perfect!

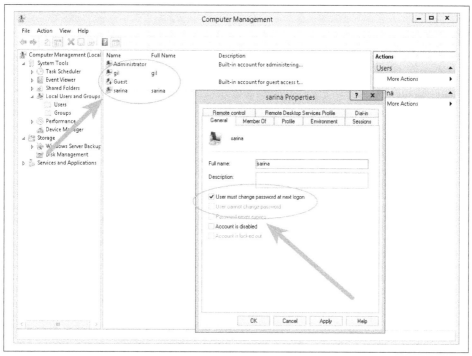

Figure 17-3. New users have been created

Conclusion

Ansible makes managing Microsoft Windows hosts almost as simple as with Linux and Unix.

Microsoft's WinRM works well, even though the execution speed is not as fast as with SSH. It will be interesting to see how the execution time will improve with native SSH support for Windows and PowerShell.

The Ansible modules for Windows are usable even though the community around them is still small. Nevertheless, Ansible is already the simplest tool for orchestrating IT across operating system borders.

## CHAPTER 18

Ansible for Network Devices

Managing and configuring network devices always makes me feel nostalgic. Log in to a console by telnet, type some commands, save the configuration to startup config, and you're done. This workflow hasn't changed much since the introduction of these devices. OK, to be fair, there were some changes, such as supporting SSH.

For a long time, we basically had two types of management strategies for network devices:

- Buy an expensive proprietary software that configures your devices.
- Develop minimal tooling around your configuration files: back up your configs locally, make some changes by editing them, and copy the result back onto the devices through the console.

However, in the last few years, we have seen some movement in this space. The first thing I noticed was that network device vendors have started to create or open their APIs for everyone. The second thing is that the so-called *DevOps* movement did not stop going lower down the stack, to the core: hardware servers, load-balancer appliances, firewall appliances, network devices, and even routers.

In my opinion, Ansible for network devices is the one of the most promising solutions to manage network devices, for three reasons:

- Ansible supports network devices with console-only access through SSH, and is not limited to vendor APIs.
- Any network operator can get productive in hours or less, as the way the modules are written is similar to what a network operator is used to doing.
- Ansible is open source software. We can use it here and now!

Status of Network Modules

Before we get our hands dirty, some words of warning: the implementation of network modules is pretty new, still in development, and marked as *preview* by Ansible. Things may change (and improve) over time. But this should not hold us back; we can already take advantage of what's there.

List of Network Vendors Supported

The first question you'll probably ask is, is my preferred vendor or network operating system supported? Here is the incomplete but already impressive list of supported network vendors and operating systems:

- Cisco ASA, IOS, IOS XR, NX-OS
- Juniper Junos OS
- Dell Networking OS 6, 9, and 10
- Cumulus
- A10 Networks
- F5 Networks
- Arista EOS
- VyOS

If your vendor is not on this list, please check the documentation for the latest list because development is proceeding quickly! At the time of writing, Ansible contains about 200 modules related to network devices.

Preparing Our Network Device

Before we can start playing with the network modules, we obviously need a network device.

I asked for a network device, and all I got was this, well, not lousy, but most likely outdated, or let's say old and noisy Cisco Catalyst 2960G Series Layer 2 switch running IOS. The device is End-of-Life since 2013. While the device might not be that remarkable, it is remarkable that this old thing is still manageable through Ansible!

First things first: before we can configure the switch by using Ansible, we must be able to connect to it. And here comes our first obstacle, as the device listens to telnet only when configured with the factory settings. We must bring it to the point that it listens for SSH connections. We really should not be using the telnet protocol for production work.

Ansible is not able to connect to network devices via telnet.

I am sure some of you may already have configured your switches and routers to listen to SSH. That said, I wouldn't call myself a typical network engineer; it took a while to figure out how to enable SSH on my Catalyst.

Enable SSH Authentication

For enabling SSH, we need to carry out a few steps. The commands we are going to use should work on most IOS devices, but they can vary a bit. However, this is nothing to worry about, as we can always get the options available on the console by typing a question mark (?).

Our Cisco switch is factory reset, and I put it into *Express Setup* mode. As I am on Linux, logging into the device by telnet is just one command away; see Example 18-1.

Example 18-1. Log in by telnet

```
$ telnet 10.0.0.1
Trying 10.0.0.1...
Connected to 10.0.0.1.
Escape character is '^]'.
Switch#
```

To configure the device, we need to get into *configuration* mode, just as in Example 18-2. Sounds obvious, doesn't it?

Example 18-2. Switch to configuration mode

```
switch1#configure
Configuring from terminal, memory, or network [terminal]? terminal
Enter configuration commands, one per line.  End with CNTL/Z.
```

The first configuration is to give it an IP, as shown in Example 18-3, so we will be able to log in afterward when all is configured.

Example 18-3. Configure a static IP

```
switch1(config)#interface vlan 1
switch1(config-if)#ip address 10.0.0.10 255.255.255.0
```

In order to generate an RSA key, we need to give it a hostname and a domain name, as shown in Example 18-4.

Example 18-4. Set a hostname and domain

```
Switch(config)#hostname switch1
switch1(config)#ip domain-name example.net
switch1(config)#
```

Once this is done, we are able generate the *crypto* key as shown in Example 18-5. At the time of this writing, the documentation recommends that we should not generate RSA keys with a size smaller than 2,048 bits.

Example 18-5. Generate RSA bits—this can take a while

```
switch1(config)#crypto key generate rsa
The name for the keys will be: switch1.example.net
Choose the size of the key modulus in the range of 360 to 4096 for your
  General Purpose Keys. Choosing a key modulus greater than 512 may take
  a few minutes.

How many bits in the modulus [512]: 4096
% Generating 4096 bit RSA keys, keys will be non-exportable...
[OK] (elapsed time was 164 seconds)

switch1(config)#
```

You may notice that we are connected to the device by telnet without any authentication. SSH, on the other hand, will ask for a username and password.

The next step, as shown in Example 18-6, is to add a new user with a username and password. Additionally, we grant it *privilege* level 15 (highest level).

> You can set the password in two ways, as `secret` or as `password`. The `password` will store it in plain text, while `secret` will store it as a hash sum, depending on your device and firmware version.

Example 18-6. Add a new user admin

```
switch1(config)#username admin privilege 15 secret s3cr3t
```

The last step, as shown in Example 18-7, is to configure the authentication model. Our switch is running in the *old model* per default. In this mode, it will prompt only for the password.

However, we want to be prompted not only for password, but also for the username; this is called the *new model of authentication, authorization, and accounting* (`aaa`).

Example 18-7. Configure the authentication model

```
switch1(config)#aaa new-model
```

In addition, we are also going to set a password for enable in Example 18-8 just to demonstrate that Ansible can handle this as well.

Example 18-8. Set a password for enable

```
switch1(config)#enable secret 3n4bl3s3cr3t
```

Once this all is done, there is no need to run this insecure plain-text telnet protocol anymore, so let's disable it, as we do in Example 18-9, on any of our 16 virtual terminals.

Example 18-9. Disable telnet on the device

```
switch1(config)#line vty 0 15
switch1(config-line)#transport input ?
  all    All protocols
  none   No protocols
  ssh    TCP/IP SSH protocol
  telnet TCP/IP Telnet protocol

switch1(config-line)#transport input ssh
switch1(config-line)#exit
```

That's it. Let's end the config and save the config as shown in Example 18-10. Note that after this step, you may lose your existing connection, but this is not a problem.

Example 18-10. Save to config to be used as startup config

```
switch1#copy running-config startup-config
Destination filename [startup-config]?
```

It is time to verify that SSH is set up and telnet is disabled, as shown in Example 18-11.

Example 18-11. Log in by SSH

```
$ telnet 10.0.0.10
Trying 10.0.0.10...
telnet: Unable to connect to remote host: Connection refused
$ ssh admin@10.0.0.10
Password:

switch01>
```

Great, it works!

How the Modules Work

Before we get to our first playbook, let's step back and talk a bit about Ansible modules. A simplified view of how Ansible works when running a playbook is that the module used in the task gets copied to the target machine and executed there.

When we look back to the network modules, this procedure would not work for a network device. They usually don't have a Python interpreter installed, or at least it is not usable for us. That is why network modules work a bit differently than ordinary Ansible modules.

We can compare them with modules dealing with HTTP APIs. Ansible modules using HTTP APIs are usually executed locally, as they run the Python code locally in which they talk by HTTP to the API. Network modules work pretty much the same way, except they do not talk HTTP but with a console!

Our First Playbook

In our first playbook, I plan to keep it simple, changing the hostname.

Because our network device is running the Cisco IOS operating system, we are going to use the `ios_config` module, which manages Cisco IOS configuration sections.

Let's create the first task, `ios_config`, in our playbook, as shown in Example 18-12.

Example 18-12. Set the hostname on Cisco Catalyst

```
---
- hosts: localhost
  gather_facts: no
  connection: local ❶
  tasks:
  - name: set a hostname
    ios_config:
      lines: hostname sw1
      provider:
        host: 10.0.0.10 ❷
        username: admin ❸
        password: s3cr3t ❹
        authorize: true ❺
        auth_pass: 3n4bl3s3cr3t ❻
```

❶   Set the connection to `local`, so every task is handled by Ansible, just like a local action.

❷ The domain name or IP address that our network device is reachable at

❸ The username to log in by SSH into the device

❹ Password user for login into the device

❺ With `authorize`, we tell the module to execute the command in privilege mode.

❻ And also pass the module the password to get into privilege mode

 Instead of passing the module arguments `username`, `password`, `authorize`, and `auth_pass` with each task, the following environment variables can be defined and will be used as a replacement: `ANSIBLE_NET_USERNAME`, `ANSIBLE_NET_PASSWORD`, `ANSIBLE_NET_AUTHORIZE`, and `ANSIBLE_NET_AUTH_PASS`.

These can help to reduce the boilerplate on each task. Keep in mind that these environment variables will be read for several network modules. However, each variable can always be overwritten by explicitly passing the module arguments, just as we did.

Is this it? Indeed, it is. Let's run this playbook:

```
$ ansible-playbook playbook.yml -v
No config file found; using defaults
[WARNING]: Host file not found: /etc/ansible/hosts

[WARNING]: provided hosts list is empty, only localhost is available

PLAY [localhost] ****************************************************************

TASK [set a hostname] **********************************************************
changed: [localhost] => {"changed": true, "updates": ["hostname sw1"],
"warnings": []}

PLAY RECAP *********************************************************************
localhost                  : ok=1    changed=1    unreachable=0    failed=0
```

Looks like it worked, but to verify, we log in to the device and double-check:

```
$ ssh admin@10.0.0.10
Password:

sw1>
```

Well, that did indeed work! We successfully executed our first playbook for our Cisco Catalyst.

Network modules are written to support idempotency. We can execute our playbook as many times as we want without changing and breaking anything!

Inventory and Variables for Network Modules

You may notice that the host target in our last playbook was defined as localhost. If we own a farm of Cisco Catalyst switches, creating a playbook for each with target localhost would not scale well and wouldn't be flexible enough, since we probably need different configurations and as a result different Ansible variables for each network device.

Let's go ahead the way we are familiar with and put the network devices into a static inventory file in Example 18-13 and save it as ./network_hosts.

Example 18-13. Hosts file containing our switches

```
[ios_switches]
sw1.example.com
```

We are now able to change the playbook target to ios_switches just the way we do in Example 18-14.

Example 18-14. Set the hostname on Cisco Catalyst

```
---
- hosts: ios_switches ❶
  gather_facts: no
  connection: local
  tasks:
  - name: set a hostname
    ios_config:
      lines: hostname sw1
      provider:
        host: 10.0.0.10
        username: admin
        password: s3cr3t
        authorize: true
        auth_pass: 3n4bl3s3cr3t
```

❶ Use ios_switches as target

Further, since we now have an inventory, we are able to use some internal Ansible variables. The variable inventory_hostname_short contains the host-part inventory

---

item (e.g., *sw1* in *sw1.example.com*). As a result, we are able to simplify our playbook as in Example 18-15.

Example 18-15. Use inventory_hostname_short for configuration

```
---
- hosts: ios_switches
  gather_facts: no
  connection: local
  tasks:
  - name: set a hostname
    ios_config:
      lines: hostname {{ inventory_hostname_short }} ❶
      provider:
        host: 10.0.0.10
        username: admin
        password: s3cr3t
        authorize: true
        auth_pass: 3n4bl3s3cr3t
```

❶ We make use of `inventory_hostname_short`.

Local Connection

It is a general pattern for network devices that playbooks always need to be executed with a local connection.

We take this setting away from the playbook and put it in a *group_vars/ios_switches* file as shown in Example 18-16.

Example 18-16. Group variable file for ios_switches

```
---
ansible_connection: local
```

Host Connection

When we look again at our playbook Example 18-15, we should also remove the configuration parameters of `ios_config`, which are likely different on each network device (e.g., the connection address `host`).

Much as we did for the *hostname*, we use an internal variable; this time it's `inventory_hostname`. In our case, `inventory_hostname` corresponds to the fully qualified domain name (FQDN) *sw1.example.com*. When this domain is resolvable by our name servers, this would be all we need. However, while we are still developing our setup, this might not be the case.

To not rely on the DNS entry, we make it a bit more flexible and create a variable net_host that is used for the connection. As a fallback, `inventory_hostname` should be used in case `net_host` is not defined.

This may sound a bit complicated, but the implementation is pretty simple. Have a look at Example 18-17.

Example 18-17. Use variable for the connection

```
---
- hosts: ios_switches
  gather_facts: no
  tasks:
  - name: set a hostname
    ios_config:
      lines: hostname {{ inventory_hostname_short }}
      provider:
        host: "{{ net_host | default(inventory_hostname) }}" ❶
        username: admin
        password: s3cr3t
        authorize: true
        auth_pass: 3n4bl3s3cr3t
```

❶ Use net_host variable and fall back to `inventory_hostname` variable for the connection.

Usually, it is a good practice to put host variables into `hosts_vars`.

Because this setting is somewhat related to connection, it is probably appropriate to put it into the inventory file *./network_hosts* as an inventory variable, just like Example 18-18.

Example 18-18. Add net_host to corresponding hosts entry

```
[ios_switches]
sw1.example.com  net_host=10.0.0.10
```

Authentication Variables

As a final step, we use variables for all authentication-related configurations. This provides the most flexibility.

The authentication configurations can be placed in `group_vars` in case all network devices in that group share the same configuration, and this is what we are going to do in Example 18-19.

Example 18-19. Group variable file for ios_switches

```
---
ansible_connection: local
net_username: admin
net_password: s3cr3t
net_authorize: true
net_auth_pass: 3n4bl3s3cr3t
```

Even when a few network devices have a different authentication configuration, these can be overwritten on the hosts_vars level.

Save the Config

It is time to save the configuration and make sure it will be used next time the device is rebooted. Luckily, the only thing to be added to our ios_config task is the parameter save with the value true.

For those of us who like to store backups, Ansible handles that as well. The Boolean parameter backup indicates that the running config should be backed up before applying any changes.

The backup will be downloaded into a file to the local directory *backup* beside your playbooks on the control host, where we run Ansible from. In case the directory *backup* has not yet been created, Ansible will create it for us:

```
$ ls backup/
switch1_config.2017-02-19@17:14:00
```

 The backup will contain the running config, not the startup config.

Our version of our playbook has now changed to Example 18-20.

Example 18-20. Final version of playbook, set hostname on Catalyst

```
---
- hosts: ios_switches
  gather_facts: no
  tasks:
  - name: set a hostname
    ios_config:
      lines: hostname {{ inventory_hostname_short }}
      provider:
        host: "{{ net_host | default(inventory_hostname) }}"
        username: "{{ net_username | default(omit) }}" ❶
```

```
        password: "{{ net_password | default(omit) }}" ❶
        authorize: "{{ net_authorize | default(omit) }}" ❶
        auth_pass: "{{ net_auth_pass | default(omit) }}" ❶
      backup: true ❷
      save: true ❸
```

❶ All these variables can be set on group_vars or host_vars level.

❷ Back up the running config into ./backup.

❸ Saves running-config to startup-config on the device.

> The parameters backup and save are handled like actions. These
> actions get executed even if no changes have been applied. I also
> noticed that the backup action does not report changed=True and
> that existing backups are automatically deleted before creating new
> ones.

Use Configs from a File

Working with the lines parameter is great for a few config tweaks. However, the way
I am used to managing devices is to have a full copy of the config saved locally as a
file. I make my modifications in the file, and copy it back into the device.

Fortunately, ios_config has another parameter for config files to the device: the src
parameter. This parameter allows us to have large static configuration parts as the file
ios_init_template.conf, as we see in Example 18-21.

Example 18-21. Example of a static IOS config as file

```
no service pad
service timestamps debug datetime msec
service timestamps log datetime msec
service password-encryption
boot-start-marker
boot-end-marker
aaa new-model
!
clock timezone CET 1 0
clock summer-time CEST recurring last Sun Mar 2:00 last Sun Oct 3:00
!
system mtu routing 1500
!
vtp mode transparent
!
ip dhcp snooping vlan 10-20
ip dhcp snooping
```

```
no ip domain-lookup
!
!
spanning-tree mode rapid-pvst
spanning-tree extend system-id
!
vlan internal allocation policy ascending
!
interface Vlan1
 no ip address
 no ip route-cache
 shutdown
!
ip default-gateway 10.0.0.1
no ip http server
no ip http secure-server
!
snmp-server community private
snmp-server community public RO
snmp-server location earth
snmp-server contact admin@example.com
!
ntp server 10.123.0.5
ntp server 10.100.222.12
!
```

No worries—I won't go through all these configurations. Instead, let's come back to our playbook of the previous section and extend it as in Example 18-22, including adding the task for using our static config from a file.

We now have two tasks configuring our network device. Using backup at each task would cause the device to make too many intermediate backups. We want only one backup of the running config, the one before any modification.

That is why we created an additional task just for the backup task at the beginning of the playbook. For the same reason, we added a handler for the save to run it only once and when something has changed.

Example 18-22. Use src with a static config file

```
---
- hosts: ios_switches
  gather_facts: no
  tasks:
  - name: backup the running config
    ios_config:
      backup: true
      provider:
        host: "{{ net_host | default(inventory_hostname) }}"
        username: "{{ net_username | default(omit) }}"
```

```
      password: "{{ net_password | default(omit) }}"
      authorize: "{{ net_authorize | default(omit) }}"
      auth_pass: "{{ net_auth_pass | default(omit) }}"

- name: init the static config
  ios_config:
    src: files/ios_init_config.conf ❶
    provider:
      host: "{{ net_host | default(inventory_hostname) }}"
      username: "{{ net_username | default(omit) }}"
      password: "{{ net_password | default(omit) }}"
      authorize: "{{ net_authorize | default(omit) }}"
      auth_pass: "{{ net_auth_pass | default(omit) }}"
  notify: save the running config ❷

- name: set a hostname
  ios_config:
    lines: hostname {{ inventory_hostname_short }}
    provider:
      host: "{{ net_host | default(inventory_hostname) }}"
      username: "{{ net_username | default(omit) }}"
      password: "{{ net_password | default(omit) }}"
      authorize: "{{ net_authorize | default(omit) }}"
      auth_pass: "{{ net_auth_pass | default(omit) }}"
  notify: save the running config ❷

handlers:
- name: save the running config
  ios_config:
    save: true
    provider:
      host: "{{ net_host | default(inventory_hostname) }}"
      username: "{{ net_username | default(omit) }}"
      password: "{{ net_password | default(omit) }}"
      authorize: "{{ net_authorize | default(omit) }}"
      auth_pass: "{{ net_auth_pass | default(omit) }}"
```

❶ Read an IOS config from a file located in *files/ios_init_config.conf*.

❷ Notify a handler to save the config.

At this point, we are already able to mix static and dynamic configs. Of course, we can extend the playbook for additional dynamic configs in the same way. However, we can even get even more advanced.

But before that, you may have noticed that there are a few large blocks of duplicate configs for the provider information. We should optimize that a bit, as shown in Example 18-23.

Example 18-23. Use src with a static config file

```
---
- hosts: ios_switches
  gather_facts: no
  vars:
    provider: ❶
      host: "{{ net_host | default(inventory_hostname) }}"
      username: "{{ net_username | default(omit) }}"
      password: "{{ net_password | default(omit) }}"
      authorize: "{{ net_authorize | default(omit) }}"
      auth_pass: "{{ net_auth_pass | default(omit) }}"
  tasks:
  - name: init the static config with backup before
    ios_config:
      backup: true ❷
      src: files/ios_init_config.conf
      provider: "{{ provider }}" ❸
    notify: save the running config

  - name: set a hostname
    ios_config:
      lines: hostname {{ inventory_hostname_short }}
      provider: "{{ provider }}" ❸
    notify: save the running config

  handlers:
  - name: save the running config
    ios_config:
      save: true
      provider: "{{ provider }}" ❸
```

❶ Use a `vars` clause with variable `provider` for the configuration in common.

❷ Because we have only one single task touching the config, we move the backup parameter to this task.

❸ Reuse the `provider` variable where needed.

> We can use `ios_config` with nothing other than the `backup` parameter to get a config template to start with.

OK, that looks good for the moment.

Templates, Templates, Templates

We have seen that the `src` parameter in `ios_config` can be used for static configs. But what about Jinja2 templates? Fortunately, `ios_config` has template support built in, as shown in Example 18-24.

Example 18-24. Use src for static config files and templates

```
---
- hosts: ios_switches
  gather_facts: no
  vars:
    provider:
      host: "{{ net_host | default(inventory_hostname) }}"
      username: "{{ net_username | default(omit) }}"
      password: "{{ net_password | default(omit) }}"
      authorize: "{{ net_authorize | default(omit) }}"
      auth_pass: "{{ net_auth_pass | default(omit) }}"
  tasks:
  - name: copy the static config
    ios_config:
      backup: true
      src: files/ios_init_config.conf.j2 ❶
      provider: "{{ provider }}"
    notify: save the running config

  handlers:
  - name: save the running config
    ios_config:
      save: true
      provider: "{{ provider }}"
```

❶ We created a template from the previous static config file and saved it as *files/ios_init_config.conf.j2* by convention.

We have turned our playbook into an adaptive Ansible IOS network device configuration playbook. All network device configurations, static and dynamic ones, can be handled within the template, as in Example 18-25.

Example 18-25. IOS config template, including dynamic configs for VLANs and interfaces

```
hostname {{ inventory_hostname_short }}

no service pad

service timestamps debug datetime msec
service timestamps log datetime msec
```

```
service password-encryption

boot-start-marker
boot-end-marker

clock timezone CET 1 0
clock summer-time CEST recurring last Sun Mar 2:00 last Sun Oct 3:00

ip dhcp snooping
no ip domain-lookup

spanning-tree mode rapid-pvst
spanning-tree extend system-id

vlan internal allocation policy ascending

!
{% if vlans is defined %} ❶
{% for vlan in vlans %}
vlan {{ vlan.id }}
 name {{ vlan.name }}
!
{% endfor %}
{% endif %}

{% if ifaces is defined %} ❶
{% for iface in ifaces %}
interface {{ iface.name}}
 description {{ iface.descr }}
{% if iface.vlans is defined %}
{% endif %}
 switchport access vlan {{ iface.vlans | join(',') }}
 spanning-tree portfast
!
{% endfor %}
{% endif %}

no ip http server
no ip http secure-server

snmp-server community public RO
snmp-server location earth
snmp-server contact admin@example.com
! add more configs here...
```

❶ Example of how to use a dynamic config within the template file

Since this is just a template, all aspects of the Jinja2 template engine can be used, including template inheritance and macros. At the time of writing, --diff does not return a diff output.

Let's run the playbook:

```
$ ansible-playbook playbook.yml -i network_hosts

PLAY [ios_switches] ********************************************************

TASK [copy the static config] *********************************************
changed: [switch1]

RUNNING HANDLER [save the running config] *********************************
changed: [switch1]

PLAY RECAP ****************************************************************
switch1                    : ok=2     changed=2    unreachable=0    failed=0
```

That was easy, wasn't it?

Gathering Facts

Collecting facts for network modules is implemented by use of a separate facts module—in our case, ios_facts.

> Use gather_facts: false in your play for network device
> playbooks.

Since we have already prepared all connection configurations in the previous section, we are ready to jump into the playbook in Example 18-26.

The ios_facts module has only one optional parameter: gather_subset. This parameter is used to limit wanted or filter unwanted facts by adding an explanation point (!). The default is !config, which corresponds to *all but config*.

Example 18-26. Collecting facts of an IOS device

```
---
- hosts: ios_switches
  gather_facts: no
  tasks:
  - name: gathering IOS facts
    ios_facts:
      gather_subset: hardware ❶
      host: "{{ net_host | default(inventory_hostname) }}"
      provider:
        username: "{{ net_username | default(omit) }}"
        password: "{{ net_password | default(omit) }}">
        authorize: "{{ net_authorize | default(omit) }}"
        auth_pass: "{{ net_auth_pass | default(omit) }}"
  - name: print out the IOS version
```

```
debug:
  var: ansible_net_version ❷
```

❶   Selecting hardware facts only

❷   All network facts start with the prefix ansible_net_

> Facts are injected to the Ansible host variables and do not need to
> be registered (e.g., register: result) on the task level.

Let's run the playbook:

```
$ ansible-playbook facts.yml -i network_hosts -v
No config file found; using defaults

PLAY [ios_switches] *********************************************************

TASK [get some facts] ******************************************************
ok: [switch1] => {"ansible_facts": {"ansible_net_filesystems": ["flash:"], "ansi
ble_net_gather_subset": ["hardware", "default"], "ansible_net_hostname": "sw1",
"ansible_net_image": "flash:c2960-lanbasek9-mz.150-1.SE/c2960-lanbasek9-mz.150-1
.SE.bin", "ansible_net_memfree_mb": 17292, "ansible_net_memtotal_mb": 20841,
"ansible_net_model": null, "ansible_net_serialnum": "FOC1132Z0ZA", "ansible_net_
version": "15.0(1)SE"}, "changed": false, "failed_commands": []}

TASK [print out the IOS version] *******************************************
ok: [switch1] => {
    "ansible_net_version": "15.0(1)SE"
}

PLAY RECAP *****************************************************************
switch1                    : ok=2    changed=0    unreachable=0    failed=0
```

Conclusion

Now you have a first impression about how to orchestrate and configure network
devices and get facts with Ansible. The ios_config, as well as the ios_facts module,
are common modules that exist with an identical feature set for different network
operation systems, (e.g., for Dell EMC Networking OS10—dellos10_config, or
Arista EOS—eos_config).

But depending on the operation system and the interface the network device provides, the amount and variety of the modules may differ quite a bit. I encourage you
to keep an eye on the docs (*http://bit.ly/2uvBe2f*) to find out more about other
modules.

## CHAPTER 19

Ansible Tower: Ansible for the Enterprise

Ansible Tower is a commercial software product originally created by Ansible, Inc. and now offered by Red Hat. Ansible Tower is implemented as a classical on-premises web service on top of Ansible. It provides a more granular user- and role-based access policy management combined with a web user interface, shown in Figure 19-1, and a RESTful API.

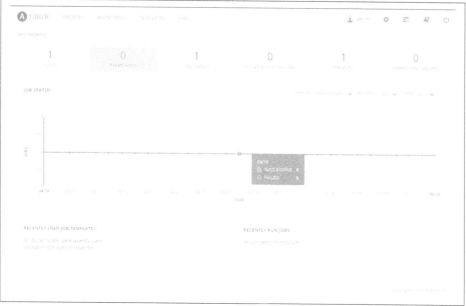

Figure 19-1. Ansible Tower dashboard

Subscription Models

Red Hat offers support as an annual subscription model with three subscription types, each with different service-level agreements (SLAs) (*https://access.redhat.com/support/offerings/production/sla*):

- Self-Support (no support and SLA)
- Standard (support and SLA: 8 × 5)
- Premium (support and SLA: 24 × 7)

All subscription levels include regular updates and releases of Ansible Tower. The Self-Support subscription model is limited to a maximum of 250 managed hosts and does not include the following features:

- Custom rebranding for login
- SAML, RADIUS, and LDAP authentication
- Multiorganization support
- Activity streams and system tracking

 After Red Hat acquired Ansible, Inc. in 2015, Red Hat committed to working on an open source version of Ansible Tower. At the time of writing, no further details and no specific timeline have been announced.

Try Ansible Tower

Red Hat provides a free trial license (*http://ansible.com/license*) with the feature set of the Self-Support subscription model for up to 10 managed hosts without expiration.

For a quick evaluation setup using Vagrant:

```
$ vagrant init ansible/tower
$ vagrant up --provider virtualbox
$ vagrant ssh
```

After we log in via SSH, we see a welcome screen similar to Example 19-1, where we can find the URL of the web interface, username, and password.

Example 19-1. Welcome screen

```
Welcome to Ansible Tower!

Log into the web interface here:

  https://10.42.0.42/

  Username: admin
  Password: JSKYmEBJATFn

The documentation for Ansible Tower is available here:

  http://www.ansible.com/tower/

For help, visit  http://support.ansible.com/
```

After login on the web interface, we are prompted for the license file, which we obtain by filling out a form and retrieving the license file by email.

 If the Vagrant machine is not reachable at *10.42.0.42*, you may need to run the following command inside the Vagrant machine to bring up the network interface associated with that IP address:

```
$ sudo systemctl restart network.service
```

What Ansible Tower Solves

Ansible Tower is not just a web user interface on top of Ansible. Ansible Tower extends Ansible's functionality in certain ways. Let's take a closer look in this section.

Access Control

In large organizations with many teams, Ansible Tower helps manage automation by organizing teams and employees into roles and giving each of them as much control of the managed hosts and devices as they need to fulfill their daily jobs.

Ansible Tower acts as a gatekeeper to hosts. When using Ansible Tower, no team or employee is required to have direct access to the managed hosts. This reduces complexity and increases security. Figure 19-2 shows Ansible Tower's web interface for user access.

Connecting Ansible Tower with existing authentication systems such as LDAP directories can reduce administrative cost per user.

Figure 19-2. Web interface for user access

Projects

A *project* in Ansible Tower terminology is nothing more than a bucket containing logically related playbooks and roles.

In classic Ansible projects, we often see that static inventories are kept along with the playbooks and roles. Ansible Tower handles inventories separately. Anything related to inventories and inventory variables kept in projects, such as group variables and host variables, will not be accessible later on.

> The target (e.g., hosts: <target>) in these playbooks is essential. Choose wisely by using a common name across playbooks. This allows you to use the playbooks with different inventories. We will discuss this further later in the chapter.

As it is a best practice, we keep our projects containing our playbooks in revision control on a source code management (SCM) system. The project management in Ansible Tower can be configured to download these projects from our SCM servers and supports major open source SCM systems such as Git, Mercurial, and Subversion.

As a fallback, even a static path can be set, where the project is stored locally on the Ansible Tower server, in case we do not want to use an SCM.

As most of our projects evolve over time, the projects on Ansible Tower server must be updated to be in sync with the SCM. But, no worries—Ansible Tower has multiple solutions for keeping projects up-to-date.

We can ensure that Ansible Tower has the latest state of our project by enabling "Update on Launch," as shown in Figure 19-3 on the project. Additionally, you can set a scheduled update job on each project to regularly update the project. Finally, you can manually update projects if you wish to maintain control of when updates happen.

Figure 19-3. Ansible Tower project SCM update options

Inventory Management

Ansible Tower allows you to manage inventories as dedicated resources. This also includes managing the access control for these inventories. A common pattern is to put the production, staging, and testing hosts into separate inventories.

Within these inventories, we will be able to add default variables and manually add groups and hosts. In addition, as shown in Figure 19-4, Ansible Tower allows you to query hosts dynamically from a source (e.g., from a VMware vCenter), and put these hosts in a group.

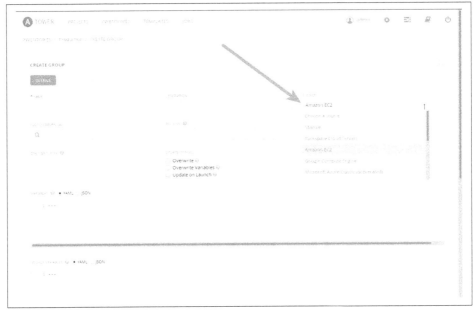

Figure 19-4. Ansible Tower inventory source

Group and host variables can be added in form fields that will overwrite defaults.

Hosts can even be temporarily disabled by clicking a button as in Figure 19-5, so they will be excluded from any job run.

Figure 19-5. Ansible Tower inventory excluded hosts

Run Jobs by Job Templates

Job templates, as shown in Figure 19-6, connect projects with inventories. They define how users are allowed to execute a playbook from a project to specific targets from a selected inventory.

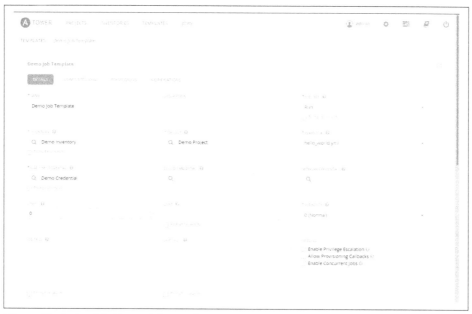

Figure 19-6. Ansible Tower job templates

Refinements on a playbook level, such as additional parameters and tags, can be applied. Further, you can specify in what *mode* the playbook will run (e.g., some users may be allowed to execute a playbook only in *check mode*, while others may be allowed to run the playbook only on a subset of hosts but in *live mode*).

On the target level, an inventory can be selected and optionally limited to some hosts or a group.

An executed job template creates a new so-called job entry, as shown in Figure 19-7.

Figure 19-7. Ansible Tower job entries

In the detail view of each job entry, shown in Figure 19-8, we find information not only about whether the job was successful but also at what date and time the job has been executed, when it finished, and who started it with which parameters.

We can even filter by play to see all the tasks and their results. All of this information is stored and kept in the database, which allows you to audit this information at any time.

Figure 19-8. Ansible Tower job detail view

RESTful API

The Ansible Tower server exposes a Representational State Transfer (REST) API that lets us integrate with existing build and deploy pipelines or continuous deployment systems.

As the API is browsable, we can inspect the whole API in our favorite browser by opening the URL *http://<tower_server>/api*:

```
$ firefox https://10.42.0.42/api
```

At the time of writing, the latest API version is v1. By clicking the appropriate link or just extend the URL to *http://<tower_server>/api/v1*, we get all the available resources as in Figure 19-9.

Figure 19-9. Ansible Tower API version 1

The latest API documentation can be found online (*http://docs.ansible.com/ansible-tower/*).

Ansible Tower CLI

So, how do we create a new user in Ansible Tower or launch a job by using nothing but the API? Of course, we could use the all-time favorite command-line (CLI) HTTP tool cURL, but Ansible has made an even more user-friendly CLI tool for us: `tower-cli`.

 Unlike the Ansible Tower application, Ansible Tower CLI is open source software published on GitHub (*https://github.com/ansible/tower-cli/*) under the Apache 2.0 license.

Installation

To install `tower-cli`, we use the Python package manager pip.

The `tower-cli` can be installed systemwide with the appropriate root permissions or, as we do, just for our local Linux user:

```
$ pip install ansible-tower-cli
```

If we choose to install on the user level, it will be installed into the path *~/.local/bin/*. Please make sure `~/.local/bin` is in our PATH.

```
$ echo 'export PATH=$PATH:$HOME/.local/bin' >> $HOME/.profile
$ source $HOME/.profile
```

Before we can access the API, we have to configure the credentials:

```
$ tower-cli config host 10.42.0.42
$ tower-cli config username admin
$ tower-cli config password JSKYmEBJATFn
```

Since Ansible Tower uses a self-signed SSL/TLS certificate preconfigured, we just skip the verification:

```
$ tower-cli config verify_ssl false
```

The default output called human provides just enough information. If we like more verbose output as a default, we probably want to change it to the yaml format. However, we can always append --format [human|json|yaml] to any command to overwrite the default:

```
$ tower-cli config format yaml
```

To verify, we simply run this:

```
$ tower-cli config
```

Create a User

Let's create a new user by using the tower-cli user command, as shown in Example 19-2. If we type this command without any further action, we will see a help output listing all actions available.

Example 19-2. Ansible Tower CLI user actions

```
$ tower-cli user
Usage: tower-cli user [OPTIONS] COMMAND [ARGS]...

  Manage users within Ansible Tower.

Options:
  --help  Show this message and exit.

Commands:
  create  Create a user.
  delete  Remove the given user.
  get     Return one and exactly one user.
  list    Return a list of users.
  modify  Modify an already existing user.
```

As it is a RESTful API, the actions (as in Example 19-2) are more or less consistent across the API, with a few exceptions. What differs per resource are the parameters and options for the resource. By running `tower-cli user create --help`, we will be shown all available parameters and options.

To create a user, only a few parameters are required:

```
$ tower-cli user create \
--username guy \
--password 's3cr3t$' \
--email 'guy@example.com' \
--first-name Guybrush \
--last-name Threepwood
```

The `tower-cli` has some logic built in, and in the default configuration, we can run the command multiple times without getting an error message. `tower-cli` queries the resource based on the key fields and will present the user we already created, as in Example 19-3.

Example 19-3. tower-cli output after creating or updating a user

```
changed: true
id: 2
type: user
url: /api/v1/users/2/
related:
  admin_of_organizations: /api/v1/users/2/admin_of_organizations/
  organizations: /api/v1/users/2/organizations/
  roles: /api/v1/users/2/roles/
  access_list: /api/v1/users/2/access_list/
  teams: /api/v1/users/2/teams/
  credentials: /api/v1/users/2/credentials/
  activity_stream: /api/v1/users/2/activity_stream/
  projects: /api/v1/users/2/projects/
created: '2017-02-05T11:15:37.275Z'
username: guy
first_name: Guybrush
last_name: Threepwood
email: guy@example.com
is_superuser: false
is_system_auditor: false
ldap_dn: ''
external_account: null
auth: []
```

However, `tower-cli` will not update the record if we change, for example, the email address. To achieve an update, we have two possibilities: appending `--force-on-exists` or explicitly using the action `modify` instead of `create`.

Launch a Job

One of the things we probably want to automate is running a job from a job template after a successful build on a continuous integration server.

The `tower-cli` makes this pretty straightforward. All we need to know is the name or ID of the job template we want to launch. Let's use the `list` action to list all available job templates:

```
$ tower-cli job_template list --format human
== ================= ========= ======= ===============
id      name         inventory project    playbook
== ================= ========= ======= ===============
 5 Demo Job Template         1       4 hello_world.yml
 7 Deploy App ..             1       5 app.yml
== ================= ========= ======= ===============
```

We have only two job templates available, and our choice is pretty easy. In a larger production-like setup, we probably see a larger set of job templates, and it would be much harder to find the wanted template. `tower_cli` has a few options to filter the output (e.g., by project, `--project <id>`; or by inventory, `--inventory`).

A more advanced way to filter a large set of job templates (e.g., "give me all job templates having this case-insensitive keyword in the name") would be to use the `--query` option.

A `--query` with the two arguments `name__icontains` and `deploy` would result in the following API URL:

```
https://10.42.0.42/api/v1/job_templates/?name__icontains=deploy
```

 All available filters can be found in the API documentation (*http://docs.ansible.com/ansible-tower/latest/html/towerapi/filtering.html*).

Running the list action with the wanted filter yields the expected result:

```
$ tower-cli job_template list --query name__icontains deploy --format human
== ============= ========= ======= ===============
id     name      inventory project    playbook
== ============= ========= ======= ===============
 7 Deploy App xy         1       4 hello_world.yml
== ============= ========= ======= ===============
```

Since we found the job template, we run it as in Example 19-4, with the action `job launch` and the argument `--job-template`, and the name or ID of the job template we selected.

Example 19-4. Launch job with tower-cli

```
$ tower-cli job launch --job-template 'Deploy App xy' --format human
Resource changed.
== ============ ======================= ======= =======
id job_template         created          status elapsed
== ============ ======================= ======= =======
11            7 2017-02-05T14:08:05.022Z pending
== ============ ======================= ======= =======
```

To monitor the job while it's running, the `tower-cli job` provides an action `monitor` with the job ID as argument. This command will run and wait until the job has finished.

```
tower-cli job monitor 11 --format human
Resource changed.
== ============ ======================= ========== =======
id job_template         created            status   elapsed
== ============ ======================= ========== =======
11            5 2017-02-05T13:57:30.504Z successful   6.486
== ============ ======================= ========== =======
```

Using a bit of command-line magic and jq (*https://stedolan.github.io/jq/*), we can even combine the launching and the monitoring in one line:

```
tower-cli job monitor $(tower-cli job launch --job-template 5 --format json | jq '.id')
```

Onward

As this chapter ends, so does our journey together. And yet, your journey with Ansible is just beginning. We hope that you'll come to enjoy working with it as much as we do, and that the next time you encounter colleagues in clear need of an automation tool, you'll show them how Ansible can make their lives easier.

SSH

Because Ansible uses SSH as its transport mechanism, you'll need to understand some of SSH's features to take advantage of them with Ansible.

Native SSH

By default, Ansible uses the native SSH client installed on your operating system. Ansible can take advantage of all the typical SSH features, including Kerberos and jump hosts. If you have an *~/.ssh/config* file with custom configurations for your SSH setup, Ansible will respect these settings.

SSH Agent

A handy program called `ssh-agent` simplifies working with SSH private keys.

When `ssh-agent` is running on your machine, you can add private keys to it by using the `ssh-add` command:

```
$ ssh-add /path/to/keyfile.pem
```

 The SSH_AUTH_SOCK environment variable must be set, or the `ssh-add` command will not be able to communicate with `ssh-agent`. See "Starting Up ssh-agent" on page 365.

You can use the `-l` or `L` flag with the `ssh_add` program to see which keys have been added to your agent, as shown in Example A-1. This example shows that there are two keys in the agent.

Example A-1. Listing the keys in the agent

```
$ ssh-add -l
2048 SHA256:o7H/I9rRZupXHJ7JnDi10RhSzeAKYiRVrlH9L/JFtfA /Users/lorin/.ssh/id_rsa
2048 SHA256:xLTmHqvHHDIdcrHiHdtoOXxq5sm9DOEVi+/jnObkKKM insecure_private_key

$ ssh-add -L
ssh-rsa AAAAB3NzaC1yc2EAAAADAQABAAAABAQDWAfog5tz4W9bPVbPDlNC8HWMfhjTgKOhpSZYI+clc
 e3/pz5viqsHDQIjzSImoVzIOTV0tOIfE8qMkqEYk7igESccCy0zN9VnD6EfYVkEx1C+xqkCtZTEVuQn
 d+4qyo222EAVkHm6bAhgyoA9nt9Um9WFO0045yHZL2Do9Z7KXTS4xOqeGF5vv7SiuKcsLjORPcWcYqC
 fYdrdUdRD9dFq7zFKmpCPJqNwDQDrXbgaTOe+H6cu2f4RrJLp88WY8voB3zJ7avv68eOgah82dovSgw
 hcsZp4SycZSTy+WqZQhzLogaifvtdgdzaooxNtsm+qRvQJyHkwdoXR6nJgt /Users/lorin/.ssh/i
 d_rsa
ssh-rsa AAAAB3NzaC1yc2EAAAABIwAAAQEA6NF8iallvQVp22WDkTkyrtvp9eWW6A8YVr+kz4TjGYe7
 gHzIw+niNltGEFHzD8+v1I2YJ6oXevct1YeS0o9HZyN1Q9qgCgzUFtdOKLv6IedplqoPkcmF0aYet2P
 kEDo3MlTBckFXPITAMzF8dJSIFo9D8HfdOV0IAdx4O7PtixWKn5y2hMNG0zQPyUecp4pzC6kivAIhyf
 HiLFR61RGL+GPXQ2MWZWFYbAGjyiYJnAmCP3NOTd0jMZEnDkbUvxhMmBYSdETk1rRgm+R4LOzFUGaHq
 HDFIPKcF96hrucXzcWyLbIbEgE980HlnVYCzRdK8jlqm8tehUc9c9WhQ== insecure_private_key
```

When you try to make a connection to a remote host, and you have ssh-agent running, the SSH client will try to use the keys stored in ssh-agent to authenticate with the host.

Using an SSH agent has several advantages:

- The SSH agent makes it easier to work with encrypted SSH private keys. If you use an encrypted SSH private key, the private key file is protected with a password. When you use this key to make an SSH connection to a host, you will be prompted to type in the password. With an encrypted private key, even if somebody got access to your private SSH key, they wouldn't be able to use it without the password. If you use an encrypted SSH private key, and you aren't using an SSH agent, then you have to type in the encryption password each time you use the private key. If you are using an SSH agent, you have to type the private-key password only when you add the key to the agent.

- If you are using Ansible to manage hosts that use different SSH keys, using an SSH agent simplifies your Ansible configuration files; you don't have to explicitly specify the ansible_private_key_file on your hosts as we did back in Example 1-1.

- If you need to make an SSH connection from your remote host to a different host (e.g., cloning a private Git repository over SSH), you can take advantage of *agent forwarding* so that you don't have to copy private SSH keys over to the remote host. We explain agent forwarding next.

Starting Up ssh-agent

How you start up the SSH agent varies depending on which operating system you're running.

macOS

macOS comes preconfigured to run `ssh-agent`, so there's nothing you need to do.

Linux

If you're running on Linux, you'll need to start up `ssh-agent` yourself and ensure that its environment variables are set correctly. If you invoke `ssh-agent` directly, it will output the environment variables you'll need to set. For example:

```
$ ssh-agent
SSH_AUTH_SOCK=/tmp/ssh-YI7PBGlkOteo/agent.2547; export SSH_AUTH_SOCK;
SSH_AGENT_PID=2548; export SSH_AGENT_PID;
echo Agent pid 2548;
```

You can automatically export these environment variables by invoking `ssh-agent` like this:

```
$ eval $(ssh-agent)
```

You'll also want to ensure that you have only one instance of `ssh-agent` running at a time. There are various helper tools on Linux, such as *Keychain* and *Gnome Keyring*, for managing `ssh-agent` startup for you, or you can modify your *.profile* file to ensure that `ssh-agent` starts up exactly once in each login shell. Configuring your account for `ssh-agent` is beyond the scope of this book, so I recommend you consult your Linux distribution's documentation for more details on how to set this up.

Agent Forwarding

If you are cloning a Git repository over SSH, you'll need to use an SSH private key recognized by your Git server. I like to avoid copying private SSH keys to my hosts, in order to limit the damage in case a host ever gets compromised.

One way to avoid copying SSH private keys around is to use the `ssh-agent` program on your local machine, with agent forwarding. If you SSH from your laptop to host *A*, and you have agent forwarding enabled, then agent forwarding allows you to SSH from host *A* to host *B* by using the private key that resides on your laptop.

Figure A-1 shows an example of agent forwarding in action. Let's say you want to check out a private repository from GitHub, using SSH. You have `ssh-agent` running on your laptop, and you've added your private key by using the `ssh-add` command.

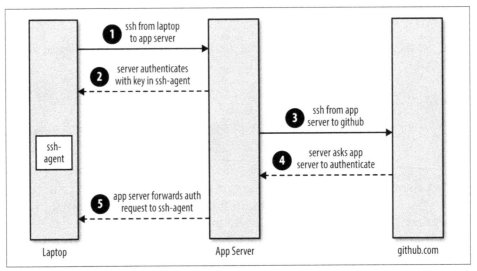

Figure A-1. Agent forwarding in action

If you were manually SSHing to the app server, you would call the ssh command with the -A flag, which enables agent forwarding:

```
$ ssh -A myuser@myappserver.example.com
```

On the app server, you check out a Git repository by using an SSH URL:

```
$ git clone git@github.com:lorin/mezzanine-example.git
```

Git connects via SSH to GitHub. The GitHub SSH server tries to authenticate against the SSH client on the app server. The app server doesn't know your private key. However, because you enabled agent forwarding, the SSH client on the app server connects back to ssh-agent running on your laptop, which handles the authentication.

There are a couple of issues you need to keep in mind in using agent forwarding with Ansible.

First, you need to tell Ansible to enable agent forwarding when it connects to remote machines, because SSH does not enable agent forwarding by default. You can enable agent forwarding for all nodes you SSH to by adding the following lines to your ~/.ssh/config file on your control machine:

```
Host *
    ForwardAgent yes
```

Or, if you want to enable agent forwarding for only a specific server, add this:

```
Host appserver.example.com
    ForwardAgent yes
```

If, instead, you want to enable agent forwarding only for Ansible, you can edit your *ansible.cfg* file by adding it to the `ssh_args` parameter in the `ssh_connection` section:

```
[ssh_connection]
ssh_args = -o ControlMaster=auto -o ControlPersist=60s -o ForwardAgent=yes
```

Here, I used the more verbose `-o ForwardAgent=yes` flag instead of the shorter `-A` flag, but it does the same thing.

The `ControlMaster` and `ControlPersist` settings are needed for a performance optimization called *SSH multiplexing*. They are on by default, but if you override the `ssh_args` variable, then you need to explicitly specify them or you will disable this performance boost. We discuss SSH multiplexing in Chapter 11.

Sudo and Agent Forwarding

When you enable agent forwarding, the remote machine sets the `SSH_AUTH_SOCK` environment variable, which contains a path to a Unix-domain socket (e.g., */tmp/ssh-FShDVu5924/agent.5924*). However, if you use `sudo`, the `SSH_AUTH_SOCK` environment variable won't carry over unless you explicitly configure `sudo` to allow this behavior.

To allow the `SSH_AUTH_SOCK` variable to carry over via `sudo` to the root user, we can add the following line either to the */etc/sudoers* file or (on Debian-based distributions like Ubuntu) to its own file in the */etc/sudoers.d* directory:

```
Defaults>root env_keep+=SSH_AUTH_SOCK
```

Let's call this file *99-keep-ssh-auth-sock-env* and put it in the files directory on our local machine.

Validating Files

The `copy` and `template` modules support a `validate` clause. This clause lets you specify a program to run against the file that Ansible will generate. Use `%s` as a placeholder for the filename. For example:

```
validate: visudo -cf %s
```

When the `validate` clause is present, Ansible will copy the file to a temporary directory first and then run the specified validation program. If the validation program returns success (0), Ansible will copy the file from the temporary location to the proper destination. If the validation program returns a nonzero return code, Ansible will return an error that looks like this:

```
failed: [myhost] => {"checksum": "ac32f572f0a670c3579ac2864cc3069ee8a19588",
"failed": true}
msg: failed to validate: rc:1 error:

FATAL: all hosts have already failed -- aborting
```

Since a bad sudoers file on a host can prevent us from accessing the host as root, it's always a good idea to validate a sudoers file by using the *visudo* program. For a cautionary tale about invalid sudoers files, see Ansible contributor Jan-Piet Mens's blog post, "Don't try this at the office: /etc/sudoers" (*http://bit.ly/1DfeQY7*).

```
- name: copy the sudoers file so we can do agent forwarding
  copy:
    src: files/99-keep-ssh-auth-sock-env
    dest: /etc/sudoers.d/99-keep-ssh-auth-sock-env
    owner: root group=root mode=0440
    validate: visudo -cf %s
```

Unfortunately, it's not currently possible to sudo as a nonroot user and use agent forwarding. For example, let's say you want to sudo from the ubuntu user to a deploy user. The problem is that the Unix-domain socket pointed to the SSH_AUTH_SOCK is owned by the ubuntu user and won't be readable or writeable by the deploy user.

As a workaround, you can always invoke the Git module as root and then change the permissions with the file module, as shown in Example A-2.

Example A-2. Cloning as root and changing permissions

```
- name: verify the config is valid sudoers file
  local_action: command visudo -cf files/99-keep-ssh-auth-sock-env
  sudo: True

- name: copy the sudoers file so we can do agent forwarding
  copy:
    src: files/99-keep-ssh-auth-sock-env
    dest: /etc/sudoers.d/99-keep-ssh-auth-sock-env
    owner: root
    group: root
    mode: "0440"
    validate: 'visudo -cf %s'
  sudo: True

- name: check out my private git repository
  git:
    repo: git@github.com:lorin/mezzanine-example.git
    dest: "{{ proj_path }}"
  sudo: True

- name: set file ownership
```

```
file:
  path: "{{ proj_path }}"
  state: directory
  recurse: yes
  owner: "{{ user }}"
  group: "{{ user }}"
sudo: True
```

Host Keys

Every host that runs an SSH server has an associated host key. The host key acts like a
signature that uniquely identifies the host. Host keys exist to prevent man-in-the-
middle attacks. If you're cloning a Git repository over SSH from GitHub, you don't
know whether the server that claims to be *github.com* is really GitHub's server, or is an
impostor that used DNS spoofing to pretend to be *github.com*. Host keys allow you to
check that the server claiming to be *github.com* really is *github.com*. This means that
you need to have the host key (a copy of what the signature should look like) before
you try to connect to the host.

Ansible will check the host key by default, although you can disable this behavior in
ansible.cfg, like this:

```
[defaults]
host_key_checking = False
```

Host-key checking also comes into play with the `git` module. Recall in Chapter 6 how
the `git` module took an `accept_hostkey` parameter:

```
- name: check out the repository on the host
  git: repo={{ repo_url }} dest={{ proj_path }} accept_hostkey=yes
```

The `git` module can hang when cloning a Git repository by using the SSH protocol if
host-key checking is enabled on the host and the Git server's SSH host key is not
known to the host.

The simplest approach is to use the `accept_hostkey` parameter to tell Git to automatically accept the host key if it isn't known, which is the approach we use in
Example 6-6.

Many people simply accept the host key and don't worry about these types of man-in-
the-middle attacks. That's what we did in our playbook, by specifying `accept_host
key=yes` as an argument when invoking the `git` module. However, if you are more
security conscious and don't want to automatically accept the host key, you can manually retrieve and verify GitHub's host key, and then add it to the systemwide */etc/ssh/known_hosts* file or, for a specific user, to the user's *~/.ssh/known_hosts*
file.

To manually verify GitHub's SSH host key, you'll need to get the SSH host-key fingerprint from the Git server by using some kind of out-of-band channel. If you're using GitHub as your Git server, you can look up its SSH key fingerprint (*http://bit.ly/1DffcxK*) on the GitHub website.

As of this writing, GitHub's base64-formatted SHA256 RSA fingerprint (newer format)[1] is `SHA256:nThbg6kXUpJWGl7E1IGOCspRomTxdCARLviKw6E5SY8`, and its hex-encoded MD5 RSA fingerprint (older format) is `16:27:ac:a5:76:28:2d:36:63:1b:56:4d:eb:df:a6:48`, but don't take our word for it—go check the website.

Next, you need to retrieve the full SSH host key. You can use the `ssh-keyscan` program to retrieve the host key associated with the host with hostname *github.com*. I like to put files that Ansible will deal with in the *files* directory, so let's do that:

```
$ mkdir files
$ ssh-keyscan github.com > files/known_hosts
```

The output looks like this:

```
github.com ssh-rsa
AAAAB3NzaC1yc2EAAAABIwAAAQEAq2A7hRGmdnm9tUDbO9IDSwBK6TbQa+PXYPCPy6rbTrTtw7PHkccK
rpp0yVhp5HdEIcKr6pLlVDBfOLX9QUsyCOV0wzfjIJNlGEYsdlLJizHhbn2mUjvSAHQqZETYP81eFzLQ
NnPHt4EVVUh7VfDESU84KezmD5QlWpXLmvU31/yMf+Se8xhHTvKSCZIFImWwoG6mbUoWf9nzpIoaSjB+
weqqUUmpaaasXVal72J+UX2B+2RPW3RcT0eOzQgqlJL3RKrTJvdsjE3JEAvGq3lGHSZXy28G3skua2Sm
Vi/w4yCE6gbODqnTWlg7+wC604ydGXA8VJiS5ap43JXiUFFAaQ==
```

For the more paranoid, the `ssh-keyscan` command supports an `-H` flag so that the hostname won't show up in the *known_hosts* file. Even if somebody gets access to your known hosts file, they can't tell what the hostnames are. When using this flag, the output looks like this:

```
|1|BI+Z8H3hzbcmTWna9R4orrwrNrg=|wCxJf50pTQ83JFzyXG4aNLxEmzc= ssh-rsa AAAAB3NzaC1y
c2EAAAABIwAAAQEAq2A7hRGmdnm9tUDbO9IDSwBK6TbQa+PXYPCPy6rbTrTtw7PHkccKrpp0yVhp5HdEI
cKr6pLlVDBfOLX9QUsyCOV0wzfjIJNlGEYsdlLJizHhbn2mUjvSAHQqZETYP81eFzLQNnPHt4EVVUh7Vf
DESU84KezmD5QlWpXLmvU31/yMf+Se8xhHTvKSCZIFImWwoG6mbUoWf9nzpIoaSjB+weqqUUmpaaasXVa
l72J+UX2B+2RPW3RcT0eOzQgqlJL3RKrTJvdsjE3JEAvGq3lGHSZXy28G3skua2SmVi/w4yCE6gbODqnT
Wlg7+wC604ydGXA8VJiS5ap43JXiUFFAaQ==
```

You then need to verify that the host key in the *files/known_hosts* file matches the fingerprint you found on GitHub. You can check with the `ssh-keygen` program:

```
$ ssh-keygen -lf files/known_hosts
```

The output should match the RSA fingerprint advertised on the website, like this:

```
2048 SHA256:nThbg6kXUpJWGl7E1IGOCspRomTxdCARLviKw6E5SY8 github.com (RSA)
```

---

1 OpenSSH 6.8 changed the default fingerprint format from hex MD5 to base64 SHA256.

Now that you are confident that you have the correct host key for your Git server, you can use the copy module to copy it to */etc/ssh/known_hosts*.

```
- name: copy system-wide known hosts
  copy: src=files/known_hosts dest=/etc/ssh/known_hosts owner=root group=root
    mode=0644
```

Alternatively, you can copy it to a specific user's *~/.ssh/known_hosts*. Example A-3 shows how to copy the known hosts file from the control machine to the remote hosts.

Example A-3. Adding known host

```
- name: ensure the ~/.ssh directory exists
  file: path=~/.ssh state=directory
- name: copy known hosts file
  copy: src=files/known_hosts dest=~/.ssh/known_hosts mode=0600
```

A Bad Host Key Can Cause Problems, Even with Key Checking Disabled

If you have disabled host-key checking in Ansible by setting host_key_checking to false in your *ansible.cfg* file, and the host key for the host that Ansible is trying to connect to does not match the key entry in your *~/.ssh/known_hosts* file, then agent forwarding won't work. Trying to clone a Git repository will then result in an error that looks like this:

```
TASK: [check out the repository on the host] ********************************
failed: [web] => {"cmd": "/usr/bin/git ls-remote git@github.com:lorin/
mezzanine- example.git -h refs/heads/HEAD", "failed": true, "rc": 128}
stderr: Permission denied (publickey).
fatal: Could not read from remote repository.

Please make sure you have the correct access rights
and the repository exists.

msg: Permission denied (publickey).
fatal: Could not read from remote repository.

Please make sure you have the correct access rights
and the repository exists.

FATAL: all hosts have already failed -- aborting
```

This can happen if you're using Vagrant, and you destroy a Vagrant machine and then create a new one, because the host key changes every time you create a new Vagrant machine. You can check whether agent forwarding is working by doing this:

```
$ ansible web -a "ssh-add -l"
```

If it's working, you'll see output like this:

```
web | success | rc=0 >>
2048 SHA256:ScSt41+elNd0YkvRXW2nGapX6AZ8MP1J1UNg/qalBUs /Users/lorin/.ssh
/id_rsa (RSA)
```

If it's not working, you'll see output like this:

```
web | FAILED | rc=2 >>
Could not open a connection to your authentication agent.
```

If this happens to you, delete the appropriate entry from your ~/.ssh/known_hosts file.

Note that because of SSH multiplexing, Ansible maintains an open SSH connection to the host for 60 seconds, and you need to wait for this connection to expire, or you won't see the effect of modifying the known_hosts file.

Clearly, a lot more work is involved in verifying an SSH host key than blindly accepting it. As is often the case, there's a trade-off between security and convenience.

Using IAM Roles for EC2 Credentials

If you're going to run Ansible inside a VPC, you can take advantage of Amazon's Identity and Access Management (IAM) roles so that you do not even need to set environment variables to pass your EC2 credentials to the instance. Amazon's IAM roles let you define users and groups and control what those users and groups are permitted to do with EC2 (e.g., get information about your running instances, create instances, create images). You can also assign IAM roles to running instances, so you can effectively say, "This instance is allowed to start other instances."

When you make requests against EC2 by using a client program that supports IAM roles, and an instance is granted permissions by an IAM role, the client will fetch the credentials from the EC2 instance metadata service (*http://amzn.to/1Cu0fTl*) and use those to make requests against the EC2 service end point.

You can create an IAM role through the Amazon Web Services (AWS) Management Console, or at the command line by using the AWS Command-Line Interface tool (AWS CLI (*http://aws.amazon.com/cli/*)).

AWS Management Console

Here's how to use the AWS Management Console to create an IAM role that has Power User Access, meaning that it is permitted to do pretty much anything with AWS except modify IAM users and groups:

1. Log in to the AWS Management Console (*https://console.aws.amazon.com*).
2. Search for and then click IAM.
3. Click "Roles at the left.
4. Click the Create New Role button.

5. Give your role a name and then click Next Step. I like to use `ansible` as the name for the role for my instance that will run Ansible.

6. Under AWS Service Roles, select Amazon EC2.

7. Search for and select PowerUserAccess, and then click Next Step.

8. Click Create Role.

Once the role is created, if you select it and click Show Policy, you should see a JSON document that looks like Example B-1.

Example B-1. IAM power user policy document

```
{
  "Version": "2012-10-17",
  "Statement": [
    {
      "Effect": "Allow",
      "NotAction": ["iam:*", "organizations:*"],
      "Resource": "*"
    },{
      "Effect": "Allow",
      "Action": "organizations:DescribeOrganization",
      "Resource": "*"
    }
  ]
}
```

When you create a role through the web interface, AWS also automatically creates an *instance profile* with the same name as the role (e.g., `ansible`), and associates the role with the instance profile name. When you create an instance with the ec2 module, if you pass the instance profile name as the `instance_profile_name` parameter, then the created instance will have the permissions of that role.

Command-Line

You can also create the role and the instance profile by using the AWS CLI tool, but it's a bit more work. You need to do the following:

1. Create a role, specifying the trust policy. The trust policy describes the entities that can assume the role and the access conditions for the role.

2. Create a policy that describes what the role is permitted to do. In our case, we want to create the equivalent of the power user, where the role can perform any AWS-related action except manipulate IAM roles and groups.

3. Create an instance profile.

4. Associate the role with the instance profile.

You'll need to create two IAM policy files first, which are in JSON format. The trust policy is shown in Example B-2. This is the same trust policy that AWS automatically generates when you create the role via the web interface.

The role policy that describes what the role is allowed to do is shown in Example B-3.

Example B-2. trust-policy.json

```
{
  "Version": "2012-10-17",
  "Statement": [
    {
      "Sid": "",
      "Effect": "Allow",
      "Principal": {
        "Service": "ec2.amazonaws.com"
      },
      "Action": "sts:AssumeRole"
    }
  ]
}
```

Example B-3. power-user.json

```
{
  "Version": "2012-10-17",
  "Statement": [
    {
      "Effect": "Allow",
      "NotAction": "iam:*",
      "Resource": "*"
    }
  ]
}
```

Example B-4 shows how to create an instance profile on the command line, after you've created the files shown in Examples B-2 and B-3.

Example B-4. Creating an instance profile at the command line

```
# Make sure that trust-policy.json and power-user.json are in the
# current directory, or change the file:// arguments to include the
# complete path

$ aws iam create-role --role-name ansible --assume-role-policy-document \
  file://trust-policy.json
$ aws iam put-role-policy --role-name ansible --policy-name \
```

```
PowerUserAccess-ansible-20170214 --policy-document file://power-user.json
$ aws iam create-instance-profile --instance-profile-name ansible
$ aws iam add-role-to-instance-profile --instance-profile-name ansible \
  --role-name ansible
```

As you can see, it's much simpler to do this via the web interface, but if you want to automate this, then you can use the command line instead. Check out the AWS Identity and Access Management User Guide (*http://docs.aws.amazon.com/IAM/latest/UserGuide*) for more details on IAM.

Once you've created the instance profile, you can then launch an EC2 instance with that instance profile. You can do this with the ec2 module by using the instance_pro file_name parameter:

```
- name: launch an instance with iam role
  ec2:
    instance_profile_name: ansible
    # Other parameters not shown
```

If you SSH into this instance, you can query the EC2 metadata service to confirm that this instance is associated with the Ansible profile. The output should look something like this:

```
$ curl http://169.254.169.254/latest/meta-data/iam/info
{
  "Code" : "Success",
  "LastUpdated" : "2014-11-17T02:44:03Z",
  "InstanceProfileArn" : "arn:aws:iam::549704298184:instance-profile/ansible",
  "InstanceProfileId" : "AIPAINM7F44YGDNIBHPYC"
}
```

You can also directly inspect the credentials, although it's not something you need to do. The Boto library will automatically retrieve these credentials when the Ansible ec2 modules or dynamic inventory script executes:

```
$ curl http://169.254.169.254/latest/meta-data/iam/security-credentials/ansible
{
  "Code" : "Success",
  "LastUpdated" : "2015-02-09T21:45:20Z",
  "Type" : "AWS-HMAC",
  "AccessKeyId" : "ASIAIYXCUETJPY42AC2Q",
  "SecretAccessKey" : "ORp9gldiymIKH9+rFtWEx8BjGRteNTQSRnLnlmWq",
  "Token" : "AQoDYXdzEGca4AMPC5W69pvtENpXjw79oH9...",
  "Expiration" : "2015-02-10T04:10:36Z"
}
```

These credentials are temporary, and Amazon will rotate them automatically for you.

You can now use this instance as your control machine, without needing to specify your credentials via environment variables. The Ansible ec2 modules will automatically retrieve the credentials from the metadata service.

Glossary

Alias

A name of a host in the inventory that is different from the actual hostname of the host.

AMI

Amazon Machine Image, a virtual machine image in the Amazon Elastic Compute Cloud, also known as *EC2*.

Ansible, Inc.

The company that manages the Ansible project.

Ansible Galaxy

A repository (*https://galaxy.ansible.com*) of Ansible roles contributed by the community.

Ansible Tower

A proprietary web-based dashboard and REST interface for controlling Ansible, sold by Ansible, Inc.

Check mode

An optional mode when running a playbook. When check mode is enabled, and when Ansible executes a playbook, it will not make any changes to remote hosts. Instead, it will simply report whether each task would have changed the state of the host. Sometimes referred to as *dry run* mode.

CIDR

Classless interdomain routing, a notation for specifying a range of IP addresses, used when defining Amazon EC2 security groups.

Configuration management

A process for ensuring that servers are in the proper state for doing their job. By *state*, we mean things like the configuration files for server applications have the correct values, the proper files are present, the correct services are running, the expected user accounts are present, permissions are set correctly, and so on.

Convergence

A property of configuration management systems whereby the system will execute multiple times against a server in order to get the server to reach the desired state, with each execution bringing the server closer to the desired state. Convergence is most closely associated with the CFEngine configuration management system. Convergence doesn't really apply to Ansible, which puts servers into desired states after a single execution.

Complex arguments

Arguments passed to modules that are of type list or dictionary.

Container

A form of server virtualization in which the virtualization is implemented at the operating system level, so that the virtual machine instance shares the same kernel as the host. Docker is the most well-known container technology.

Control machine
The computer that you run Ansible on that is used to control the remote hosts.

Control socket
A Unix domain socket that SSH clients use to connect to a remote host when SSH multiplexing is enabled.

ControlPersist
A synonym for SSH multiplexing.

Declarative
A type of programming language in which the programmer describes the desired output, not the procedure for how to compute the output. Ansible's playbooks are declarative. SQL is another example of a declarative language. Contrast with *procedural* languages, such as Java and Python.

Deployment
The process of bringing software up onto a live system.

DevOps
IT buzzword that gained popularity in the mid-2010s.

Dry run
See *Check mode*.

DSL
Domain-specific language. In systems that use DSLs, the user interacts with the systems by writing text files in the domain-specific language and then runs those files through the system. DSLs are not as powerful as general-purpose programming languages, but (if designed well) they are easier to read and write than general-purpose programming languages. Ansible exposes a DSL that uses YAML syntax.

Dynamic inventory
Source that provides Ansible with information about hosts and groups at playbook execution time.

EBS
Elastic Block Store. On Amazon EC2, an EBS refers to a persistent disk that can be attached to instances.

Fact
A variable that contains information about a specific host.

Glob
A pattern used by Unix shells to match against filenames. For example, `*.txt` is a glob that matches all files that end in `.txt`.

Group
A named collection of hosts.

Handler
Similar to a task, except that handlers execute only in response to a task that is configured to notify the handler on change of state.

Host
A remote server managed by Ansible.

IAM
Identity and Access Management, a feature of Amazon's Elastic Compute Cloud that allows you to manage user and group permissions.

Idempotent
An action is idempotent if executing the action multiple times has the same effect as executing it once.

Instance
A virtual machine. The term is commonly used to refer to a virtual machine running inside an infrastructure-as-a-service cloud, such as Amazon's Elastic Cloud Compute (EC2).

Inventory
The list of hosts and groups.

Lookups
Code that executes on the control machine to obtain some configuration data needed by Ansible while a playbook is running.

Module

Ansible script that performs one specific task. Examples include creating a user account, installing a package, or starting a service. Most Ansible modules are idempotent.

Orchestration

Performing a series of tasks in a well-specified order on a collection of servers. Orchestration is often needed for performing deployments.

Pattern

Ansible syntax for describing which hosts to run a play against.

Play

Associates a set of hosts with a list of tasks to perform on that host.

Playbook

An Ansible script. It specifies a list of plays and a collection of hosts to execute the plays against.

Registered variable

A variable created by using the `register` clause in a task.

Role

An Ansible mechanism for bundling together a collection of tasks, handlers, files, templates, and variables.

For example, an `nginx` role might contain tasks for installing the Nginx package, generating the Nginx configuration file, copying TLS certificate files, and starting the Nginx service.

SSH multiplexing

A feature of the OpenSSH SSH client that can reduce the time it takes to make an SSH connection when making multiple SSH connections to the same machine. Ansible uses SSH multiplexing by default to improve performance.

Task

The unit of work in an Ansible play. A task specifies a module and its arguments, as well as an optional name and some additional optional parameters.

TLS

Transport Layer Security, a protocol used to secure communications between web servers and browsers. TLS superseded an earlier protocol called *Secure Sockets Layer* (SSL). Many people refer to TLS incorrectly as SSL.

Transport

The protocol and implementation Ansible uses to connect to the remote host. The default transport is SSH.

Vault

A mechanism used by Ansible for encrypting sensitive data on disk. Typically used to safely store secret data in a version-control system.

Vagrant

A tool for managing virtual machines, intended for use by developers to create reproducible development environments.

Virtualenv

A mechanism for installing Python packages into an environment that can be activated and deactivated. Enables a user to install Python packages without root access and without polluting the global Python package library on the machine.

VPC

Virtual Private Cloud. A term used by Amazon EC2 to describe an isolated network you can create for your EC2 instances.

Bibliography

Hashimoto, Mitchell. *Vagrant: Up and Running*. O'Reilly Media, 2013.

Hunt, Andrew; Thomas, David. *The Pragmatic Programmer: From Journeyman to Master*. Addison-Wesley, 1999.

Jaynes, Matt. *Taste Test: Puppet, Chef, Salt, Ansible*. Publisher, 2014.

Kleppmann, Martin. *Designing Data-Intensive Applications*. O'Reilly Media, 2015.

Kurniawan, Yan. *Ansible for AWS*. Leanpub, 2016.

Limoncelli, Thomas A.; Hogan, Christina J.; Chalup, Strata R. *The Practice of Cloud System Administration: Designing and Operating Large Distributed Systems*. Addison-Wesley Professional, 2014.

Mell, Peter; Grance, Timothy. *The NIST Definition of Cloud Computing*. NIST Special Publication 800-145, 2011.

OpenSSH/Cookbook/Multiplexing, Wikibooks, *http://bit.ly/1bpeV0y*, October 28, 2014.

Shafer, Andrew Clay. *Agile Infrastructure in Web Operations: Keeping the Data on Time*. O'Reilly Media, 2010.

Index

register clause, 70
    and modules with facts for returned values,
        77
registry (Docker images), 283
    publishing images to multiple registries, 304
    pushing our image to, 288, 290
regular expressions, search_regex parameter,
    267
remote servers, 3
repo_url variable, 101
required option, 223
required_one_of parameter, 227
requirements.txt file, 103
    example file, 103
    installing packages from, 104
requiretty option, disabling, 207
rescue clause, 168
REST API
    Amazon EC2, 246
    Ansible Tower, 357
reverse proxy, 91
roles, 8, 127-141
    Ansible Galaxy, 139-141
    basic structure, 127
    creating role files and directories with
        ansible-galaxy, 138
    database role for deploying the database,
        130-133
    defining variables in, 133
    dependent, 138
        one-way dependency, 185
        SSL role, 185
    example, database and mezzanine roles, 128
    ghost-nginx, creating for Dockerized appli-
        cation, 298
    in Ansible Tower projects, 352
    include_role clause, 164
    mezzanine role for deploying Mezzanine,
        133-137
    tasks executing before or after roles, 130
    using in playbooks, 128-130
roles_path setting, 128
root user, 18, 33
    adding become clause to selected tasks, 98
    Postgres user, 108
route53 module, 280
routing table for a VPC, 271
RSA keys, generating, 331
run_command method arguments, 229

run_once clause, 176

S

save parameter, 339, 340
scaffolding, 138
scaling
    Ansible's up and down scalability, 127
    scaling down with Ansible, 6
script module, 113
    using instead of writing your own module,
        216
search_regex argument, 267
secret access key (Amazon EC2), 248
secret variables, 96
security groups, 261-263
    associated with EC2 instances, 258
    IP addresses permitted to connect to an
        instance, 262
    Packer and, 279
    ports, 263
    rule parameters, 262
security updates on Windows, playbook for,
    322
selective plugin, 197
sequences in YAML, 29
serial clause, 166
    list of serials, 175
    passing a percentage to rather than a fixed
        value, 175
    using to restrict number of hosts, 174
    using with max_fail_percentage, 175
servers
    setting up a server for testing, 11-19
    treating as pets versus cattle, 55
services, 91
settings.py file, 108
setup module, 75
    facts output by, 75
    invoking explicitly to gather facts, 189
set_fact module, 78
set_fs_attributes_if_different method, 228
shebang (!), 236
shebangs, 27
shell module
    changed key, 71
    output structure, 72
shells
    ansible_shell_type parameter, 50

About the Authors

Lorin Hochstein was born and raised in Montreal, Quebec, though you'd never guess he was a Canadian by his accent, other than his occasional tendency to say "close the light." He is a recovering academic, having spent two years on the tenure track as an assistant professor of computer science and engineering at the University of Nebraska-Lincoln, and another four years as a computer scientist at the University of Southern California's Information Sciences Institute. He earned his BEng in Computer Engineering at McGill University, his MS in Electrical Engineering at Boston University, and his PhD in Computer Science at the University of Maryland, College Park. He is currently a Senior Software Engineer at Netflix, where he works on the Chaos Engineering team.

René Moser lives in Switzerland with his wife and three kids, likes simple things that work and scale, and earned an Advanced Diploma of Higher Education in IT. He has been engaged in the open source community for more than 15 years, recently as an Ansible Core Contributor and author of over 40 Ansible modules, as well as a member of the Project Management Committee and Committer of Apache CloudStack. He is currently a System Engineer at SWISS TXT.

Colophon

The animal on the cover of *Ansible: Up and Running* is a Holstein Friesian *(Bos primigenius)*, often shortened to Holstein in North America and Friesian in Europe. This breed of cattle originated in Europe in what is now the Netherlands, bred with the goal of obtaining animals that could exclusively eat grass—the area's most abundant resource—resulting in a high-producing, black-and-white dairy cow. Holstein Friesians were introduced to the United States from 1621 to 1664, but American breeders didn't become interested in the breed until the 1830s.

Holsteins are known for their large size, distinct black-and-white markings, and high production of milk. The black and white coloring is a result of artificial selection by the breeders. Healthy calves weigh 90–100 pounds at birth; mature Holsteins can weigh up to 1,280 pounds and stand at 58 inches tall. Heifers of this breed are typically bred by 13 to 15 months; their gestation period is 9½ months.

This breed of cattle averages about 2,022 gallons of milk per year; pedigree animals average 2,146 gallons per year, and can produce up to 6,898 gallons in a lifetime.

In September 2000, the Holstein became the center of controversy when one of its own, Hanoverhill Starbuck, was cloned from frozen fibroblast cells recovered one month before his death, birthing Starbuck II. The cloned calf was born 21 years and 5 months after the original Starbuck.

Learn from experts.
Find the answers you need.

Sign up for a **10-day free trial** to get **unlimited access** to all of the content on Safari, including Learning Paths, interactive tutorials, and curated playlists that draw from thousands of ebooks and training videos on a wide range of topics, including data, design, DevOps, management, business—and much more.

Start your free trial at:
oreilly.com/safari

(No credit card required.)

CPSIA information can be obtained
at www.ICGtesting.com
Printed in the USA
BVHW081418230119
538451BV00021B/1141/P